PRECARITY AND AGEING

Understanding Insecurity
and Risk in Later Life

Edited by
Amanda Grenier, Chris Phillipson
and Richard A. Settersten Jr

P

First published in Great Britain in 2021 by

Policy Press, an imprint of
Bristol University Press
University of Bristol
1-9 Old Park Hill
Bristol
BS2 8BB
UK
t: +44 (0)117 954 5940
e: bup-info@bristol.ac.uk

Details of international sales and distribution partners are available at
policy.bristoluniversitypress.co.uk

© Bristol University Press 2021

British Library Cataloguing in Publication Data
A catalogue record for this book is available from the British Library

ISBN 978-1-4473-4086-7 (paperback)
ISBN 978-1-4473-4085-0 (hardback)
ISBN 978-1-4473-4088-1 (ePub)
ISBN 978-1-4473-4087-4 (ePDF)

The right of Amanda Grenier, Chris Phillipson and Richard A. Settersten Jr to be identified as editors of this work has been asserted by them in accordance with the Copyright, Designs and Patents Act 1988.

All rights reserved: no part of this publication may be reproduced, stored in a retrieval system, or transmitted in any form or by any means, electronic, mechanical, photocopying, recording, or otherwise without the prior permission of Bristol University Press.

Every reasonable effort has been made to obtain permission to reproduce copyrighted material. If, however, anyone knows of an oversight, please contact the publisher.

The statements and opinions contained within this publication are solely those of the editors and contributors and not of the University of Bristol or Bristol University Press. The University of Bristol and Bristol University Press disclaim responsibility for any injury to persons or property resulting from any material published in this publication.

Bristol University Press works to counter discrimination on grounds of gender, race, disability, age and sexuality.

Cover design: Dave Worth
Front cover image: Shutterstock

Contents

List of figures and tables		v
Notes on contributors		vii
Editors' acknowledgements		ix
Series editors' preface		xi
1	Precarity and ageing: new perspectives for social gerontology *Amanda Grenier, Chris Phillipson and Richard A. Settersten Jr*	1

PART I: Life course perspectives on precarity

2	How life course dynamics matter for precarity in later life *Richard A. Settersten Jr*	19
3	Precarious life, human development and the life course: critical intersections *Stephen Katz*	41

PART II: Precarity across situations

4	Rereading frailty through a lens of precarity: an explication of politics and the human condition of vulnerability *Amanda Grenier*	69
5	Older workers and ontological precarity: between precarious employment, precarious welfare and precarious households *David Lain, Laura Airey, Wendy Loretto and Sarah Vickerstaff*	91
6	Precarity, migration and ageing *Karen Kobayashi and Mushira Mohsin Khan*	115
7	A framework to identify precarity in the social sciences: insights from qualitative research *Elena Portacolone*	147

PART III: Austerity, care and social responses to precarity

8	Reconstructing dependency: precarity, precariousness and care in old age *Michael Fine*	169
9	From precarious employment to precarious retirement: neoliberal health and long-term care in the United States *Larry Polivka and Baozhen Luo*	191

| 10 | Austerity and precarity: individual and collective agency in later life
Chris Phillipson | 215 |
| 11 | Conclusion: Precarity and ageing in the 21st century
Chris Phillipson, Amanda Grenier and Richard A. Settersten Jr | 237 |

Index 247

List of figures and tables

Figures
5.1	Mapping the interactions between precarious employment, welfare states and households	97
5.2	Positioning individuals between precarious employment, welfare states and households	101
6.1	Number of immigrants and immigration rate (1852–2014)	118

Table
5.1	Demographic information of the interviewees	99

Notes on contributors

Laura Airey is a postdoctoral research fellow at the University of Edinburgh Business School, UK.

Michael Fine is Honorary Professor in the Department of Sociology at Macquarie University in Sydney, Australia.

Amanda Grenier is Professor and Norman and Honey Schipper Chair in Gerontological Social Work at the University of Toronto and Baycrest Hospital, Canada.

Stephen Katz is Professor (Emeritus) of Sociology and founding member of the Trent Center for Aging and Society at Trent University in Peterborough, Canada.

Mushira Mohsin Khan is a doctoral candidate in the Department of Sociology and a student affiliate with the Institute on Aging and Lifelong Health at the University of Victoria, British Columbia, Canada.

Karen Kobayashi is Professor of Sociology and a research affiliate with the Institute on Aging and Lifelong Health at the University of Victoria, British Columbia, Canada.

David Lain is Senior Lecturer in Employment Studies at Newcastle University Business School, UK.

Wendy Loretto is Dean and Professor of Organisational Behaviour at the University of Edinburgh Business School, UK.

Baozhen Luo is Associate Professor in Sociology at Western Washington University, USA.

Chris Phillipson is Professor of Sociology and Social Gerontology at the University of Manchester, UK.

Larry Polivka is Director of the Claude Pepper Center at Florida State University, USA and Scholar-in-Residence with the Claude Pepper Foundation, Inc.

Elena Portacolone is Assistant Professor of Sociology at the Institute for Health & Aging and a Pepper Center Scholar at the University of California, San Francisco, USA.

Richard A. Settersten Jr is Barbara E. Knudson Endowed Chair and Professor of Human Development and Family Sciences at Oregon State University, USA.

Sarah Vickerstaff is Professor of Work and Employment at the University of Kent's School of Social Policy, Sociology and Social Research, UK.

Editors' acknowledgements

This collection emerged from discussions on the concept of precarity with regard to ageing and late life. Professor Grenier wishes to thank the Canadian Social Sciences and Humanities Research Council for its award of an Insight Grant for the project *Precarity and Aging: Unequal Experiences in Contemporary Late Life* (grant number 435-2016-0933). We also wish to thank Equity Burke at the Gilbrea Centre for Studies in Aging at McMaster University for her assistance with the collection.

Series editors' preface

Chris Phillipson (University of Manchester, UK)
Toni Calasanti (Virginia Tech, USA)
Thomas Scharf (Newcastle University, UK)

Global ageing and the increasing numbers of older people in all world regions raise new issues and concerns for consideration by academics, policy makers and health and social care professionals around the world. Ageing in a Global Context is a book series, published by Policy Press in association with the British Society of Gerontology, that aims to influence and transform debates in what is a fast-moving field in research and policy. The series seeks to achieve this in three main ways. First, the series publishes books which rethink key questions shaping debates in the study of ageing. This has become particularly important given the restructuring of welfare states, especially in the Global North, alongside the complex nature of population change. Each of these elements opens up the need to explore themes which reach beyond traditional perspectives in social gerontology. Second, the series represents a response to the impact of globalization and related processes, which are contributing to the erosion of the national boundaries that originally framed the study of ageing. This is reflected in the increasing scope and breadth of issues that are explored in contributions to the series, for example: the impact of transnational migration, growing ethnic and cultural diversity, new types of inequality, and themes relating to ageing in different environmental contexts. Third, a key concern of the series is to explore interdisciplinary connections in gerontology. Contributions provide a critical assessment of the disciplinary boundaries and territories influencing the study of ageing, creating in the process new perspectives and approaches relevant to the 21st century.

Against this background, we are grateful to the editors of this book, Amanda Grenier, Chris Phillipson and Richard A. Settersten Jr, whose book aligns so closely to the aims of the Ageing in a Global Context series. Exploring the emerging topic of precarity and ageing, the book offers a fundamentally new perspective on the ways in which later life is shaped within the context of a redefined welfare model and deepening inequalities. With a strong conceptual grounding in critical gerontology, the book's chapters, written by leading scholars from a range of countries, considers the multiple and intersecting pathways that lead to precarity in older age, the different spheres of life that are becoming more precarious under the influence of profound structural change, and the role of social policy in framing and responding to precarity. Taken together, the book makes a key contribution to conceptual, empirical and policy-relevant understandings of what is becoming a key topic in social gerontology. The book is likely to be read very widely, becoming a key text for academics, policy makers and a range of professionals who share a passion to study and understand better how ageing is changing within an increasingly globalized context.

1

Precarity and ageing: new perspectives for social gerontology

Amanda Grenier, Chris Phillipson and Richard A. Settersten Jr

Introduction

This book examines some of the challenges facing older people, given a context of rising life expectancy, cuts to the welfare state, and widening economic and social inequalities. Although cultural representations and policy discourses depict older people as a group healthier and more prosperous than ever, many older people experience ageing amid insecurities that emerge in later life or are carried forward as a consequence of earlier disadvantage. At the same time, responsibility is now placed upon individuals and/or their families to secure support for many of the vulnerabilities associated with old age. The purpose of this book is to examine the potential of a new approach to thinking about the risks facing older people, drawing on debates in the field of 'precarity' and 'precariousness'.

This book examines precarity and ageing from a range of disciplinary backgrounds, critical perspectives and contexts. The collection of chapters develops a distinctive approach to understanding the changing cultural, economic and social circumstances that create precarity for different groups of older people. This book explores what insights the concept of precarity might bring to an understanding of ageing across the life course, especially in the context of the radical sociopolitical changes affecting the lives of older people. In doing so, it draws attention to altered forms of ageing, but also to changing social and cultural contexts, and to realities that challenge the assumption that older people will be protected by existing social programmes or whatever resources can be marshalled privately.

This chapter sets the foundation for the book, with an exploration of the concept of precarity and its relevance to the field of ageing. It establishes precarity as a lens, or a means, for drawing attention to insecurity and risk in later life. The chapter begins with a discussion of the concept of precarity and precariousness in fields such as geography and labour studies, and how the concept has been applied to ageing and late life. It then poses a series of questions to guide reflection and ground the debates pursued by authors, followed by a brief overview of the chapters ahead.

What do we mean by precarity?

To date, the concept of precarity has been used to highlight new forms of risk and rising insecurities in the context of global economic and social change (Gallie et al, 2003; Schram, 2015). A number of fields of study have drawn attention to precarity and precariousness, although rarely with regard to ageing or late life. Discussions of precarity are most prominent in labour studies, migration, sociology and geography, and in the context of international social movements (Avant, 2017; Bowe, 2008; Lewchuk, 2017; Lewchuk et al, 2008; Lewis et al, 2015; Oxman-Martinez et al, 2005; Vosko, 2006; Waite, 2009). Although some variations exist in associated meanings, 'precarity' is used most often to refer to the insecurities, unwanted risks and hazards of contemporary life, typically associated with globalization and neoliberal economic and social policies (Standing, 2010; 2012; Waite, 2009).

There are a number of contributions of particular assistance in helping to situate the concept of precarity in relation to ageing, and which extend the analysis beyond the immediate association with labour. First, writing from a geographical perspective, Waite (2009, p 426) refers to precarity as 'life worlds characterised by uncertainty and insecurity', and as a concept that implies 'both a condition and a possible rallying point for resistance'. Second, Millar (2017) delineates three different approaches to precarity: as a condition (as developed by Bourdieu); as a category or class (following Standing); and as an ontological condition (as in, for example, Butler).[1] Third, one of the most widely cited references to precarity, and more specifically precariousness, is that of Butler (2009, p 25), who views it as a 'politically induced condition in which certain populations suffer from failing social and economic networks of support and become differentially exposed to injury, violence, and death'.

The research literature draws an important distinction between the terms 'precarity' and 'precariousness'. The Oxford English Dictionary (OED) records and guides the use of the English language, providing insight into cultural frames of reference, meaning and experience. Although the concept of precarity has become widely used in labour and migration studies, and is one we use throughout this volume, it does not appear in the OED. In academic scholarship and research, precarity is often used in ways that combine 'precarious' and 'proletariat' (Standing, 2010; see also Bodnar, 2006). The definition of 'precarious', however, which does appear in the OED, gives insight into more flexible readings of precarity, such as those noted by Millar (2017), and to differences that are important for the various contributors to this book. Accordingly, 'precarious, adj.' is defined as both 'a right, tenancy' (that is, something held or enjoyed by the favour of and at the pleasure of another person) and a condition whereby one is 'vulnerable to the will or decision of others'. The uses of the concept 'precarious' range from 'a line of argument, inference, opinion, etc. [that is] insecurely founded or reasoned, doubtful, dubious', to something 'dependent on chance or circumstance; uncertain; liable to fail; exposed to risk, hazardous; insecure, unstable', to something 'subject to or fraught with physical danger or insecurity; at risk of falling, collapse, or similar accident; unsound, unsafe, rickety' ('precarious, adj.', nd).

These distinctions in language offer encouraging directions where our assessment of precarity and precariousness with regard to ageing and late life is concerned. Drawing on frames of reference within social sciences, approaches to precarity and precariousness can be considered to include both a structural element, often denoted by the term 'precarity', and a philosophical or interpretive strand, which more often employs the language of 'precariousness'. Although these broad and diverse sets of thought are sometimes viewed as theoretically incompatible, they need not be. Instead, as suggested by a number of authors in this volume, the diverse approaches to precarity and precariousness offer complementary, intersecting and equally necessary windows into insecurity and risk in relation to ageing and late life.[2]

The exploration of precarity and ageing thus represents an important link to other research that is focused exclusively on earlier segments of the life course but pays little to no attention to later life. Our challenge to these fields is to raise their awareness that processes of disadvantage and inequality must be understood across a much longer time horizon, and that dynamics from earlier periods are carried forward into later decades. That is, experiences related to work, migration or poverty do not end at the point of retirement age. A focus on precarity and precariousness, as will be argued throughout the subsequent chapters, provides an important means to open new discussions with interdisciplinary scholars studying related issues in earlier life periods. As such, the analysis reaches beyond the aim of raising awareness of the lifelong nature and implications of those phenomena, stretching into how researchers might work together to consider solutions to improve the later well-being of younger populations as they grow older.

The chapters in this volume join with those of a relatively small number of international contributions that are beginning to apply precarity to the topic of ageing. For example, other applications have highlighted precarious historical circumstances such as the 'Great Recession' (Craciun et al, 2015; Craciun and Flick, 2016; see also Craciun, 2019), ageing and employment (Bohle et al, 2010; Hum and Simpson, 2010), care work (Baines et al, 2014), financial insecurity and/or exclusion (Craciun and Flick, 2014), disability and citizenship (Knight, 2014) and increasing inequality in the G20 countries (Biggs, 2014; Grundy and Laliberte Rudman, 2018; Porter, 2015). Other research has illuminated how older people get caught in the 'precarity trap' of 'flexible' and lower-income status positions, as well as highlights the extent to which older people may come to rely upon precarious workers as carers (Baines et al, 2014; Standing, 2010).

Each of the chapters in this volume helps to bring much-needed attention to the question of how precarity and precariousness in late life might differ from that in earlier life periods. In this context, it is experiences such as the increased likelihood of living alone, of managing chronic illness, disability, frailty and dementia, or of needing care, that are likely to become increasingly important (see Grenier et al, 2017; Knight, 2014; Portacolone, 2013). Consistent with observations made by Butler (2009), extending the analysis of precarity to the later years naturally moves into questions of 'what it means to be human' and to live a 'devalued life' in a variety of contexts, including those relating to health and social care (see Grenier et al, 2017).

Precarity and critical perspectives on ageing populations

An important rationale for the book has been the concern to develop new approaches to understanding ageing, given a context of radical economic and social change. Current approaches to ageing emerged at a time of economic growth in Western economies. As such, the models that presently guide our understandings of change throughout the life course are based on assumptions of economic stability and the continued development of the welfare state (albeit with a mix of private and public funding). Judt (2005; 2012) makes the point that

> the chief basis of the support for state-funded welfare and social services lay in the popular sense that these

> corresponded to the proper tasks of government. The postwar state across Europe was a 'social' state, with an implicit (and often constitutionally explicit) responsibility for the well-being of its citizens. It had an obligation to provide not only the institutions and services necessary for a well-regulated, safe and prosperous land, but also to *improve* the condition of the population, as measured by a broad and expanding range of indices. (Judt, 2005, p 76)

The outcome, it was hoped, would be a more cohesive society with no category of person excluded or less 'deserving'. But challenges to the 'welfare' or 'social' state, together with the impact of economic recession, have dislodged the main pillars around which approaches to ageing were constructed. This context of rising insecurity, combined with increasing longevity that signals a need for more extended forms of health and social care, raises questions about the relevance of existing paradigms and approaches in social gerontology. At the same time, it suggests that the possibilities for achieving the intended goals of fairness and citizenship may be breaking down under conditions of economic and social crisis. While contemporary conditions are rapidly altering ageing and the realities of late life, there is a gap in the state of knowledge of and approaches to understanding risk and vulnerability during this period of the life course.

Approaching understandings of ageing from the perspective of precarity provides a point of reconnection with critical gerontology. In the late 1970s and early 1980s, critical gerontology emerged to provide a critique both of the type of welfare state that had emerged over the postwar period (Estes, 1979; Townsend, 1981), and of the widening social inequalities that subsequently emerged with the combination of globalization and neoliberalism (Baars et al, 2006). Moving into the 21st century, critical gerontology developed new strands, illustrated by the emergence of cultural gerontology and attention to questions associated with lifestyles, meanings and identity in later life (Gilleard and Higgs, 2000; Twigg and Martin, 2015). But despite the strengths of this approach and the continued contribution from other critical perspectives, critical gerontology struggled to develop effective responses to the various crises introduced by the post-2008 financial recession. The reasons for this are complex but almost certainly reflect the challenge posed by the relatively rapid decline of the welfare state that accompanied austerity (notably in Europe), the influence of new positive perspectives in gerontology (such as ideas associated with 'active' or 'successful' ageing), and intersecting forms of inequality that affect groups such as women, migrants and older workers (Phillipson, 2013).

This book should be seen as a response to the challenges posed by the combination of changes to the welfare state and the need for new perspectives in critical and social gerontology. The arguments from the various contributors are developed in three main ways. First, the book extends existing research on precarity to consider ageing, the life course and late life. In particular, it expands the discussion of precarity beyond labour and people of working age, and explores a range of experiences that make precarity a particularly relevant feature of ageing and later life. The various chapters illustrate how contemporary conditions – such as threats to pensions, austerity, structural inequalities and flexible labour relations – create trajectories that extend into late life. That is, taking a 'long view' of the life course, authors demonstrate how the accumulation of disadvantage may not only widen the inequality gap between groups of older people, but heighten precarity in later life.

Second, the book considers precarity in relation to related concepts of *risk, social exclusion, inequality, disadvantage, marginalization* and *vulnerability*. The different chapters highlight the need to critically analyse these concepts in order to increase clarity in their definitions and boundaries and, ultimately, in their measurement. This is a crucial exercise for advancing the concept of precarity in the development of theory and its application to work in the field of ageing. Throughout the detailed examples in the collection, authors explore the potentials and pitfalls of precarity, and assess the extent to which this concept may (or may not) assist with understanding the complex range of changes that affect older people in everyday life (such as living arrangements and family statuses, migration and immigration, illness and disability, and needs related to getting and giving care).

Third, the book adds to the emerging illustrations of perspectives that bridge structural, cultural and interpretive approaches to ageing and late life. The investigation of precarity, itself with structural, philosophical and interpretative strands, provides a conceptual case for testing the boundaries of critical and cultural gerontology. As such, the detailed exploration of precarity simultaneously represents an attempt to extend the theoretical base of critical gerontology and the substantive focus on disadvantage and inequality, and a reconsideration of existing responses. In doing so, it offers insight into the areas that may produce the greatest discrepancies between policy frameworks, institutional or organizational practices, and the lives of older people, thereby underscoring the urgency of addressing insecurities, risks and vulnerabilities carried across the life course and into late life.

Guiding questions and key themes of the book

This collection resulted from ongoing exchanges in the context of research grants and conferences among a group of people studying disadvantage and inequality in late life.[3] As we designed the collection, we strategically invited major scholars working in the targeted topic areas that would reveal the sources, consequences and experiences of precarity in different domains of life and sectors of society. To frame our inquiry, we set out a number of guiding questions:

- How might understandings of precarity and precariousness be extended to late life? Does precarity offer a new lens to understand insecurity, risk and vulnerability in late life?
- Is precarity a new form of ageing? To what extent has late life become precarious?
- How does an approach guided by precarity and/or precariousness differ from existing approaches to inequality and ageing? What are the potentials and/or pitfalls of precarity?
- How does precarity and/or precariousness align (or not) with other relevant concepts, such as risk, social exclusion or vulnerability?
- Is precarity a worthwhile concept from which to advance understandings of ageing and the life course, and can it help build a foundation for change?

The contents of the volume, as a whole, emphasize five larger themes. First, precarity often has *spill over* effects – from one period of life, from one domain and from one level to another. Second, precarity often has *social* origins and consequences – which implies human agency, brings about a potential for malleability and implies openness to chance, intervention and/or response. Third, precarity, and particularly precariousness, is often felt acutely in and expressed through social relationships, at particular transitional moments, and in contexts, making it an *interpersonal* phenomenon. Fourth, precarity is often experienced in intersectional ways, and at social locations that include age, ability, gender, ethnicity, migration status, race and socioeconomic status. As such, the analysis that results from precarity and precariousness reveals that there are both different ways that precarity is experienced by older people across a range of social locations and geographic contexts, and an inherent potential to address structures or social trajectories of risk. Finally, because precarity has a natural association with social policies and matters of inequality, it is also an inherently *political* phenomenon – something that becomes acutely visible in the illustrations throughout the collection as a whole.

The collection is divided into three parts. The first following this chapter, consisting of contributions from Settersten and Katz, focuses on life course perspectives on precarity. These chapters set out a conceptual context for the study of precarity in relation to ageing and the life course. The second part, with chapters by Grenier, Lain et al, Kobayashi and Khan, and Portacolone, provides detailed investigations of precarity across a range of situations, including frailty, employment, migration and living alone. The third and final part, with chapters by Fine, Polivka and Luo, and Phillipson, focuses on the terrain of austerity, care and social relationships, and in particular how changes in social responses experienced in relation to the need for care may deepen precarity. The concluding chapter by Phillipson et al draws together the themes of the book and provides a discussion of the mutually enriching contributions that a focus on precarity makes to ageing, and ageing to understandings of precarity and precariousness.

What's ahead in the book

The collection consists of 11 chapters covering a range of topics and contexts. While topics such as the life course, migration, labour, frailty and care abound within gerontology, they are rarely pursued from a critical perspective, and even less so as an attempt to link them with theory on ageing, inequality and late life. Together, the contributions of each chapter offer new angles and fresh insights into insecurity and risk in late life.

Chapter 2 (Settersten) examines precarity and ageing through the lens of the life course. The chapter begins by describing how precarity in later life is connected to three distinct dimensions: time (experiences in prior life periods), life domains (experiences in education, work, family, health and wealth) and levels (such as individual, relational, institutional and demographic). It also generates specific lessons for assessing how life course dynamics matter for precarity in late life, revealing how the final decades of life are a time of heightened precarity; how precarity stems from life transitions, other people and social environments; how individuals' skills and capacities create precarity or their responses to it; and the significance of subjective evaluations and anticipation in affecting personal experiences with precarity. Because precarity is part of the human condition, some aspects of it are also universal.

Chapter 3 (Katz) draws on a figurative methodology to explore human development and the life course as precarious forms of life. Biopolitical governance and neoliberal policies have produced discourses and interventions organized around individualized risks and health crises that encourage the public to engage in 'a will to health' around lifestyle, exercise, diet, sexuality, environment, childrearing and ageing in order to manage issues of life, security and risk associated with various life course transitions. The chapter outlines the critical and ethical issues for ageing populations, and examines the crisis-laden personification of problems through the figures of the obese child, the unstable adolescent, the despairing mid-lifer and the cognitively impaired older adult. The chapter considers and compares the suggested responses of resilience and resistance, highlighting the need for individuals to refuse to be subjugated as precarious subjects, and imagining new future strategies for radical and non-precarious life course trajectories.

Chapter 4 (Grenier), providing the transition into the second part of the book, reconsiders frailty through the lens of precarity. In this chapter, Grenier argues for the need to shift the focus from frailty as an individual biomedical and corporeal risk to the insecurities and vulnerabilities that are produced and sustained in neoliberal contexts of care. The chapter outlines the problems and limitations of existing approaches to frailty, including how approaches currently overlook the political and relational aspects of frailty and vulnerability that are central to older people's experiences. It examines precarity as a lens for analysing and resituating frailty in the political context of care, and for framing frailty in relation to the construction of devalued subjects. It exposes frailty as a shared experience of vulnerability, as socially, culturally, economically and politically situated, and as a result of political systems that deepen vulnerability.

Chapter 5 (Lain, Airey, Loretto and Vickerstaff) explores and theorizes the notion of 'ontological precarity' as a means to extend debates on precarity and older workers. Focusing on the idea that precarity is a lived experience rather than simply a labour outcome, the chapter views precarity as a useful concept for making sense of the position of older workers. Drawing on qualitative research with older workers and, in this case, female workers in a case study of the hospitality industry, it probes the concept of 'ontological precarity' as an individual experience of anxiety that stems from being subject to precarious work on a daily basis. The chapter presents a new framework that accounts for the intersections between the three separate domains of precarious employment, precarious welfare and precarious households, thereby highlighting the relationship between sociopolitical conditions, employment contexts and individual life course trajectories. It points to the especially problematic discrepancies between policy decisions, such as the rising state pension ages, and the concern that 'in-work precarity' will become more widespread.

Chapter 6 (Kobayashi and Khan) provides a discussion of precarity, migration and ageing. The chapter begins by introducing key economic, psychosocial and cultural markers of precarity in older immigrants. Drawing on media stories and qualitative research with stakeholders who work with older immigrants in Canada, it highlights the politics of precarity for this population, including systemic racism and discrimination, immigration policy, and health and social care practices. It builds on existing research to suggest that precarity be conceptualized and analysed as a complex multidimensional construct. Especially important is the need to capture both objective measures and interpretive aspects of the experience, lifestyle behaviours and health in context (including changes between country of birth and country of residence over time), and gender and migration status. The authors conclude by pointing to the need for continued critical reflection on precarity, ageing and migration, and to a number of practical measures that could be used to prevent disadvantage in late life.

Chapter 7 (Portacolone) proposes a framework for identifying and assessing precarity across a range of settings. The chapter begins by setting the context for precarity and the challenges of understanding and measuring precarity. To illustrate these challenges, it turns to two qualitative studies on living alone in old age, emphasizing four specific markers of precarity that could be used to build a framework: uncertainty, limited access to appropriate services, the importance of maintaining independence, and cumulative pressures. The chapter underscores the need to link research-based insights with programmes, policies and practices in an effort to alter the negative experiences of precarity among older people.

Chapter 8 (Fine) provides the entry into the third part of the book. The chapter considers precarity and precariousness in relation to existing scholarship and critical theory on care. Despite improvements in population health and increasing life expectancies over the 20th and 21st centuries, the need for supportive care on an ongoing basis or in critical periods continues to increase with age. Without appropriate social responses, life itself can be curtailed or cease to be viable. Drawing on the work of philosopher Eva Kittay and other scholars, the chapter develops theoretical perspectives on formal and informal provision of care, exploring how economic and political changes have restructured patterns of dependency for both those in receipt of care and those who provide it. It also comments on how the marketization of care has led to significant increases in precarity, especially for those with life histories of social disadvantage and marginalization. Understanding the care of older people as precarious helps to make visible the otherwise hidden links between the global reach of precarious work and the uncertain and unevenly distributed risks of needing care in late life.

Extending the analysis of care, Chapter 9 (Polivka and Luo) illustrates how precarity has been generated by the spread of corporatization to publicly funded health care programmes and by the emergence of neoliberal health and long-term care, particularly in the United States. Building on the work of Standing, the chapter focuses on the growing 'precariat' of low-wage workers with few if any retirement and health benefits and with no guarantees regarding continuing employment. Anchored in Streeck's theory of the neoliberal consolidation state, the chapter provides an in-depth treatment of how changes in US health care programmes have created precarity, and warns of the effects of similar trends towards neoliberal long-term care in several European countries that seem certain to result in growing precarity among older people in those nations as well.

Chapter 10 (Phillipson) focuses on how economic and social pressures have created precarious environments for growing old in the 21st century. This chapter examines the rise of precarity in the lives of older people, beginning with how experiences of ageing have been isolated from institutions that were once central to the provision of support in later life, and how older people have been affected by changes to the welfare state. The chapter establishes the link between precarity, the impacts of globalization and the financial crisis, and responses that are increasingly organized around austerity politics characterized by declining social supports, as well as a 'decline of the social' more generally. It underscores the problems of making individuals personally responsible for managing life course transitions, of lowering expectations, and of the erosion of public support based on the moral case for welfare. At the same time, it emphasizes the importance of collective responses to ageing, consisting of universal basic services, substantive equality and citizenship.

The concluding chapter by Phillipson, Grenier and Settersten provides an overview of the arguments developed throughout the book together with the linkages that exist between the chapters. Drawing on the various perspectives presented, it turns attention to the lives of older people in the context of austerity and precarious institutions. It then summarizes what ageing can bring to the study of precarity and vice versa, including reaching beyond the insecurities provided by the labour market in early periods of life, developing a deeper understanding of cumulative disadvantages and ontological vulnerabilities, and the importance of drawing upon other frameworks for change such as those associated with maintaining human rights. The chapter concludes with the importance of pushing the boundaries of critical scholarship to gain new insights into our understanding of the nature of precarity and ageing, and the challenges associated with living in a precarious world.

Ageing in new times: understanding risk and insecurity

This book is offered as a response to the tension that has emerged between longevity on the one hand and a more unequal old age on the other. This must itself be linked to the weakening of key institutions undergirding old age, notably in relation to retirement and the welfare state. The stakes are now high in terms of future support for older people. As Gray (2010, p 5) has observed: 'A roll-back of the state of the magnitude [currently underway] will leave people more exposed to the turbulence of world markets than they have been for generations. Inevitably, they will seek protection.' Yet such assistance will inevitably be different from that which shaped the lives of older people in the second half of the 20th century. The evidence suggests a more divided old age, with prosperity for some matched by deep poverty for others.

Society is now faced with a different type of ageing, underpinned by changing cultural and economic forces and responses. These are transforming the landscape around which the social construction of ageing has traditionally been built. The purpose of this book is to examine the new risks and insecurities facing older people, but also the potential for new forms of solidarity that need to be built within the context of ageing societies. Social gerontology has been slow to respond to the structural changes facing older people, with the dismantling of the institutions that defined social ageing in the 20th century. Acknowledging 'precarity' and the 'precariousness' of old age is an initial response to this changed environment, one requiring new theories and policies to be developed within social and critical gerontology.

Notes

1. Millar (2017, pp 7–8) concludes her analysis of these three approaches to precarity by arguing that, despite relevant critique, precarity retains both an analytic and a political value because it can open questions about the relationship between forms of labour and the fragile conditions of life. It is precisely this analysis that becomes extremely relevant for ageing, and in particular the intersections of the impacts of labour (or care) over time and the need for various forms of support in late life.
2. Most discussions of precarity have tended to focus on labour. Our approach, by linking these with scholarship on care and vulnerability from a range of perspectives, but most notably cultural studies (Butler), aims to extend current understandings of insecurity and risk as applied to the study of ageing and late life (see Butler, 2006; 2009; Butler and Athanasiou, 2013; Standing, 2011; 2012).
3. Some of the contributors and the material discussed in this volume are part of work funded by an Insight Grant from the Canadian Social Sciences and Humanities Research Council: Grenier, A. (PI), Rudman, D., Kobayashi, K.M, Marier, P. and Phillipson, C. (2016–21) *Precarity and Aging: Unequal Experiences in Contemporary Late Life*, grant number 435-2016-0933.

References

Avant, R. (2017) *The Wealth of Humans*, London: Allen Lane.

Baars, J., Dannefer, D., Phillipson, C. and Walker, A. (eds) (2006) *Aging, Globalization and Inequality: the New Critical Gerontology*, Amityville, NY: Baywood.

Baines, D., Cunningham, I., Campey, J. and Shields, J. (2014) 'Not profiting from precarity: the work of nonprofit service delivery and the creation of precariousness', *Just Labour*, 22: 74–93.

Biggs, S. (2014) 'Precarious ageing versus the policy of indifference: international trends and the G20', *Australasian Journal on Ageing*, 33(4): 226–8.

Bodnar, C. (2006) 'Taking it to the streets: French cultural worker resistance and the creation of a precariat movement', *Canadian Journal of Communication*, 31(3): 675–94.

Bohle, P., Pitts, C. and Quinlan, M. (2010) 'Time to call it quits? The safety and health of older workers', *International Journal of Health Services*, 40(1): 23–41.

Bowe, J. (2008) *Nobodies: Modern American Slave Labor and the Dark Side of the New Global Economy*, New York: Random House.

Butler, J. (2006) *Precarious Life: The Powers of Mourning and Violence*, London: Verso.

Butler, J. (2009) *Frames of War: When Is Life Grievable?*, London: Verso.

Butler, J. and Athanasiou, A. (2013) *Dispossession: The Performative in the Political*, Hoboken, NJ: John Wiley & Sons.

Craciun, C. (2019) *Positive Aging and Precarity: Theory, Policy, and Social Reality within a Comparative German Context*, New York: Springer.

Craciun, C. and Flick, U. (2014) '"I will never be the granny with rosy cheeks": perceptions of aging in precarious and financially secure middle-aged Germans', *Journal of Aging Studies*, 29: 78–87.

Craciun, C. and Flick, U. (2016) 'Aging in precarious times: exploring the role of gender in shaping views on aging', *Journal of Women & Aging*, 28(6): 530–9.

Craciun, C., Gellert, P. and Flick, U. (2015) 'Aging in precarious times: positive views on aging in middle-aged Germans with secure and insecure pension plans', *Ageing International*, 40(3): 201–18.

Estes, C.L. (1979) *The Aging Enterprise*, San Francisco: Jossey Bass.

Gallie, D., Paugam, S. and Jacobs, S. (2003) 'Unemployment, poverty and social isolation: is there a vicious circle of social exclusion?', *European Societies*, 5(1): 1–32.

Gilleard, C. and Higgs, P. (2000) *Cultures of Ageing: Self, Citizen and the Body*. London: Routledge.

Gray, J. (2010) 'Progressive, like the 1980s', *London Review of Books*, 32(20): 3–7.

Grenier, A., Lloyd, L. and Phillipson, C. (2017) 'Precarity in late life: rethinking dementia as a "frailed" old age', *Sociology of Health & Illness*, 39(2): 318–30.

Grundy, J. and Laliberte Rudman, D. (2018) 'Deciphering deservedness: Canadian employment insurance reforms in historical perspective', *Social Policy & Administration*, 52(3): 809–25.

Hum, D. and Simpson, W. (2010) 'The declining retirement prospects of immigrant men', *Canadian Public Policy*, 36(3): 287–305.

Judt, T. (2005) *Postwar: A History of Europe since 1945*. London: William Heinemann.

Judt, T. with Snyder, T. (2012) *Thinking the Twentieth Century*, London: William Heinemann.

Knight, A. (2014) 'Disability as vulnerability: redistributing precariousness in democratic ways', *The Journal of Politics*, 76(1): 15–26.

Lewchuk, W. (2017) 'Precarious jobs: where are they, and how do they affect well-being?', *Economic and Labour Relations Review*, 28(3): 402–19.

Lewchuk, W., Clarke, M. and De Wolff, A. (2008) 'Working without commitments: precarious employment and health', *Work, Employment and Society*, 22(3): 387–406.

Lewis, H., Dwyer, P., Hodkinson, S. and Waite, L. (2015) *Precarious Lives: Forced Labour, Exploitation and Asylum*, Bristol: Policy Press.

Millar, K.M. (2017) 'Toward a critical politics of precarity', *Sociology Compass*, 11(6): e12483.

Oxman-Martinez, J., Hanley, J., Lach, L., Khanlou, N., Weerasinghe, S. and Agnew, V. (2005) 'Intersection of Canadian policy parameters affecting women with precarious immigration status: a baseline for understanding barriers to health', *Journal of Immigrant and Minority Health*, 7(4): 247–58.

Phillipson, C. (2013) *Ageing*, Cambridge: Polity.

Portacolone, E. (2013) 'The notion of precariousness among older adults living alone in the U.S.', *Journal of Aging Studies*, 27(2): 166–74.

Porter, A. (2015) 'Austerity, social program restructuring, and the erosion of democracy: examining the 2012 employment insurance reforms', *Canadian Review of Social Policy*, 71: 21–52.

'precarious, adj.' (def. 1) (nd) *OED Online*, available from: https://www.oed.com/view/Entry/149548?redirectedFrom=precarious& [Accessed 23 August 2019].

Schram, S.F. (2015) *The Return of Ordinary Capitalism: Neoliberalism, Precarity, Occupy*, Oxford: Oxford University Press.

Standing, G. (2011) *The Precariat: The New Dangerous Class*, London: Bloomsbury Academic.

Standing, G. (2012) 'The precariat: from denizens to citizens?', *Polity*, 44(4): 588–608.

Townsend, P. (1981) 'The structured dependency of the elderly: a creation of social policy in the twenty-first century', *Ageing & Society*, 1(1): 5–28.

Twigg, J. and Martin, W. (2015) 'The challenge of cultural gerontology', *The Gerontologist*, 55(3): 353–9.

Vosko, L.F. (ed.) (2006) *Precarious Employment: Understanding Labour Market Insecurity in Canada*, Montreal: McGill–Queen's University Press.

Waite, L. (2009) 'A place and space for a critical geography of precarity?', *Geography Compass*, 3(1), 412–33.

PART I

Life course perspectives on precarity

2

How life course dynamics matter for precarity in later life

Richard A. Settersten Jr

Introduction

What can a life course perspective reveal about precarity? The 'personological' paradigm of life course research (Dannefer and Settersten, 2010) attempts to account for how individuals' past experiences affect later ones. However, a life course perspective on ageing is much more than understanding the shadow of the past or studying a phenomenon over time. The 'institutional' paradigm of life course research (Dannefer and Settersten, 2010) emphasizes the role of *social* forces in opening and closing opportunities and structuring pathways through life. Both of these paradigms provide important lessons for understanding precarity: when, where, how and for whom precarity occurs, and what legacies precarity carries in the lives of individuals, families and societies. I begin with three broad propositions informed by these paradigms – that there is a need to understand precarity across levels, domains and time (inspired by Bernardi et al's (2019) 'life course cube') – before turning to more specific insights about how life course dynamics matter for precarity in later life.

Precarity occurs across multiple, often interacting, 'levels'

Understanding precarity relies on explicitly differentiating between three distinct and interacting levels of analysis: inner-individual, individual and supra-individual (Bernardi et al, 2019). The inner-individual level comprises variables like genetic, biological, physiological and psychological attributes (such as dispositions, values, attitudes and subjective well-being). The individual level comprises 'biographical' variables that reflect social and behavioural statuses and outcomes – such as education, whom one lives with or where one lives, social class, or special legal rights or social privileges (such as citizenship or gender) – and which affect the type and amount of resources an individual has to invest or to act. The supra-individual level comprises attributes of the external sociocultural environments in which an individual's behaviour takes place, environments that potentially affect individual opportunities, choices and behaviours. These range from the immediate environment (such as personal and professional relationships and networks) to larger social institutions (such as educational and health care systems or workplaces), together with more distal contexts (such as the economy, culture, demography, and historical events and periods of social change).

These levels, and the interactions between them, are key spaces for understanding precarity. For instance, precarity might stem from interactions between the supra and individual levels. Consider demography. First, declining fertility, combined with increases in life expectancy, have created longer and more interdependent relationships among family members. Second, increases in divorce and family complexity alter marriage markets and gender roles (for example, shared custody arrangements may bring opportunities for fathers to devote more time to care, and for mothers to devote more time to work or activities outside the household). In both cases, relationships can create precarity or protect people from it. As another example of an interaction between the supra and individual levels, a cultural 'regime' related to gender – in which women's social integration is ensured primarily through the family and men's is ensured primarily through the labour market – differentially weights the childcare and career responsibilities of mothers and fathers. This creates different types of precarity for men and women, and at potentially different times in life.

Similarly, as an example of how precarity might stem from interactions between the supra and inner-individual levels, consider the field of epigenetics. Epigenetic studies are important for understanding precarity because they reveal ripple effects across multiple generations that are largely invisible. Animal and emerging human research suggests that exposure to environmental toxins, nutritional deficits and parental stress during gametogenesis, gestation and early life can alter gene expression, increasing the risk of health problems over the life course and potentially altering health trajectories of subsequent generations (see, for example, Hanson and Skinner, 2016).

A particularly powerful illustration is that a grandparent's or great-grandparent's history of malnutrition (due to population-level deprivation or personal food insecurity) affects the outcomes of subsequent generations, producing higher rates of obesity or diabetes and underscoring the idea that 'you are what your grandmother ate'.

Research is expanding this idea beyond nutrition to drinking, smoking, nurturing and other behaviours (Hurley, 2015). Similarly, life course theory undergirds the popular 'fetal origins' or 'Barker' hypothesis (Barker, 1998), which connects low birth weight and later life coronary heart disease. This hypothesis is being extended to epigenetic questions about the influence of prenatal and early childhood nutrition on later-life high blood pressure, stroke, osteoporosis, premature ageing and ovarian cancer (see, for instance, Heindel and Vandenberg, 2015).

Precarity occurs in multiple, often interacting, life domains

A life course perspective points to the fact that precarity can occur in multiple life domains, including employment, family, education, physical and mental health, and leisure (Bernardi et al, 2019). People can experience precarity in multiple domains simultaneously. Precarity in one domain can interact with or spill over into others. So, too, can precarity in one domain be reduced or offset by the strength or stability of other domains (see further Chapter 5). Low-wage work or unemployment, for example, restricts or diminishes income, which in turn affects options for housing, neighbourhood, school or health care. Compromised physical or mental health may limit an individual's daily activities or social engagement. The resources an individual allocates towards addressing precarity in one domain may leave fewer resources for other domains, such as when the time necessary for the treatment of an illness or disability leaves one unable to work or to work only sporadically. An individual may be well positioned in employment, such as being a partner in a law firm or a doctor in a family practice, but be overloaded in ways that undermine mental health, eliminate physical activity or leisure, or fracture family relationships. It is easy to think about the precarity caused by work, income loss or strain, but these latter examples reveal that the 'time binds' associated with having to simultaneously manage life's multiple domains create precarity as well. For other illustrations of cross-domain dynamics, particularly with regard to interactions between stressors and resources, see Spini et al, 2017.

Precarity must be understood 'the long way'

A long view of precarity means paying attention to the relevance of the past – not just the shadows of the recent past, but also the far-away past – in determining the present. 'Path dependency' processes occur when the probability of a particular event or the direction of a change in a person's life is conditioned by their longer life history (Bernardi et al, 2019). Part of that history may involve experiences with precarity that restrict future pathways.

A good example from life course research that relates to precarity is the notion of cumulative disadvantage or advantage (Dannefer, 2018); in particular, the idea that early-life socioeconomic hardship or privilege can pile up and be compounded over time. For populations, these differences may be the result of social processes that provide opportunities to some groups, and exclude or restrict opportunities to others. For individuals, adverse childhood experiences (various kinds of abuse, neglect, violence and risk) may create mental health or other problems that, in turn, result in school dropout, placement in foster care or encounters with the juvenile justice system. These, in turn, channel the life course, reinforcing certain paths and eliminating other possibilities, and creating lives of recurring precarity, albeit in new forms as individuals grow up and older.

The notion of a 'turning point' is also important for understanding precarity from a life course perspective. Turning points are experiences that change the direction of a person's life trajectory, making a distinct turn – in the case of precarity, a potentially costly downward turn. However, a turning point is not always negative; it can also signal an upward turn, which is equally important for understanding precarity. For example, military service in the Second World War allowed many men from disadvantaged backgrounds to 'knife off' (Sampson and Laub, 1996) the hardship of their Depression pasts, thereby reducing precarity in their lives and putting in place more resources and opportunities for positive outcomes (Spiro et al, 2016).

A turning point can occur for multiple reasons (Bernardi et al, 2019). It can be the result of a conscious action taken in order to (or as an attempt to) alter the pathway's direction. It can be due to an external shock, such as an economic depression or recession, that changes the conditions for gaining or maintaining individual well-being in the future. It can occur when an individual's life reaches a critical or tenuous state in which even small changes or fluctuations create uncertainty or instability that could send it in quite different directions.

People can also be at risk of precarity based on factors that remain latent until a later point. To continue with the example of military service, many veterans of the Second World War, even those who saw serious combat, were for decades able to keep the ill effects of their experiences at bay. However, as ageing taxed their physical and psychological reserves, the negative effects of earlier service, including symptoms of long-term trauma, suddenly emerged in later life (Sprio et al, 2016).

Similarly, activities that create precarity in one period of life may not be forever damning and may even serve to protect an individual from precarity later on. Continuing again with the example of military service, the intensity and duration of combat during the Second World War or the Korean War was often the source of negative psychological outcomes early in life, but it was also the source of positive psychological outcomes and evaluations later in life (Settersten et al, 2012). The growth that stemmed from trauma, to a certain point, increased veterans' capacity to adapt and be resilient in the face of ageing. One can imagine other examples where life course statuses might create conditions of precarity at an earlier point but protect individuals from precarity at a later point, and vice versa – where statuses are protective early in life but create precarity later on. For example, earlier childbirth or higher fertility might result in opportunity costs to education and work, significantly lowering social and financial capital up front but increasing options for family-based care and social support later on. In contrast, delayed childbirth and lower fertility might result in greater social and financial capital up front but shrink family-based care and support options later on.

Later life is a time of heightened precarity

Taking a long view of precarity sensitizes us to the fact that precarity can occur in all periods of life. However, there are aspects of later life that make it especially primed for precarity. These years are embodied with so much possibility, yet their potentials, if they are to be realized, depend on some 'Big Ifs' (Settersten, 2017) that cannot be predicted or controlled. These contingencies relate to health, resources and life itself: *if* we are still alive and healthy, can manage financially, can live independently, have support from children, and so on. As these contingencies come undone, so do the futures that have been counted on.

'Old age' spans multiple decades, and often encompasses earlier and later phases that are extremely different and capture the growing precarity that accompanies ageing. This is reflected in what historian Laslett (1989) called the 'third' and 'fourth' ages of life, which are sometimes conceptualized as being about age but are ultimately about functional statuses and the ideas associated with these statuses. The third age can last several decades, and is viewed as a time of opportunity and activity because most people are in good health and have fewer childcare or work responsibilities. The fourth age, in contrast, may involve encounters with illness and disability.

The transition from the third to fourth age is difficult, but not necessarily permanent, for many people. Individuals can move out of the fourth age and back into the third, for example, if debilitating conditions are cured or go into remission. Significant others, like partners or children, may also go through this transition. An interesting case study comes from German gerontologist Ines Himmelsbach (2015), who described a woman from her study whose husband was critically ill. Although this woman was initially healthy, she was also in a sort of fourth age because of her husband's condition: she was deeply entrenched in caregiving and bound to the house, and her own health and well-being was compromised in the process. When her husband died, she was able to regain her health and freedom and resume meaningful roles and social activity – moving 'backwards' (forwards, in a sense) to the third age. This possibility of reversibility is a reminder that, while empirical research often measures these phases using retirement status or age 65 for the third age, and age 80 or 85 for the fourth age, there is a danger in doing so. Age itself is not what marks movement from one phase to the next, but instead changes in one's statuses and circumstances (see also Grenier, 2012). In addition, it may be the third age rather than the fourth that captures precarity in a deep psychological sense, for it is at this point that people have growing awareness that they cannot take their health or their life for granted, and that the terms of their lives could change suddenly and drastically.

Life transitions are sources of precarity

Life transitions, even positive ones, heighten precarity because these are times when selves and social roles are in flux (Settersten and Thogmartin, 2018). Consider major adult transitions such as completing degrees or training, finding work, forming a partnership or marriage, becoming a parent, divorcing, changing jobs, retiring, or being widowed. These transitions alter social networks and supports. Their timing (the age at which they occur) or their duration are often considered key dimensions that determine how the transition is experienced or the consequences that result. From a cultural standpoint, some transitions may be socially contested or negatively sanctioned – such as cohabitation or same-sex marriage – and therefore explicitly create precarity because people are marginalized, have limited social supports, or are denied legal protections.

Life course research reveals that life transitions and trajectories have become highly individualized, suggesting that there are growing 'flexibilities' for people of every age, including those who are in their later years, to live in ways that are more congruent with their personal interests and wishes and less bound to social norms (see also Chapter 3). But these flexibilities also generate growing precarities because 'do it yourself biographies', to use Beck's (2000) phrase, are more vulnerable to breakdown. One must ask what happens over time to the mental health of individuals when there is no shared framework within which to assess themselves and others.

Later life might be characterized as a phase in which individuals are trying to *minimize* difficult transitions – and therefore minimize or postpone precarity. Indeed, popular models of 'successful' ageing (see, for example, Rowe and Kahn, 1998) see the later years as a time for maintaining stability in function, avoiding illness, remaining socially engaged and ageing 'in place' (staying in one's home and community) as long as possible. This latter point – which is ultimately about delaying entry into assisted living or nursing homes – provides an 'institutionalized' aspect to health transitions as declining health status may trigger movement into new care environments. Retirement also adds an institutional element to later life, as individuals separate from organizations or move through a succession of 'bridge jobs'. What is ultimately normative about later life – declining health, at some point, followed by death – is not generally welcomed. Life becomes more precarious. One or two key transitions – such as a major health incident or the loss of a spouse – can trigger a cascade of experiences that create precarity.

Physical and cognitive losses can threaten or undermine an individual's ability to manage transitions. That is, these losses heighten personal vulnerability. Encounters with illness and disability make planning difficult because individuals face an increasingly uncertain future. A central aspect of this experience is that people become strangers to their bodies – bodies they no longer recognize, that do not match their sense of self, and that are unpredictable and let them down (Hagestad and Settersten, 2017). It is important, however, to put the precarity of contemporary old age in historical perspective: it is much like the precariousness that earlier generations experienced as a natural part of the *whole* life span (Hagestad and Settersten, 2017). Then, illness, disability and death often came early and throughout life. In this regard, human beings are, in many places of the world, in a relatively privileged position today.

Precarity is a characteristic of environments or stems from environments

Precarity exists in the social world and social spaces, and results from the interactions between people and precarious worlds. Precarity can be addressed by social institutions and policies (as a response to precarity, offering a set of often minimal protections) or created by institutions and policies (as when there are few or no protections offered).

As individuals grow up and older, their lives join with and are challenged by changing environments: family settings, schools, communities, workplaces, generations in families and age groups in the population. There are whole bodies of literature on how these and other settings can have negative and positive effects on people, creating precarity or affecting responses to it. Two distal environments that have profound but often invisible implications for precarity are history and demography.

History

The lives of individuals and entire cohorts unfold within a slice of national and world history that leaves them with vulnerabilities and strengths. The last century was punctuated by major historical events and social change related to war, economic hardship and prosperity, health epidemics, civil rights reforms, and innovations in medicine, communication and transportation. The lives of whole populations can be altered amid large-scale changes in political administrations (think of the discord and disruption associated with voter approval of Britain's exit from the European Union or the election of Donald Trump as US president), recessions and depressions, wars, or events like 9/11. Lives are swept up in changes that are not desired or expected. What people took for granted is suddenly in question, rupturing how they understand and see the world and marking their lives in before-and-after terms. These events and changes may therefore be 'hidden variables' (Spiro et al, 2016) that exist beneath the knowledge base on ageing, thereby shaping the precarity that people may experience or feel as they grow older.

It is not just one's own cohort that lurks as a force in their life; other cohorts affect them too. Cohort influences might be especially felt through intergenerational family relationships. For example, consciously or not, individuals have been shaped by the historical influences that affected their parents or grandparents, who transmitted values and expectations based on earlier times and places. Generational mentalities carry the imprint of depressions and recessions, wars, epidemics and pandemics, food insecurity, educational opportunities, gender ideologies, racism, and other factors. Differences in basic worldviews across generations – including ideas about what is 'normal' for or to be expected of men and women in different periods of life – are the source of friction in family relationships.

Demography

With respect to demography, the 'first demographic transition' (see, for instance, Kirk, 1996) from the 18th century onwards made lives longer and more predictable. Little more than a century ago, the possibility of death lurked in all periods of life. Today, in ageing societies, death occurs largely in old age. This 'revolution' *reduced* precarity in life. And yet, this process has brought about a new kind of precarity: the denial of finitude (Hagestad and Settersten, 2017). That is, longevity has created a sense that people do not die. We have more distance from death because we have fewer social experiences with it, often not until well into adulthood, and even then, it may catch us off guard and unprepared. Because relationships have the potential to be long lasting, losses are felt more acutely. In some places, such as the United States, the denial of death is a pervasive cultural phenomenon. There are also recent alarming signs of a reversal in life expectancy in the United States, reflecting increases in injuries, suicides and Alzheimer's disease, as well as drug and alcohol abuse, many of which are taken to be dire signs of widespread despair (Kochanek et al, 2017; Woolf and Aron, 2018).

Although the gap in the length of men's and women's lives has begun to close, mortality at every age is higher for males and the sex ratio naturally declines with age (Howden and Meyer, 2011). To be very old, then, continues more often to be a female experience. The longstanding sex differential in mortality affects individual ageing through the composition of social networks and the presence of a spouse. For example, women more often experience widowhood, not only because men die earlier but because women tend to marry older men. The naturally declining sex ratio, which shifts significantly in the 70s and sharply in the 80s, means that the social worlds of older people, as well as care institutions, are heavily populated with women. As a result of demographic change, women's social 'convoys' (Kahn and Antonucci, 1980) are more characterized by co-longevity and relationships of long duration than is the case for men. This gives women more potential sources of support in later life and more 'co-biographers' throughout life, to use Bertaux's (1981) term.

What is known as the 'epidemiological transition' (see, for example, Omran, 2005) has also affected precarity, as causes of death shifted from infectious disease to lifestyle-related illnesses. This has created distinct themes of precarity for older men and women. That is, men more often die with little or no warning from an acute illness, whereas women more often live for many years with chronic illnesses (Hagestad and Settersten, 2017).

The 'second demographic revolution' (for instance, see Lesthaeghe, 2014), from the 1970s onwards, has also created new kinds of precarity for many groups of people: sub-replacement fertility, a multitude of living arrangements other than marriage, a disconnection between marriage and procreation, and within-country geographic mobility and selective migration from origin to destination countries. These bring important implications for precarity and ageing, in that the family relationships of older people may have become, and continue to become, more fragile or unavailable, or more inactive, because family members have uncertain relationships or are at greater distance from one another.

Precarity is rooted in social dynamics related to gender, social class and inequality

Because life course experiences are heavily gendered, so too is precarity. This chapter has described some of the ways that demography interacts with gender to create different worlds of precarity for ageing women and men. There are other important trends to highlight as well.

Men and women attach different social meanings to age and ageing, use different guidelines to measure the progress of their lives, and are subject to different expectations and evaluations (Settersten and Hagestad, 2015). These differences create unique precarity for men and women. For example, there are strong and persistent cultural differences in the valuation of ageing bodies, including the 'double standard' of ageing in which the physical signs of ageing often accentuate a man's social capital but for women take it away (Bell, 1970; Sontag, 1972). This creates precarity for women because it results in harsher self and social judgements, and undermines their well-being. Although the double standard disadvantages women, ageing can also bring a loss of male attractiveness, because of the cultural premium on youthfulness. Physical frailty may be harder for men, because they place a premium on strength and independence.

One cannot help but wonder whether women's lifelong experiences in more diverse and multiple roles might make it easier for them to adjust to change and manage the precarity that comes with ageing. Although women's earlier investments in family life often take tolls on their careers and economic well-being, these investments may bring social dividends to women in later life, as they are more likely than men to be embedded in larger and supportive networks. In younger generations, the 'new father' who is more invested in fathering may not only improve the well-being of his children. New fathers may also become new kinds of older men: men who are more socially integrated and have deeper connections to children, family and community. These relationships may in the future offer greater protection to men in later life.

For subpopulations of men today, however, some fathers are not intensely involved with or committed to their children. Divorce is particularly important to understand because it often leads to a loss or restriction of fathers' ties to children. It is similarly important to understand the risks that come to childless men. Children have traditionally been key to integrating men into social networks, and fatherhood is a gateway to psychological growth and identity development (Settersten et al, 2014). For these men, absent or detached relations may increase their precarity as they grow older.

Later life itself offers novel powers and possibilities for men's relationships. Aged men seem to begin to care less about the judgements of other men and about masculinity and manhood, and are more able to reclaim their more feminine sides, becoming more nurturing and emotionally expressive (see, for example, the classic work of Gutmann, 1987). These shifts bring greater freedom and time for men to be present in relationships. Cohorts of young adult men today also have more fluid attitudes about masculinity and femininity. Together, these may in the future reduce precarity in the lives of older men.

Trends in women's educational attainment, employment and earnings suggest that women's lives are converging with and in some cases surpassing those of men, despite the fact that in other dimensions, such as economic standing, their aggregate status remains lower. To date, women's family relationships have been more active and positive, and have offered greater protection, than those of men. It is possible, however, that women's greater educational attainment and increased commitment to work will over time risk some of the family protections they have traditionally known. Regardless, future cohorts of older women will be different from past cohorts because of their educational, work and family experiences. There is much to learn about whether older women in the future will face new kinds of precarity as a result.

There are many signals that men are facing new vulnerabilities in employment, education and other arenas. For example, in young adulthood, like other life periods, many of the crisis stories are often about men: dropping out of high school and college, unemployment, disconnectedness (not in school, work or the military), suicide, alcohol and substance abuse, high-risk sexual behaviour, homicide, non-sexual assault, anger and emotion regulation, and imprisonment (Settersten, 2015b). Because young men's precarity is so high, it is important to monitor their precarity as they grow older. This is not to say that young women are not vulnerable. For example, young women are at risk for depression, sexual assault and intimate partner violence, and eating disorders, among other things. It is instead to say that the task of reducing precarity in the life course is reducing the negative impact of a gendered life course on both men and women. This can occur through improving opportunities and outcomes for women, as well as for many subgroups of men whose disadvantage and vulnerability spills over and creates precarity for women and children.

It is important, however, not to overly homogenize 'men' and 'women', as many of the trends discussed in this chapter differ dramatically for particular subgroups – especially by social class and by race or ethnicity. An exploration of precarity must probe how the differential attainments and experiences of these subgroups earlier in life will leave individuals in different financial, social and psychological standing in the later years. Social class has powerful effects on the life course and ageing, creating significant 'cleavages' within societies, to use Martin Kohli's (2015) term. Consistent with an 'intersectional' approach, inequalities generated by social class are often amplified or manifested differently for people based on inequalities related to gender, race and ethnicity.

Unlike during the 'generational equity' debate that surfaced a few decades ago, which attempted to pit children and older people against one another in a struggle for public resources (see Quadagno, 1989), it seems more likely that subgroups of older people will have greater competing needs – especially across wealth and health categories. The most vulnerable of older people not only have fewer choices; they have fewer capacities and resources to draw on as they make those choices, further exacerbating their vulnerabilities. These and other divisions will make the life course and ageing even greater sources of political regulation and conflict, and of public controversy and struggle (see further Chapter 10; also Kohli, 2015).

Precarity is exacerbated by neoliberal emphases on 'choice' and 'responsibility'

Welfare states are important in understanding precarity because, in providing different packages of resources, they create stronger or weaker scaffolding as individuals move through life's final decades. The ethos of liberal market welfare state regimes, like the United States, underscores the notion that life outcomes are personal choices and responsibilities. That is, beyond basic protections provided by old-age policies, the later years are to be managed using whatever resources a person has or can marshal for their own well-being. This is especially true of the vast space between childhood and old age, when there are limited and temporary supports – such as unemployment and its consequences for finances or health insurance. The neoliberal emphasis on personal responsibility seems likely only to grow as public resources dwindle and are in question economically and politically (see Chapter 10).

Gerontologists and ageing advocacy organizations have, ironically, contributed to the potential precarity of the later years by reinforcing the perspective that individuals are personally responsible for their ageing outcomes. In particular, these groups have been prophets of 'productive,' 'active' and 'successful' ageing. This is exemplified by current talk of the need to 'disrupt ageing' through personal choices, a view promoted by the CEO of AARP (Jenkins, 2016) and endorsed by the Gerontological Society of America. This sentiment also undergirds the commercial 'anti-ageing' industry (Flatt et al, 2013).

These perspectives are often well intended, in that they hope to promote health and healthy behaviours. But they are problematic because they suggest that precarity in the domain of health can largely be avoided and need not exist at all – if only individuals made the right choices. People *do* make choices and engage in behaviour that can help or hurt them, which is consistent with the significance of human 'agency' as a concept in life course research (for example, see Hitlin and Kwon, 2016). These messages about positive ageing can, however, be damning because they deny the natural and real dark sides of ageing – not only normative physical and cognitive declines that are difficult for most people, but also serious or debilitating conditions. These dark sides must be acknowledged if individuals, families and whole societies are to prepare for and better manage them. The precarity people face may be heightened if individuals inappropriately blame themselves for things that are not their fault or in their control.

Precarity is interpersonal

A life course perspective reveals that intimate social relationships, especially family relationships, are often the key places where precarity is felt, expressed and given meaning. For this reason, families are primary spaces in which precarity can be spread or transmitted to others. Following this line of thinking, most 'personal' experiences of precarity are therefore actually *interpersonal*. Indeed, one's well-being across the many decades of adult life is inextricably dependent on the choices, behaviours and resources of others, and, by the same token, the welfare of others is inextricably dependent on one's own (see, for instance, Settersten, 2015a; 2018). Relationships significantly constrain life, but they also bring life much of its meaning. The later years are no exception.

This reality of interdependence – what Elder (1994) called 'linked lives' – stands in direct contrast to one of the most cherished cultural values in the United States and many other places: independence. Ageing enters this dynamic because it threatens independence. There is a mistaken assumption on the part of the public and government that once people have reached adulthood, they are fully independent until later life, when failing health may make it necessary to depend on others. Relying on care from others is at times even described as a 'burden' because it violates this cultural value (see also Chapter 8).

The reality, however, is that most of the resources and supports for managing life's changes come from families. When families have limited resources and supports to offer one another, the precarity that people face is accentuated. How precarity is experienced in one generation can spill over into others, and what happens in one generation affects the flow of time, money and effort to other generations. If individuals have supportive, reliable and resourced relationships, interdependence can provide stability and continuity in later life. We are not only at the 'will of our bodies', to adapt Frank's (1991) phrase, but also at the will of other people, whose functioning and availability condition the support we might receive. It is also important not to limit considerations of interdependence to the here and now, but to appreciate the impact that ideas of reciprocity may have across long periods with regard to the precariousness of ageing: you helped me out 50 years ago, so now it is my turn; or, I helped you out 50 years ago, so now it is your turn (Hagestad and Settersten, 2017).

Earlier this chapter gave examples from epigenetics that reveal how an individual's precarity can be influenced by the experiences of generations before them. In addition, it is important not to have overly romanticized notions of what families do: many of the risks that people carry, and the negative things they experience, may stem from family relationships that have been absent, neglectful or abusive. Precarity can also stem from 'unlinked lives' (Settersten, 2015a) and the things that are lost or gained as relationships come to an end or are severed. These things are not just about what parents do to minor children and youth and the legacies of these experiences for later precarity. They are about how earlier absence, neglect and abuse can continue or emerge anew in people's later years. Indeed, it is circumstances like these, or when a person is *not* embedded in a supportive fabric of interdependent lives, that produce what Hagestad and Settersten (2017, p 143) call the 'most naked forms of precariousness'.

The characteristics of individuals create precarity or affect responses to it

The increased variability and freedom in the life course, described earlier, has also resulted in precarity. When one's life is their own to make, for better or for worse, personal characteristics become increasingly important for fostering positive outcomes and managing precarity. These more psychological or social-psychological capacities of individuals include:

- *Fluid self-definitions*: development during later life, as in earlier life periods, may be facilitated by being open and committed to cultivating multiple selves. The later years would seem to offer opportunities for individuals to reclaim selves they left behind or to try on selves they have longed to explore. Fluid and dynamic self-definitions may foster adaptation during a precarious period of life.
- The ability to *plan for and set realistic goals* – but also to be flexible and open to new and unexpected experiences. This includes knowing when to disengage or relinquish a goal that is not attainable and when to make accommodations.
- *Reflective capacity and self-regulation*: possessing self-awareness and the ability to take others into account, and to control and adjust emotions and behaviour accordingly.
- *Moderate risk-taking*: having too strong a propensity towards risky decision-making and behaviour might more often create precarity, but being too risk-averse might leave individuals trapped in precarity and unable to alter their life circumstances. People are often irrational and unpredictable. The dwindling and uncertain

time horizon that comes with ageing is also likely to affect decisions and behaviours, in some cases increasing caution (such as wanting to use one's remaining time carefully) and in other cases decreasing it (such as wanting to live more freely and worry less).
- *Self-efficacy*: being able to manage disappointment and be persistent when confronted with setbacks, foreclosed opportunities or failures.
- *Comfort with ambiguity*: because being in a precarious state inherently means that one is in a period of flux or risk, and without a clear pathway or timetable to resolution or restoration.
- The *capacity for intimacy and close social relationships*: to make and maintain healthy, supportive relationships with others.
- The *capacity for inter-group relationships*: to be able to understand and relate to various social, political and cultural groups in a diverse society and world.

Some argue that characteristics like these are inherent in individuals, but there is good evidence to show that many can be modelled and cultivated. Not having these characteristics would seem to create precarity or make precarity more difficult to manage, just as being in precarious states might affect an individual's ability to acquire or activate these characteristics. As noted earlier, these types of skills can also grow out of difficult, even traumatic, experiences.

Precarity involves processes that occur in the mind

Precarity is not just about a process or status that is an 'objective reality' that can be seen or described from the outside. It is something that is 'subjectively' experienced by the person or people going through it. Understanding the subjective realm is important because it is not always what happens to individuals per se that matters, but instead how individuals interpret and respond to those experiences. This idea is persistent in literature on stressful or traumatic life experiences. Drawing again on the example of combat during the Second World War, veterans' recollections (or reconstructions) of their military experiences over their lives proved to be more important than their actual experiences in predicting their later-life health and well-being (Settersten et al, 2012; 2018).

Perceptions are therefore an important piece in the puzzle of precarity: the extent to which people recognize their precarity, how they understand or explain it, and what they anticipate its possible outcomes to be will influence its effects. On the one hand, as the philosopher Seneca once noted, individuals may 'suffer more often in imagination than in reality'. On the other hand, individuals may face precarity and not be conscious of or fully comprehend the gravity of their circumstances. In addition, individuals may fail to see how their precarity is fuelled by factors that lie outside of them, or to recognize that the circumstances of their lives are not unique to them but are instead shared with many other people – what Mills (1959) called the need for a 'sociological imagination'. Some precarity is also invisible from the outside: for example, the personal hardships of members of marginalized or stigmatized groups may not be shared with others for fear of social or legal repercussions, as might occur in the case of immigrants without documentation or LGBTQ+ families.

Any treatment of precarity as a subjective state thus requires attention to *anticipation*. The failing health and death of parents and loved ones, and even of oneself, are good examples. Historical declines in morbidity and mortality have made major illnesses and death more predictable in that they are now largely confined to later life, as noted earlier. We cannot know, however, exactly how long we and others will live or have good health, and we probably overestimate it. Still, our or their ages may prompt us to think in more conscious ways about the time left, which may lead to a change in behaviour or perspective now. As Neugarten (1968) noted 50 years ago, a growing 'awareness of middle age' for individuals between the ages of 40 and 60 brings a cognitive shift, as people start thinking in terms of *time left to live* rather than *time since birth*. This, too, can create a sense of precarity as time horizons dwindle.

Many life experiences are influenced by cultural ideas and regulated by social expectations about what is to happen in life's different phases. These contribute to what sociologists call 'anticipatory socialization': they convey a sense of what lies ahead, even many years into the future, and provide a chance for people to get ready. In later life, these changes might include retiring, encountering illness and disability, needing to provide care to or receive it from others, being widowed, or preparing to die.

Many normative experiences are so valued and desired that not being able to achieve them, for whatever reason, can make their loss difficult and create precarity – such as an inability to find a life partner or have children. Actively rejecting these statuses can leave individuals feeling marginalized or ostracized. When social scripts are strong, people are aware of their departure from them and others recognize it too. Support groups, for example, are often designed for people who find themselves in non-normative circumstances, and are meant to buffer the resulting precarity that individuals experience or feel.

Earlier I suggested that precarity must be understood in relation to the 'shadow of the past'. So too must it be understood in relation to the 'shadow of the future' (Bernardi et al, 2019). The predictability of a long-time horizon, at least in many countries today, has made planning more possible, and human beings have an inherent need for predictability. The obsession with planning in the Western world can be seen in the fact that each period of life brings some preoccupation with what might happen in the next. For example, mid-career employees are focused on retirement and health care planning; retirees may be focused on estate planning and funeral planning.

Planning would seem to both diminish and heighten precarity: when one faces or feels precarity, it is difficult, if not impossible, to plan; and when one cannot plan, one feels precarity. Planning may help offset the likelihood that individuals will find themselves in precarious circumstances, or help manage their response to it; and yet, planning too rigidly may create precarity when things do not unfold as anticipated.

Conclusion

Precarity is at the heart of human experience and, as such, is universal. In every period of life, all people face some minimal types and levels of precarity simply in being alive and in having to navigate an ever-changing world. At the same time, precarity is particularistic: some kinds of precarity, and experiences associated with it, may be unique in different periods of life, and some people and groups clearly have more of it, or more serious types, than others. As outlined throughout this chapter, these differences can be the result of social processes that reinforce or reproduce it. This chapter has generated a number of lessons for understanding precarity from a life course perspective:

- precarity occurs across multiple, often interacting, 'levels';
- precarity occurs in multiple, often interacting, domains;
- precarity must be understood 'the long way';
- later life is a time of heightened precarity;
- life transitions are sources of precarity;
- precarity is a characteristic of environments or stems from environments;
- precarity is rooted in social dynamics related to gender, social class and other sources of inequality;
- precarity is exacerbated by neoliberal emphases on 'choice' and 'responsibility';
- precarity is interpersonal;

- the characteristics of individuals create precarity or affect responses to it;
- precarity involves processes that occur in the mind;
- precarity is part of the human condition – and therefore universal.

These lessons demand an examination of the precursors and consequences of precarity; precarity as independent, mediating and dependent variables; and precarity as point-in-time states versus longer processes that involve lead up, adjustment and recovery. They emphasize that precarity brings both short- and long-term effects, and that effects can, surprisingly, sometimes be positive as well as negative. They show that precarity is not only the result of an individual's active choices, but often the result of 'choices' that are created for or forced upon them. Actions in earlier periods of life are often aimed at minimizing or eliminating potential precarity in subsequent periods, just as actions in later periods are often about minimizing or eliminating the effects of earlier precarity. These lessons reveal that precarity is felt, expressed and given meaning in relationships with others, especially in the family context. Precarity is also something experienced by whole groups, and something around which people can find solidarity and take collective action.

Acknowledgements

The topics of several sections of this chapter evolved from Settersten (2015a; 2017; 2018) and Settersten and Thogmartin (2018), which are cited in the References, were published by Taylor & Francis or Oxford University Press, and are extended here to the concept of precarity. I also wish to thank a few special others who, through collaboration and publications cited here, have provided a foundation from which to develop some of these reflections: Laura Bernardi, Johannes Huinink and Gunhild Hagestad.

References

Barker, D.J. (1998) 'In utero programming of chronic disease', *Clinical Science*, 95(2): 115–28.

Beck, U. (2000) 'Living your own life in a runaway world: individualization, globalization, and politics', in W. Hutton and A. Giddens (eds) *Global Capitalism*, New York: The New Press, pp 164–74.

Bell, I.P. (1970) 'The double standard', *Trans-action*, 8(1/2): 75–80.

Bernardi, L., Huinink, J. and Settersten, R.A., Jr (2019) 'The life course cube: a tool for studying lives', *Advances in Life Course Research*, advance online publication, available from: https://doi.org/10.1016/j.alcr.2018.11.004 [Accessed 13 August 2019].

Bertaux, D. (ed.) (1981) *Biography and Society: the Life History Approach in the Social Sciences*, Beverly Hills, Sage.

Dannefer, D. (2018) 'Systemic and reflexive: foundations of cumulative dis/advantage and life-course processes', *Journals of Gerontology Series B: Psychological Sciences & Social Sciences*, advance online publication, available from: https://doi.org/10.1093/geronb/gby118 [Accessed 13 August 2019].

Dannefer, W.D. and Settersten, R.A., Jr (2010) 'The study of the life course: implications for social gerontology', in W.D. Dannefer and C. Phillipson (eds) *International Handbook of Social Gerontology*, London: Sage, pp 3–19.

Elder, G.H., Jr (1994) 'Time, agency, and social change: perspectives on the life course', *Social Psychology Quarterly*, 57(1): 4–15.

Flatt, M.A., Settersten, R.A., Jr, Ponsaran, R. and Fishman, J.R. (2013) 'Are "anti-ageing medicine" and "successful ageing" two sides of the same coin? Views of anti-ageing practitioners', *Journals of Gerontology Series B: Psychological Sciences & Social Sciences*, 68(6): 944–55.

Frank, A.W. (1991) *At the Will of the Body: Reflections on Illness*, Boston: Houghton Mifflin.

Grenier, A. (2012) *Transitions and the Lifecourse: Challenging the Constructions of 'Growing Old'*, Bristol: Policy Press.

Gutmann, D. (1987) *Reclaimed Powers: Toward a New Psychology of Men and Women in Later Life*, New York: Basic Books.

Hagestad, G.O. and Settersten, R.A., Jr (2017) 'Ageing: it's interpersonal! Reflections from two life course migrants', *The Gerontologist*, 57(1): 136–44.

Hanson, M.A. and Skinner, M.K. (2016) 'Developmental origins of epigenetic transgenerational inheritance', *Environmental Epigenetics*, 2(1): 1–9.

Heindel, J.J. and Vandenberg, L.N. (2015) 'Developmental origins of health and disease: a paradigm for understanding disease cause and prevention', *Current Opinion in Pediatrics*, 27(2): 248–53.

Himmelsbach, I. (2015) 'Transitions of health and (in)dependent living', *Transitions in the Life Course Conference*, Goethe University, 27 April, Frankfurt.

Hitlin, S. and Kwon, H.W. (2016) 'Agency across the life course', in M.J. Shanahan, J.T. Mortimer and M.K. Johnson (eds) *Handbook of the Life Course: Vol. 2*, New York: Springer, pp 431–49.

Howden, L.M. and Meyer, J.A. (2011) *Age and Sex Composition: 2010 U.S. Census Briefs (C2010BR-03)*, Washington, DC: US Census Bureau.

Hurley, D. (2015) 'Grandma's experiences leave a mark on your genes', *Discover* [online], June 25, available from: http://discovermagazine.com/2013/may/13-grandmas-experiences-leave-epigenetic-mark-on-your-genes [Accessed 9 August 2019].

Jenkins, J.A. (2016) *Disrupt Aging: A Bold New Path to Living Your Best Life at Every Age*, New York: PublicAffairs.

Kahn, R.L. and Antonucci, T. (1980) 'Convoys over the life course: attachment, roles, and social support', in P.B. Baltes and O.G. Brim (eds) *Life-Span Development and Behaviour: Vol. 3*, New York: Academic Press, pp 254–83.

Kirk, D. (1996) 'Demographic transition theory', *Population Studies*, 50(3): 361–87.

Kochanek, K.D., Murphy, S.L., Xu, J.Q. and Arias, E. (2017) *NCHS Data Brief Number 293: Mortality in the United States, 2016*, Hyattsville, MD: National Center for Health Statistics [online], available from: https://www.cdc.gov/nchs/products/databriefs/db293.htm [Accessed 13 August 2019].

Kohli, M. (2015) 'Cleavages in ageing societies: generation, age, or class?', in M. Bernd (ed) *The Future of Welfare in a Global Europe*, Vienna: Ashgate, pp 327–51.

Laslett, P. (1989) *A Fresh Map of Life: The Emergence of the Third Age*, London: Weidenfeld and Nicolson.

Lesthaeghe, R. (2014) 'The second demographic transition: a concise overview of its development', *Proceedings of the National Academy of Sciences of the United States of America*, 111(51): 18112–15.

Mills, C.W. (1959) *The Sociological Imagination*, New York: Oxford University Press.

Neugarten, B.L. (1968) 'The awareness of middle age', in B.L. Neugarten (ed) *Middle Age and Ageing: A Reader in Social Psychology*, Chicago: University of Chicago Press, pp 93–98.

Omran, A.R. (2005) 'The epidemiologic transition: a theory of the epidemiology of population change', *Milbank Quarterly*, 83(4): 731–57.

Quadagno, J. (1989) 'Generational equity and the politics of the welfare state', *Politics and Society*, 17(3): 353–76.

Rowe, J.W. and Kahn, R.L. (1998) *Successful Ageing*, New York: Dell.

Sampson, R.J. and Laub, J.H. (1996) 'Socioeconomic achievement in the life course of disadvantaged men: military service as a turning point, circa 1940–1965', *American Sociological Review*, 61(3): 347–67.

Settersten, R.A., Jr (2015a) 'Relationships in time and the life course: the significance of linked lives', *Research in Human Development*, 12(3/4): 217–23.

Settersten, R.A., Jr (2015b) 'The new landscape of early adulthood: implications for broad-access higher education', in M.L. Stevens and M. Kirst (eds) *Remaking College: Broad-Access Higher Education for a New Era*, Palo Alto, CA: Stanford University Press, pp 113–33.

Settersten, R.A., Jr (2017) 'Some things I have learned about aging by studying the life course', *Innovation in Aging*, 1(2): 1–7.

Settersten, R.A., Jr (2018) 'Nine ways that social relationships matter for the life course', in D.F. Alwin, D.H. Felmlee and D.A. Kreager (eds) *Social Networks and the Life Course: Integrating the Development of Human Lives and Social Relational Networks*, New York: Springer, pp 27–40.

Settersten, R.A., Jr and Hagestad, G.O. (2015) 'Subjective ageing and new complexities of the life course', *Annual Review of Gerontology and Geriatrics*, 35(1): 29–53.

Settersten, R.A., Jr and Thogmartin, A. (2018) 'Flux: insights into the social aspects of life transitions', *Research in Human Development*, 15(3/4): 360–73.

Settersten, R.A., Jr, Day, J., Elder, G.H., Jr and Waldinger, R.J. (2012) 'Men's appraisals of their military experiences in World War II: a 40-year perspective', *Research in Human Development*, 9(3): 248–71.

Settersten, R.A., Jr, Day, J.K., Cancel-Tirado, D. and Driscoll, D.M. (2014) 'Fathers' accounts of struggle and growth in early adulthood: an exploratory study of disadvantaged men', *New Directions for Child and Adolescent Development*, 2014(143): 73–89.

Settersten, R.A., Jr, Recksiedler, C., Godlewski, B. and Elder, G.H., Jr (2018) 'Two faces of wartime experience: veterans' appraisals and collective memories in later life', in A. Spiro, R.A. Settersten, Jr. and C.M. Aldwin (eds) *Long-Term Outcomes of Military Service: the Health and Well-Being of Aging Veterans*, Washington, DC: American Psychological Association Press, pp 19–36.

Sontag, S. (1972) 'The double standard of ageing', *Saturday Review*, 23 September, pp 29–38.

Spini, D., Bernardi, L. and Oris, M. (2017) 'Toward a life course framework for studying vulnerability', *Research in Human Development*, 14(1): 5–25.

Spiro, A., III, Settersten, R.A., Jr and Aldwin, C.M. (2016) 'Long-term outcomes of military service in aging and the life course: a positive re-envisioning', *The Gerontologist*, 56(1): 5–13.

Woolf, S.H. and Aron, L. (2018) 'Failing health of the United States', *BMJ*, 360: k496.

3

Precarious life, human development and the life course: critical intersections

Stephen Katz

Introduction

In this chapter, I explore human development and the life course as precarious forms of life. The first part reviews the literature on precarity to draw out some of the critical and ethical issues related to ageing populations. The second part follows with an examination of how figures of the obese child, unstable adolescent, despairing mid-lifer and cognitively impaired older adult are examples of crisis-laden personifications of social problems. The two parts are connected through an approach similar to what Imogen Tyler (2008, p 18) calls a 'figurative methodology', whereby 'social classifications' are generated by 'representational struggles' that in turn are 'played out in highly condensed figurative forms':

> A figurative methodology makes it possible to describe – zoom in on – appearances of a figure within specific media and contexts, whilst also insisting that it is through the repetition of a figure across different media that specific figures acquire accreted form and accrue affective value in ways that have significant social and political impact. (Tyler, 2008, p 19)

While these figurative forms for Tyler are British class-making identities, here they are age-making ones. Rather than adhering to any one biological, psychological or gerontological model, my perspective on human development and the life course focuses on their discursive and interchangeable meanings in the social sphere, where the human sciences, public health politics and cultural narratives about ageing have converged.

The chapter's conclusions consider and compare resilience and resistance as two responses to life course precarity. Resilience, in ageing research and associated professional practices, typically refers to the natural capacity of individuals, families and communities to cope with and *bounce back* from adversity. As such, resilience offers a corrective to passive and pathologizing stereotypes of older adults as deficient in adaptability, agency and resourcefulness. However, this meaning also implies that any failure to manage vulnerability, frailty, disability and dependency is because of a lack of personal resilience rather than the social determinants of liveability. In this way the resilience literature reiterates the *successful and healthy ageing* models it claims to supersede. My conclusions advocate a second response, however, which is to refuse to be the subjects we have become, to pursue alternative paths that contest dominant global life course hierarchies and their fashioning of age identities through crisis, precarity and resilience, and to imagine new strategies for radical and non-precarious life course trajectories into the future. Here and throughout the chapter I am inspired by the ideas of Michel Foucault and his followers on the relation between power and knowledge and the governing of bodily and populational life.

Critical trends in precarity thinking

Political, economic and environmental commentators increasingly use the terms 'precarious', 'precariousness' and 'precarity' to identify the growing conditions of instability, risk and dislocation that are affecting human communities around the world, contributing to a popular literature on the unpredictable and uncontrollable forces of *uncertainty*, such as natural disasters, economic volatility, climate change and global terrorism. However, more critical writers have captured such conditions with expressions such as 'liquid times' (Bauman, 2007), 'the risk society' (Beck, 1992), 'the precariat' (Standing, 2011) and 'geontopower' (Povinelli, 2016),[1] and explain the upsurge in global precarity as a consequence of capitalist predatory economies and the deregulating tendencies of neoliberal governance, especially since the 1990s. Saskia Sassen (2014) and Elizabeth Povinelli (2011) go further in their work on global precarity to bring into relief the alarming scope of human suffering and destruction of living environments.

For Sassen (2014), the 'subterranean' hyper-profiting trends of global financial power operate beneath and around nations, economies and trade zones, and manifest in areas such as refugee camps and urban slums and through punishing debt and austerity programmes imposed on struggling countries. These trends, disregarded by conventional economists and planners, drive the expulsions of people from their homes, resources and social belongings. Meanwhile, the flow of wealth from poor to rich grows unconscionably, with a 60 per cent growth in the wealth of the 1 per cent at the top globally from the 1980s into the 2000s (Sassen, 2014, p 13). In Sassen's analysis, these developments are materialized in the tearing apart of local economies and sustainable communities. For example, in the United States an estimated 9.3 million home foreclosure evictions between 2005 and 2010 (Sassen, 2014, p 127) created an uprooted population whose assets were exhausted rather than protected, yet who seemed, like other vulnerable and expelled populations, to disappear and 'become invisible to formal measurements' (Sassen, 2014, p 37).

Povinelli's (2011) radical conceptualization of 'abandonment' complements Sassen's work by addressing the survival of expelled peoples. For Povinelli (2011, p 22), the neoliberal and postcolonial devaluation of 'any form of life that is not organized on the basis of market values' means that expelled and abandoned people are penalized for being 'a potential security risk' and deserving of being 'actively attacked and rooted out of the state and national psyche'. Destined for abandonment, devalued lives are also denied a future or inclusion in the future, and are forced to live in a different social tense. Povinelli's case study is Australian Aboriginal communities abandoned to precarious life – not out of choice, but because 'they were born at the far end of liberal capitalism's exhaust system'. Thus, they live in the 'seams' and 'gray economy' of big finance capital, where precarious life is parsed into daily and trivial non-events that normalize risk and insecurity (Povinelli, 2011, p 129).

The menace of expulsion and abandonment are but two examples of the precarity wrought by the runaway capitalization of life and dismantling of welfare states. These are problems that affect ageing populations most directly through the corporate control of pension provisions, rising property costs and residential dislocation, privatized care and medical systems, labour uncertainty and anti-unionism, and forced migration of families and fragmentation of their traditional bonds of support. In his writing on these and other global issues of ageing, Chris Phillipson enumerates how capital strategies have not only skewed the needs of ageing populations as unaffordable, but also deliberately limited their public tax-based support in favour of private markets that profit from abdicating responsibility for older people (Phillipson, 2009; 2010; 2013). As a result, few political organizations are able or willing to work on behalf of older people and challenge the deleterious effects of global capital on their lives (Estes and Wallace, 2010, p 516).

The work of Sassen, Povinelli, Phillipson and others produces a diagram of precarity that draws together the various subterranean chains of economic exploitation and deprivation that engulf human (and non-human) populations and endanger their survival and prospects for longevity. However, this diagram is vague about the precarity of life itself and the intrinsic nature of human suffering, both central issues of caregiving for older people. Here Judith Butler (2004; 2016) has been at the forefront of a philosophical inquiry that asserts 'precariousness' as 'part of living' because 'it implies dependency on others and social supports to make life liveable and sustainable' (Butler, 2016, p 14). If life is naturally precarious, the problem to be resolved is that the distribution of precariousness must also be equitable, reciprocal and life-affirming. Put another way, if all lives are to be recognized as worthwhile, then the precariousness within them must also be recognized and supported, rather than exploited and excluded. Butler's arguments offer to ageing research a shift in perspective about fragility, dependency and impairment, one that acknowledges these conditions as probable for all of us throughout the life course, rather than reducing them to the *expected* medical outcomes of ageing decline. Thus, it is our cultural reaction and shunning of precarity, as well suffering in general in old age (Gilleard, 2018), that has isolated older people as 'other' and justified their exclusion from social participation.

The position advocated by Butler is a positive one for changing our ageing society, because if precarity and vulnerability are understood to be interdependently shared at the core of human sociality, then the politics of recognition, ethics of inclusion and practices of care can flow more compassionately and equitably (see also Chapter 8). As Grenier et al (2017a) argue in their adaptation of Butler's work, the connective tissue of precarity across all ages creates a relational model that could alter care practices and the terms by which we (de)value people with dementia in particular. Furthermore, 'the social and political conditions which shape a devaluing of subjects by means of their physical or cognitive impairments, can serve to reinforce precarity, and deflect attention from the disadvantages that accumulate and affect late life' (Grenier et al, 2017a, p 325). Butler also differentiates precarity from precariousness, with the former term designating 'that politically induced condition in which certain populations suffer from failing social and economic networks of support and become differentially exposed to injury, violence, and death' (Butler, 2016, p 25). Together, precariousness and precarity can foster solidarity among groups opposing the state, an argument borne out in Lorey's (2017) insightful work on a Spanish collective care community and its resistance to a governmental regime that rules through insecurity and precarity.

However, the problem with Butler's perspective is that precariousness and precarity blur together through an undergirding of precarious life as a universalizing ontological condition. While for Butler, this conceptual strategy is justified in order to advocate an ethical and relational model of precarity, the question of how life itself becomes precarious, outside of the politics and discourses that frame it as such, remains open and important to address given this chapter's constructive approach to the life course. Based on this argument, Michel Foucault's work on the government of life provides an important response because of his claim that biological life, as we have come to know both it and ourselves through it, is a modern phenomenon.

In his writing on the 'art' of government or governmentality (1991) and the 'bio-politics of the population' (1980), Foucault delineates how, during the 18th and 19th centuries, Western states grew powerful through their control over the health, security and productivity of their populations. Using governmental data-collecting technologies such as statistics, surveys, health records, settlement maps and population censuses, state bureaucracies brought human existence into the political field.[2] Nikolas Rose (1990), drawing on Foucault, in his inventive study of British social psychology, explains that 'with the entry of the population into political thought, rule takes as its object such phenomena as the numbers of subjects, their ages, their longevity, their sicknesses and types of death, their habits and vices, their rates of reproduction.' Hence 'the birth and history of the knowledges of subjectivity and intersubjectivity are intrinsically bound up with programmes which, in order to govern subjects, have found that they need to know them' (Rose, 1990, p 5). While text-craft provided state-craft with the means to render living populations into knowable, manageable and governable subjects, the genres and styles of governmental text-craft also found their way into what Foucault calls 'non-obvious' documents, such as training manuals, urban laws, education guides and codes of conduct (Foucault, 1977). The influence of 'non-obvious' and factually ordinary texts and documents is a feature of modern expertise in general, and in ageing studies is found in medical atlases, health inventories, policy reports and *state-of-the-art* research texts, as well as popular advice and lifestyle media (see Katz, 2000; Pickard, 2016).

This part of the chapter has reviewed critical ideas about global precarity and its processes of expulsion and abandonment, and the nature and origins of precarious life itself, noting where these are relevant to issues of ageing. The ethical position advanced by Judith Butler – that all life is precarious and therefore should be acknowledged as such in political and social practice – leaves open the question of how life itself became precarious, which Foucault's work addresses in its historicization of the government of life as an object of power and knowledge. Taken together, these theoretical threads provide the background to the next part of this chapter on figures of crisis and precarious life within the life course.

The life course and its crises

The 'life course' is a key idea in gerontology, popular for being both a sociological entry point into research on ageing and for broadening such research beyond earlier biological, psychological and evolutionary models of human development. Glen Elder is widely credited as a pioneer of this approach. His book *Children of the Great Depression* (1974) documents the (American) life course as a complex historical and fluid intersection of individuals, cohorts, families and generations. Since the 1990s, the sociology of the life course has grown to become a gerontological subfield of its own, which critical writers have expanded to include analyses of policy, diversity and inequality (Calasanti and Slevin, 2006; Dannefer, 2003; Grenier, 2012; Settersten, 2003), while anthropologists have deconstructed the notion of a universal life course itself (Sokolovsky, 2009). Criticisms of life course research, while too numerous to summarize here, have also surfaced and questioned researchers' assumptions that changes in age and changes in time are reciprocal and can be predicted by maps of life course trajectories, transitions, pathways and strategies (see Dannefer and Kelley-Moore, 2009). Gilleard and Higgs (2016) further point out that, in their haste to distance themselves from the earlier human development models, life course researchers have often neglected issues relating to subjective agency, identity and experience.

In the context of precarity, these criticisms are valuable because they lead to inquiries about the kinds of discourses and truths that *underlie* the mapping and trajectories of those life course stages identified as risky and precarious. Indeed, the life course can be investigated in a very different way if the making of precarious life is seen as its constituting principle within a web of global powers and expert discourses, as the previous section argued. One way to see how this principle has developed in real terms is through a figurative methodology that zooms in on specific identities that have come to embody precarious life across the life course. This chapter focuses on childhood obesity, adolescence instability, mid-life despair and old-age cognitive (memory) impairment as illustrations.[3] The following sections review key contributions in each case, and the lessons they offer for understanding the critical intersections between precarious lives, human development and the life course.

Childhood and the crisis of obesity

Obesity and the Limits of Shame (Seeman and Luciani, 2011) is one of a growing number of publications about childhood obesity as a leading cause of global health problems such as diabetes and cardiovascular disease, as well as their escalating costs. The book reports that in the United States, childhood obesity rates have nearly quadrupled in the past three decades, as have rates of associated chronic diseases, with 32 per cent of American children considered overweight or obese (with those terms frequently intermixed). The resulting life course trajectory – that fat children become fat adults who bear more fat children – is creating a 'globesity' epidemic where, for every four malnourished adults in the world, five children are overweight (although undernourished people can also be obese). The scope of the epidemic has fuelled an industry of advice books, fat codes, weight charts, calorie apps, diet journals, 'before-and-after' social media sites and, unfortunately, bullying cultures of 'fat-shaming'.

In schools, as Deana Leahy (2009) points out, the biopolitical crisis is funnelled into obesity education aimed at children, where teachers frame children as 'health learners' around nutrition, exercise and weight. But this learning also disrupts children's sense of themselves as they see fatness – their own and that of others – with a new disgust. Indeed, a child's school lunchbox itself has become transformed into an object of surveillance. Yet, as schools update their health programmes, overhaul their cafeteria lunches, limit soda-pop vending machines and push children to become self-regulating dietitians, they struggle to contain the real sources of food-related precarious health in their communities, such as junk food industry monopolies, lack of fresh-food stores in poorer areas, shrinking urban green spaces and toxic environments, the elimination of school meals and physical exercise programmes, and the privatization of food and water-safety protection. Bombarded with virtuous disciplining at school, children then come home to television shows such as the moralizing *Jamie's School Dinners* or the humiliating *The Biggest Loser* and *Honey, We're Killing the Kids* (Rich, 2011), where parents, mostly mothers of course, are demonized for failing both their children and society at large. Meanwhile, for the privileged white family, their flabby child's body has become a data stream of medical risk factors that threaten to denigrate the family's status in terms of race, sex and class (see LeBesco, 2010).

Obesity has thus turned childhood into a precarious time of life in which parents, schools, the media and public health policymakers are tasked to intervene and control. It involves a medicalized rendering of the life of the child's body into measurements of calorie intake, weight gain and fat deposits that translate into moral orders of social belonging or abandonment. One could argue that childhood has always been a precarious stage, as is evident from the historical data on childhood diseases and mortality rates. But as children in industrialized countries are surviving deadly infectious diseases and are freed from the life-shortening labours of the past, it is the precarious figure of the child itself, whose traditional innocence has disappeared into uncontrollable appetite and addiction to sedentary entertainment, that has become a cause of public health burden and global insecurity, and a threat to longevity and healthy ageing now and into the future.

Puberty, adolescence and the crisis of youth

However, one grows out of obese-risk childhood, and moves into the next stage of risk and crisis. The life course transition to adolescent 'youth' has always been identified as crisis-laden since the invention of modern adolescence. This view is encapsulated by psychologist G. Stanley Hall (1844–1924) in his encyclopedic two-volume work, *Adolescence: Its Psychology and Its Relations to Physiology, Anthropology, Sociology, Sex, Crime, Religion and Education* (1904), the full title of which represents the extent of professional interest in the new adolescence. Hall's book, about human development between the ages of 13 and 18, was a contradictory blend of Victorian morals and modern science that characterized adolescence as overwhelmed by delinquent thrill-seeking, emotional vulnerability, susceptibility to media influences, the importance of peer relationships, rapid biological development (puberty), mood swings and 'relational aggression' (among adolescent girls).

In some circles *Adolescence* was considered a work of genius, and in others a work of madness. It was even banned in some places because of Hall's liberal views on adolescent sexual desire. Yet, it is impressive that the two-volume work sold over 25,000 copies in its first printing and attracted an international readership of reformers, educators, criminologists and child psychologists, who together created the 'troubled teen' as a figure of instability, one that would feature in media, literary and consumer images of youth. Most important, Hall's work influenced educational policies, such as those that matched secondary school grades in the United States to his three stages of adolescence (Chudacoff, 1989, p 68) and lengthened the schooling period so that adolescents could be prepared to cope with the newly discovered instabilities of their life stage.

The psychological precarity of adolescence was deeply connected to the construction of the physical risks of puberty itself, which Celia Roberts, in her study of 'puberty in crisis' (2015), traces to the textual production of medical atlases such as *The Adolescent Period: a Graphic and Pictorial Atlas* (Shuttleworth, 1938) and later the *Atlas of Children's Growth* (Tanner and Whitehouse, 1982). To create his atlas, British paediatrician James Mourilyn Tanner did his research on the Harpenden Longitudinal Study in the UK, between 1948 and 1971, comprising mostly poor and institutionalized children.[4] Tanner's and other atlases were filled with images of puberty that, as Roberts says, 'were literally scientific objects – they were not intended as illustrative representations but were themselves to be measured' (Roberts, 2015, p 70). Circulated and treated as inventories of the vulnerability and frailty of youth, the atlases became discursive authorities on puberty. Tanner also invented the 'Tanner scale' to universalize measured growth around puberty and, from its publication in 1962, this became the gold standard for puberty studies, only to be superseded later by pharmaceutical companies promoting hormone treatments for cases of 'early' female puberty.

Hall's *Adolescence* and Tanner's atlas and scale are two of many examples of how the life sciences discursively manufactured and relayed the crises and risks of adolescence and puberty that would manifest in redemptive campaigns such as those to prevent teenage pregnancy, drug use, smoking and school-leaving (see Barcelos, 2014). As with childhood obesity, here the figure of the unstable and precarious life of the adolescent is an opportune terminal point for the scientific, educational and political interests that invest in controlling young life, while sidelining the realities of violence, abuse, poverty, environmental degradation and social deprivation that actually threaten it.[5]

Mid-life and the crisis of despair

Of the many stages and concepts associated with adulthood, the 'mid-life crisis' endures as one of the most popular and dramatic expressions of how the uncertainties of mid-life adult employment, security, family life and health became psychologically distilled into a personal despair over the waning of youth. While there is a long history of 'prime of life' models in the sciences and politics of industry, reproduction, war and national energies, the modern mid-life crisis, beginning in the 1950s, became a new kind of life course dilemma of individual post-prime stagnation. By the 1970s, despite the scattered and unreliable research, the mid-life crisis had become a sufficiently serious problem to warrant therapeutic treatment, reflected in bestsellers such as Gail Sheehy's *Passages: Predictable Crises of Adult Life* (1974).[6]

But it was Erik and Joan Erikson who, inspired by Jaques' famous speech in Shakespeare's *As You Like It* (about the Renaissance conception of the seven stages of man), constructed an eight-stage diagram of the life course that marked out a lengthy middle age as a time of psychosocial crisis. The Eriksons wrote during their own middle age, as did Eliott Jaques, the Canadian psychoanalyst who invented the term 'mid-life crisis' (at age 38) with his article 'Death and the mid life crisis' (1965). For Jaques, the mid-life crisis was premised on the depressing realization that more years of life now lay behind than ahead. But for the Eriksons, in their books *Childhood and Society* (Erikson, 1950), *Identity and the Life Cycle* (Erikson, 1959) and *The Life Cycle Completed* (Erikson, 1982), mid-life became part of a more complicated scheme of stages and conflicts, when adult life could be both productive and positive. Like Hall's *Adolescence*, Erikson's *Childhood and Society* was a scientific text that had tremendous popular appeal, selling 30,000 copies yearly from its publication and a total of 3.2 million copies by 1990 (not including used book market sales). The Eriksons, Jaques and their associates had succeeded in migrating middle age from an earlier eclectic circle of scientists and psychologists to the centre of attention for postwar states and publics worried about mid-life ageing decline (Gullette, 1988; 2004).[7]

As Patricia Cohen (2012) has elaborated, mid-life continues to be a field of research that attracts large funding organizations, such as the MacArthur Foundation, which funded Bert Brim's programme *Network on Midlife* in 1989, and itself became a vast repository of surveys, interviews, databanks and publications. When the American National Institute on Aging took over the MacArthur Foundation project in 2002, renaming it *The Midlife in the United States* (MIDUS), it proceeded to fund another US$26 million project to include neurological and cognitive as aspects as well, now putting the middle-aged brain under the microscope of crisis. MIDUS also extended mid-life to 25–72 years of age, as its later surveys covered not only health but also emotional, financial, employment and family risk, in addition to well-being. As with younger life, the publicity around mid-life as a crisis has continued to attract funding, intervention, media attention, commercialization and surveillance. Indeed, the despairing mid-life voyager, who, like the fat child or the troubled teen, is expected to self-manage their life in socially valuable ways, but now also harbours the globalized precarity of unstable work and unemployment, the accumulation of social inequalities (Grenier et al, 2017b), as well as potential homelessness (Grenier et al, 2016) and living alone in isolation (Portacolone, 2013). And as with other discourses of precarious life, the discourses of the mid-life and its crises have collapsed the social prevention of these trajectories into the presumed resourcefulness of an individual figure.

Old age and the crisis of cognitive memory decline

Today, as life expectancy lengthens and life-extending medical interventions expand for more affluent populations, chronological age has become less meaningful in both gerontology and post-traditional society in general. Certainly, the age of 65 has ceased to symbolize the entry into old age, even if earlier pension movements were based on it. In gerontological research, these and other conventional markers have lost their certainty and validity as researchers struggle to come up with alternative measures and definitions of ageing (Moreira, 2015; 2016). Meanwhile, a commercialized seniors culture has emerged to promote anti-ageing lifestyle, diet and activity regimes that accord with gerontological models of successful and healthy ageing. As many critical writers have pointed out, we now live in a society that bifurcates later life into opposing realms of independence and dependence, ability and disability, and resilience and frailty (Katz and Calasanti, 2015). Thus, the realities of old age – or the 'fourth age' – are to be avoided and shunned as a kind of 'black hole' (Gilleard and Higgs, 2010) that threatens to engulf those who fail to prevent decline or compensate for their vulnerability.

While debates about the status of physical, functional and chronological markers of the ageing body ensue, I would argue that measures of *cognitive health* have become more prominent, especially in the shadow of what has been termed the 'epidemic' of Alzheimer's disease. In particular, the loss of recall memory is increasingly taken to indicate the risk of a possible slide from a healthy and active third age to a dependent and incapable fourth age.[8] Thus, the maintenance of memory has become a vital aspect of successful, active and basically ageless identities (Swinnen and Schweda, 2015; Whitehouse and

George, 2008; Williams et al, 2012). Consumer culture has also reacted with new products for cognitive and brain optimizing products (such as brain stimulants and exercises) that promise to enhance *cognitive reserve* and *plasticity* while delaying brain decline (Rose and Abi-Rachid, 2013; Thornton, 2011).

In this context, it is not surprising that new pre-dementia conditions for older adults, such as mild cognitive impairment (MCI), have emerged as feared cross-boundary disease categories between normal 'forgetfulness' and memory 'deficit' (Katz and Peters, 2015; Lock, 2013). Overall, it seems that the social determinants of precarity in late life have vaporized into a crisis of memory and brain ageing, popularly represented by the figure of the confused and addle-minded senior, while dementia is cruelly represented by images of an endless funeral, a silent tsunami, a millennium demon, a time bomb and a mind robber (Behuniak, 2011; Zeilig, 2014). And despite the heavy investments in neuroscientific and dementia research, too many people with Alzheimer's disease remain isolated, neglected and abandoned, leading critics to argue for a new ethics of care (Basting, 2009; Kontos et al, 2017). However, there is also a need to critique how brain ageing, as a signifier of late-life precarity and risk, has been singled out as a threat to the continuity of the life course itself, and how the construction of old age as cognitively unstable further sediments the crisis-model of human development connecting later to earlier times of life. It is little wonder that older people are released from the restrictions of chronological age only to face the frightening uncertainties of cognitive decline, and face even greater pressures to be risk-averse, health-smart and, as the next section discusses, resilient.

Conclusion

This chapter has identified specific frameworks of precarity and figures of precarious life to make the argument that models of human development and the life course have been popular and professional resources for folding the risks of social insecurity into personal dilemmas of crisis and insecurity. This is not simply an unpredictable process, as popular interpretations may imply, but a traceable historical one, and now part of a very deliberate strategy to control and contain life itself between global capital and neoliberal governance. By way of a conclusion, the remainder of this chapter considers the question of resistance to the forces of precarity, beginning with a critique of resilience, since resilience has become the basis of an industry of educational, policy and research programmes and literatures aimed at countering the risks and harms of precarity, particularly for older people.

The resilient self

Resilience is typically defined as the individual or systematic ability to cope with, adapt to or *bounce back* from adversity. While ecology is one source of resilience research (Holling, 1973), it was in childhood studies (Werner and Smith, 1982; 1992; 2001) that the concept of resilience became revelatory because researchers could use it to measure how some children could cope better with poverty, violence and abuse than others.[9] As Henderson and Denny (2015, p 356) argue, 'the concept of resilience rests on a moment of renewal in the knowledge of children's development, when the question was turned from negative developmental outcomes and the identification risk factors to a conscious pursuit of explanations for the unexpected: the surprising "adaptations" and "self-righting" trajectories in high-risk groups'. Furthermore, if research could identify the risks and vulnerabilities of childhood, then it could also prepare and train children to be resilient as they mature into adulthood (Goldstein and Brooks, 2013).

The formative research on resilience offered optimistic and pragmatic models of how precarious life carried its own capacity for internal recovery, applicable to a range of vulnerable groups including survivors of catastrophes and wars. These models are also part of a knowledge world of global reports, planning policies and research centres: for example, the Stockholm Resilience Centre (Stockholm University), the World Health Organization (Europe) report on *Mental Health, Resilience and Inequalities* (Friedli, 2009) and the Bellagio Initiative background paper on resilience (Martin-Breen and Anderies, 2011). The Bellagio paper's authors offer a statement of goals that clearly represents the resilience model: 'to build resilience that enhances individual, community and institutional capacity to survive, adapt, and grow in the face of acute crises and chronic stresses' and 'to promote growth with equity so that poor and vulnerable people have more access to opportunities that improve their lives' (Martin-Breen and Anderies, 2011, front page). These kinds of statements frame living populations and communities both as inevitably prone to crises and stress, and, where properly supported, as naturally resilient to them. As Rose and Lentzos (2017, p 11) say, 'resilience seems perfectly suited to our present'.

Thus, it is not surprising that resilience has become a potent idea in gerontology. Articles from the Gerontological Society of America journals with resilience in the title have almost tripled in number every three years since 2008. The idea of resilience promotes a positive and democratic approach to coping with old age that veers away from the idealistic and bifurcating models of successful and healthy ageing. While not everybody can age healthfully or successfully, they can age resiliently and even find new ways of flourishing in the face of disability and frailty. Researchers typically approach resilience with the use of psychometric scales to measure resilient physical, cognitive, emotional and experiential categories (see Randall et al, 2015; Wild et al, 2013). However, qualitative research has also focused on cultivating resilience, including the development of a discourse where research subjects identify and report themselves as resilient. For example, in their evaluation of a resilience education programme, Fullen and Gorby note that, 'although group members expressed a limited understanding of the term resilience at the outset of the program, by its conclusion many group members were referring to themselves or others in the group as resilient' (Fullen and Gorby, 2016, p 668). A similar study of Australian older adults facing disabling circumstances (Ottmann and Maragoudaki, 2015) concludes that professionals and health workers can best help their clients learn to identify their 'assets' of resilience and encourage clients through a 'resilience repertoire'.

The issue of self-reporting and *becoming* resilient introduces the first of two critical problems with the resilience model: first, its shaping of precarity and adversity as conditions lacking in resilience; second, its assumption that individuals can learn a capacity for resilience.

On the first of these, the argument is that if catastrophe arises, it can be excused as an absence of resilience or signal a need for it (Moser, 1998). This means that, however positive and self-empowering resilience education may be for an older individual, it still creates a division between being resilient and failing to cope. Wild et al (2013, p 154) caution that gerontological researchers need to be 'wary of the potential for resilience to be used as a euphemistic buzz-word for transferring responsibility or blaming victims', and that such reflexivity 'must also extend to the tendency of some resilience researchers to romanticize the "assets" and capabilities of the individual as "survivor", while underplaying the very real struggle and disadvantage associated with living with chronic adversity'. I would also argue, along with Henderson and Denny (2015), that even where life course resilience is contextualized as relational and collective, it remains in the end an individual trait:

> The developmental self of resilience may be relational, embedded in affective and effective relationships, but this

> self is not for that matter a social being. Relationships are meaningful within resilience science to the extent that they are capable of reducing later vulnerability in the individual. They are investments in agency in the context of a life course, agency that is manifested in an individual's healthy choices and, when his or her life enters into relationship 'ecologies' with others, in affective interactions that promote individual competencies. (Henderson and Denny, 2015, p 360)

The second problem with the resilience model, in assuming that individuals can learn to mobilize a capacity for personal resilience, is that it shares a design for life and survivability with other personal capacities celebrated for a neoliberal age, such as adaptability, plasticity, responsibility, empowerment and entrepreneurship (Maasen and Sutter, 2007; Pitts-Taylor, 2010; 2016; Rose, 2007). These capacities are extolled for absorbing the neoliberal withdrawal of social protections and mediating the predatory effects of late capitalism (see also Chapter 10). Indeed, the metaphors used to describe the resilient individual, such as 'assets, gains and losses', 'reserves', 'human capital' and 'balances', are themselves redolent of neoliberal market discourse.

The critique of resilience in neoliberal society is one of the main themes of Evans and Reid's (2014, p 2) scathing review that claims resilience makes us forgo the hope for real security and embrace 'the necessity of our exposure to dangers of all kinds as a means by which to live well'. Their arguments have particular relevance to the life course because, as they comment, 'if the social state promised to take care of life from cradle to grave, resilience logically inverts this by foregrounding the catastrophic such that every stage of the subject's development appears to be fraught with potential hazards that always and already threaten what existence may become' (Evans and Reid, 2014, p 99). For the fat child, troubled teen, vulnerable mid-lifer and cognitively ageing elder, resilience illuminates their presumed precarity by offering to resolve it. It also confines the ageing subject to a permanent conflict between being resilient-fit or facing the risk of devaluation.

Being other than ourselves

If resilience is part of the problem, rather than the solution to precarious life, then how might we imagine resistance to it differently? In a view of the world presented as chaotic and ungovernable, the idealization of resilience not only blurs the lines between accommodation and real resistance (Schott, 2013), but it also depoliticizes victimization, violence and vulnerability by transforming these into opportunities for coping and bouncing back (to normal?). In this way, ageism, for example, becomes less a problem of social exclusion and abandonment than one of non-resilient subjects who fail to cope with it. But what if we resist the tossing of our lives between precarity and resilience as if this was part of the natural and unchanging churning of life itself? What if instead we relocated our true capacities for adaptability, coping and resilience to the caring, relational and resourceful communities that defy precarity and abandonment, akin to Sassen (2014) and Povinelli (2011), advocating that resistance lay in the ability of expelled and abandoned groups to develop their own social belongings and economic spaces (see further Chapter 10)? Judith Butler, again, argues that it is the ethical obligation of peoples and governments to recognize and democratize precarity in ways that value all life as liveable, sustainable and, if lost, grievable.

However, as in my earlier discussion of Foucault's contributions, a critique of precariousness needs to take account of how life itself became precarious. Therefore, I suggest that we imagine other ways of life itself, what it means to have a life, and the means by which we measure, predict, manage and narrate it apart from the hierarchical life course models of fractured identity crises, unstable figures and risky trajectories. To this end, Foucault's thinking is again valuable for its reflections on radical subjectivity:

> Maybe the target nowadays is not to discover what we are, but to refuse what we are. We have to imagine and to build up what we could be to get rid of this kind of political 'double bind,' which is the simultaneous individualization and totalization of modern power structures.
>
> The conclusion would be that the political, ethical, social, philosophical problem of our days is not to try to liberate the individual from the state, and from the state's institutions, but to liberate us both from the state and from the type of individualization which is linked to the state. We have to promote new forms of subjectivity through the refusal of this kind of individuality which has been imposed on us for several centuries. (Foucault, 1983, p 216)

Foucault is not suggesting that a person can simply refuse to be poor, homeless, alone or old, but that the political expectations and responsibilities that personalize such conditions be refused.

His proposal that we 'refuse what we are' and 'promote new forms of subjectivity' resonates with a renewed imagination about ageing and the life course. If, for example, cognitive impairment or dementia for older adults became less-feared matters of personal decline and more integrated into community care and life-affirming environments, then the restrictive disease-models and terrifying public images that separate and isolate old age as either precarious or resilient might also be refused, as would our fear of a catastrophic future marked by what Kathleen Woodward (2009, p 217) calls 'statistical panic' – an affective reaction to 'the omnipresent discourse of risk'. Therefore, part of 'living otherwise' embraces a commitment to pursuing collective security, stability and social belonging in a shared future tense as the true bulwarks against precarity, risk, abandonment and expulsion. Helen Small, in her masterful book *The Long Life* (2007), elucidates the long history of philosophical and literary thinkers who coalesced their concerns about history, morality, knowledge, justice and purpose into the question of 'what it means to live a *good* life' (Small, 2007, p 21; emphasis in original). Today we inherit the legacy of these thinkers as we struggle to think about what constitutes a good and long life in its development and longevity. To this end, this chapter has explored how a critique of precarious life, in its ageing figurations and discourses of truth, might contribute to this legacy.

Notes

1. 'Geontopower' is Povinelli's term for signifying a reordered relationship between non-life ('geos') and being ('ontology') in an era of late liberal governance, whose extraordinary forms of violence, ability to threaten biological existence and creation of synthetic forms of life on a global scale have perforated 'the boundary between the autonomy of Life and its opposition to and difference from Nonlife' (2016, p 14), in order to exploit both. Paolo Palladino also explores new relations of life, death and ageing in the biological and medical sciences (Palladino, 2016).
2. There is a large literature on these governmental technologies, but two seminal texts that detail the history of statistical and factual knowledges are *A History of the Modern Fact* by Mary Poovey (1998) and *The Taming of Chance* by Ian Hacking (1990).
3. There are other life course figures that could be included and have been analysed in ways similar to what I am proposing here, especially those that intersect gender identities. For example, Pickard examines the 'new', 'go' or 'can-do' girl as a figure that expresses the contradiction between neoliberal entrepreneurial success and conformance to feminine ideals (Pickard, 2016; 2018). Wilson and Yochim (2017) critique new figurations

4   of the family mother, who must compensate for collapsing support systems, failing schools, unsafe environments and displaced communities as 'the naturalized caregivers and keepers of the domestic realm that underwrite precarization and make it possible' (Wilson and Yochim, 2017, p 22).

4   The close relationship between the rise of the human sciences and their research on poor and helpless institutionalized populations is a familiar theme of Foucault's work on asylums, hospitals and prisons. My own work draws on his to document how the poor and abandoned older women stuck in 19th-century Paris' immense Salpêtrière Hospital became the research subjects for Jean-Martin Charcot and his foundational geriatrics text, *Clinical Lectures on the Diseases of Old Age* (Charcot and Loomis, 1881; Katz, 1999). On the connection between discourse and power in human development research, see Erica Burman (2007).

5   Dale Dannefer has been a leading critic of the *undersocialization* of the life course and the tendency in gerontology towards the personological *microfication* of macrosocial inequalities (Hagestad and Dannefer, 2001). In a recent article, Dannefer and Huang (2017) include a discussion about precarity and youth, criticizing how life course researchers have misconstrued agency as a matter of individual choice and thus obscured the role of social structure and potential for collective engagement with precarity. Settersten and Ray (2010) also argue for a balanced approach to the uncertainties of young life with their insightful study of the advantageous strategies of young people who choose slower paths to adulthood.

6   In gerontology, middle age became a specialized area when Bernice Neugarten (1968; 1974) created the terms 'early' 'middle' and 'late' life, and Peter Laslett (1987) wedged the 'third age' between the younger adulthood (second) and older (fourth) ages as a new and positive period of independence, learning, vitality and self-care. However, this scholarship was not necessarily related to mid-life as a crisis, but aimed at countering negative narratives of decline.

7   For women, mid-life was also constructed as a precarious biological crisis because of the menopause, which was medicalized as a health disaster requiring lifelong oestrogen replacement therapy (HRT), a problem fomented by Robert A. Wilson's blockbuster text, *Feminine Forever* (1966). For more on the HRT market as well as the pharmaceutical industry's promotion of testosterone and Viagra to treat male andropause (or viropause), see Marshall and Katz (2006).

8   There is an interesting history to how memory became a feature of brain function and thereafter linked to assumptions that ageing and memory loss were correlated as part of the general state of senility (Ballenger, 2006; Danziger, 2008; Draaisma, 2000). Gerontological advocates, such

as Robert N. Butler, urged replacing senility with Alzheimer's disease as an affliction apart from, but not necessarily part of, the ageing process. As such, Alzheimer's became deserving of public funding, research and hope for a cure, developments that paradoxically may have further stigmatized older people.

9 Emily E. Werner and Ruth S. Smith began with their research with children in Hawaii (1977), where adversity and survival were obviously very real social threats. It is also interesting to note that facing adversity itself has an historical dimension in terms of shifts in meaning from fortitude to vulnerability (Furedi, 2007).

References

Ballenger, J.F. (2006) *Self, Senility, and Alzheimer's Disease in Modern America: a History*, Baltimore: Johns Hopkins University Press.

Barcelos, C.A. (2014) 'Producing (potentially) pregnant teen bodies: biopower and adolescent pregnancy in the USA', *Critical Public Health*, 24(4): 476–88.

Basting, A.D. (2009) *Forget Memory: Creating Better Lives for People with Dementia*, Baltimore: Johns Hopkins University Press.

Bauman, Z. (2007) *Liquid Times: Living in an Age of Uncertainty*, Cambridge: Polity.

Beck, U. (1992) *Risk Society: towards a New Modernity*, translated by M. Ritter, London: Sage.

Behuniak, S.M. (2011) 'The living dead? The construction of people with Alzheimer's disease as zombies', *Ageing & Society*, 31(1): 70–92.

Burman, E. (2007) *Deconstructing Developmental Psychology* (2nd edn), London: Routledge.

Butler, J. (2004) *Precarious Life: The Powers of Mourning and Violence*, London: Verso.

Butler, J. (2016) *Frames of War: When Is Life Grievable?*, London: Verso.

Calasanti, T.M. and Slevin, K.F. (eds) (2006) *Age Matters: Realigning Feminist Thinking*, New York: Routledge.

Charcot, J.M. and Loomis, A.L. (1881) *Clinical Lectures on the Diseases of Old Age*, translated by L.H. Hunt, New York: William Wood.

Chudacoff, H.P. (1989) *How Old Are You? Age Consciousness in American Culture*, Princeton: Princeton University Press.

Cohen, P. (2012) *In Our Prime: the Invention of Middle Age*, New York: Scribner.

Dannefer, D. (2003) 'Whose life course is it anyway? Diversity and "linked lives" in global perspective', in R.A. Settersten Jr (ed.) *Invitation to the Life Course: Toward New Understandings of Later Life*, Amityville, NY: Baywood, pp 259–68.

Dannefer, D. and Kelley-Moore, J.A. (2009) 'Theorizing the life course: new twists in the paths', in V.L. Bengston, D. Gans, N.M. Putney and M. Silverstein (eds) *Handbook of Theories of Aging* (2nd edn), New York: Springer, pp 389–411.

Dannefer, D. and Huang, W. (2017) 'Precarity, inequality, and the problem of agency in the study of the life course', *Innovation in Aging*, 1(3): 1–10.

Danziger, K. (2008) *Marking the Mind: a History of Memory*, Cambridge: Cambridge University Press.

Draaisma, D. (2000) *Metaphors of Memory: a History of Ideas about the Mind*, translated by P. Vincent, Cambridge: Cambridge University Press.

Elder, G.H., Jr (1974) *Children of the Great Depression: Social Change in Life Experience*, Chicago: Chicago University Press.

Erikson, E.H. (1950) *Childhood and Society*, New York: W.W. Norton.

Erikson, E.H. (1959) *Identity and the Life Cycle: Selected Papers*, New York: International Universities Press.

Erikson, E.H. (1982) *The Life Cycle Completed: a Review*, New York: Norton.

Estes, C.L. and Wallace, S.P. (2010) 'Globalisation, social policy, and ageing: a North American perspective', in D. Dannefer and C. Phillipson (eds) *The Sage Handbook of Social Gerontology*, London: Sage, pp 513–24.

Evans, B. and Reid, J. (2014) *Resilient Life: the Art of Living Dangerously*, Cambridge: Polity.

Foucault, M. (1977) 'Nietzsche, genealogy, history', in *Language, Counter-Memory, Practice: Selected Essays and Interviews*, edited by D.L. Bouchard, translated by D.F. Bouchard and S. Simon, Ithaca: Cornell University Press, pp 139–64.

Foucault, M. (1980) *The History of Sexuality: Vol. 1, an Introduction*, translated by R. Hurley, New York: Vintage.

Foucault, M. (1983) 'Afterword: the subject and power', in H.L. Dreyfus and P. Rabinow, *Michel Foucault: beyond Structuralism and Hermeneutics* (2nd edn), Chicago: University of Chicago Press, pp 208–26.

Foucault, M. (1991) 'Governmentality', in G. Burchell, C. Gordon and P. Miller (eds) *The Foucault Effect: Studies in Governmentality*, Chicago: University of Chicago Press, pp 87–104.

Friedli, L. (2009) *Mental Health, Resilience and Inequalities*, Copenhagen: World Health Organization Regional Office for Europe [online], available from: https://apps.who.int/iris/handle/10665/107925 [Accessed 13 August 2019].

Fullen, M.C. and Gorby, S.R. (2016) 'Reframing resilience: pilot evaluation of a program to promote resilience in marginalized older adults', *Educational Gerontology*, 42(9): 660–71.

Furedi, F. (2007) 'From the narrative of the Blitz to the rhetoric of vulnerability', *Cultural Sociology*, 1(2): 235–54.

Gilleard, C. (2018) 'Suffering: the darker side of ageing', *Journal of Aging Studies*, 44: 28–33.

Gilleard, C. and Higgs, P. (2010) 'Ageing without agency: theorizing the fourth age', *Aging & Mental Health*, 14(2): 121–8.

Gilleard, C. and Higgs, P. (2016) 'Connecting life span development with the sociology of the life course: a new direction', *Sociology*, 50(2): 301–15.

Goldstein, S. and Brooks, R.B. (eds) (2013) *Handbook of Resilience in Children*, New York: Springer.

Grenier, A. (2012) *Transitions and the Lifecourse: Challenging the Constructions of 'Growing Old'*, Bristol: Policy Press.

Grenier, A., Barken, R. and McGrath, C. (2016) 'Homelessness and aging: the contradictory ordering of "house" and "home"', *Journal of Aging Studies*, 39: 73–80.

Grenier, A., Lloyd, L. and Phillipson, C. (2017a) 'Precarity in late life: rethinking dementia as a "frailed" old age', *Sociology of Health & Illness*, 39(2): 318–30.

Grenier, A, Phillipson, C., Laliberte Rudman, D., Hatzifilalithis, S., Kobayashi, K. and Marier, P. (2017b) 'Precarity in late life: understanding new forms of risk and insecurity', *Journal of Aging Studies*, 43: 9–14.

Gullette, M.M. (1988) *Safe at Last in the Middle Years: the Invention of the Midlife Progress Novel*, Berkeley: University of California Press.

Gullette, M.M. (2004) *Aged by Culture*, Chicago: University of Chicago Press.

Hacking, I. (1990) *The Taming of Chance*, Cambridge: Cambridge University Press.

Hagestad, G. and Dannefer, D. (2001) 'Concepts and theories of aging: beyond microfication in social science approaches', in R.H. Binstock and L.K. George, *Handbook of Aging and the Social Sciences* (5th edn), San Diego: Academic Press, pp 3–21.

Hall, G.S. (1904) *Adolescence: Its Psychology and Its Relations to Physiology, Anthropology, Sociology, Sex, Crime, Religion and Education* (2 vols), New York: D. Appleton.

Henderson, J. and Denny, K. (2015) 'The resilient child, human development and the "postdemocracy"', *Biosocieties*, 10(3): 352–78.

Holling, C.S. (1973) 'Resilience and stability of ecological systems', *Annual Review of Ecology and Systematics*, 4: 1–23.

Jaques, E. (1965) 'Death and the mid-life crisis', *International Journal of Psychoanalysis*, 46(4): 502–14.

Katz, S. (1999) 'Charcot's older women: bodies of knowledge at the interface of aging studies and women's studies', in K. Woodward (ed.) *Figuring Age: Women, Bodies, Generations*, Bloomington: Indiana University Press, pp 112–27.

Katz, S. (2000) 'Reflections on the gerontological handbook and the rhetoric of the text', in T.R. Cole, R. Kastenbaum and R.E. Ray (eds) *Handbook of the Humanities and Aging* (2nd edn), New York: Springer, pp 405–18.

Katz, S. and Calasanti, T. (2015) 'Critical perspectives on successful aging: does it "appeal more than it illuminates"?', *The Gerontologist*, (55)1: 26–33.

Katz, S. and Peters, K.R. (eds) (2015) 'Special issue: voices from the field: expert reflections on mild cognitive impairment', *Dementia*, 14(3).

Kontos P., Miller, K.-L. and Kontos, A.P. (2017) 'Relational citizenship: supporting embodied selfhood and relationality in dementia care', *Sociology of Health & Illness*, 39(2): 182–98.

Laslett, P. (1987) 'The emergence of the third age', *Ageing & Society*, 7(2): 133–60.

Leahy, D. (2009) 'Disgusting pedagogies', in J. Wright and V. Harwood (eds) *Biopolitics and the 'Obesity Epidemic': Governing Bodies*, London: Routledge, pp 172–82.

LeBesco, K. (2010) 'Fat panic and the new morality', in J.M. Metzl and A. Kirkland (eds) *Against Health: How Health Became the New Morality*, New York: New York University Press, pp 72–82.

Lock, M. (2013) *The Alzheimer Conundrum: Entanglements of Dementia and Aging*, Princeton: Princeton University Press.

Lorey, I. (2017) *State of Insecurity: Government of the Precarious*, translated by A. Derieg, London: Verso.

Maasen, S. and Sutter, B. (eds) (2007) *On Willing Selves: Neoliberal Politics vis-à-vis the Neuroscientific Challenge*, Basingstoke: Palgrave Macmillan.

Marshall, B.L. and Katz, S. (2006) 'From androgyny to androgens: resexing the aging body', in T.M. Calasanti and K.F. Slevin (eds) *Age Matters: Realigning Feminist Thinking*, New York: Routledge, pp 75–97.

Martin-Breen, P. and Anderies, J.M. (2011) *Resilience: a Literature Review*, Brighton: Institute of Development Studies, Bellagio Initiative [online], available from: https://opendocs.ids.ac.uk/opendocs/handle/123456789/3692 [Accessed 13 August 2019].

Moreira, T. (2015) 'Unsettling standards: the biological age controversy', *Sociological Quarterly*, 56(1): 18–39.

Moreira, T. (2016) 'De-standardising ageing? Shifting regimes of age measurement', *Ageing & Society*, 36(7): 1407–33.

Moser, C.O.N. (1998) 'The asset vulnerability framework: reassessing urban poverty reduction strategies', *World Development*, 26(1): 1–19.

Neugarten, B.L. (ed.) (1968) *Middle Age and Aging: a Reader in Social Psychology*, Chicago: University of Chicago Press.

Neugarten, B.L. (1974) 'Age groups in American society and the rise of the young-old', *Annals of the American Academy of Political and Social Science*, 415(1): 187–98.

Ottmann, G. and Maragoudaki, M. (2015) 'Fostering resilience later in life: a narrative approach involving people facing disabling circumstances, carers and members of minority groups', *Ageing & Society*, 35(10): 2071–99.

Palladino, P. (2016) *Biopolitics and the Philosophy of Death*, London: Bloomsbury Academic.

Phillipson, C. (2009) 'Reconstructing theories of ageing: the impact of globalization on critical gerontology', in V. Bengston, D. Gans, N.M. Putney and M. Silverstein (eds) *Handbook of Theories of Aging*, New York: Springer, pp 615–28.

Phillipson, C. (2010) 'Ageing and urban society: growing old in the "century of the city"', in D. Dannefer and C. Phillipson (eds) *The Sage Handbook of Social Gerontology*, London: Sage, pp 597–606.

Phillipson, C. (2013) 'Ageing and class in a globalised world', in M. Formosa and P. Higgs (eds) *Social Class in Later Life: Power, Identity and Lifestyle*, Bristol: Policy Press, pp 33–51.

Pickard, S. (2016) *Age Studies: a Sociological Examination of How We Age and Are Aged through the Life Course*, London: Sage.

Pickard, S. (2018) *Age, Gender and Sexuality through the Life Course: the Girl in Time*, London: Routledge.

Pitts-Taylor, V. (2010) 'The plastic brain: neoliberalism and the neuronal self', *Health*, 14(6): 635–52.

Pitts-Taylor, V. (2016) *The Brain's Body: Neuroscience and Corporeal Politics*, Durham, NC: Duke University Press.

Poovey, M. (1998) *A History of the Modern Fact: Problems of Knowledge in the Sciences of Wealth and Society*, Chicago: University of Chicago Press.

Portacolone E. (2013) 'The notion of precariousness among older adults living alone in the U.S.', *Journal of Aging Studies*, 27(2): 166–74.

Povinelli, E.A. (2011) *Economies of Abandonment: Social Belonging and Endurance in Late Liberalism*, Durham, NC: Duke University Press.

Povinelli, E.A. (2016) *Geontologies: a Requiem to Late Liberalism*, Durham, NC: Duke University Press.

Randall, W., Baldwin, C., McKenzie-Mohr, S., McKim, E. and Furlong, D. (2015) 'Narrative and resilience: a comparative analysis of how older adults story their lives', *Journal of Aging Studies*, 34: 155–61.

Rich, E. (2011) '"I see her being obesed!": public pedagogy, reality media and the obesity crisis', *Health*, 15(1): 3–21.

Roberts, C. (2015) *Puberty in Crisis: the Sociology of Early Sexual Development*, Cambridge: Cambridge University Press.

Rose, N. (1990) *Governing the Soul: the Shaping of the Private Self*, London: Routledge.

Rose, N. (2007) *The Politics of Life: Biomedicine, Power, and Subjectivity in the Twenty-First Century*, Princeton: Princeton University Press.

Rose, N. and Abi-Rached, J.M. (2013) *Neuro: the New Brain Sciences and the Management of the Mind*, Princeton: Princeton University Press.

Rose, N. and Lentzos, F. (2017) 'Making us resilient: responsible citizens for uncertain times', in S. Trnka and C. Trundle (eds) *Competing Responsibilities: the Ethics and Politics of Contemporary Life*, Durham, NC: Duke University Press, pp 27–48.

Sassen, S. (2014) *Expulsions: Brutality and Complexity in the Global Economy*, Cambridge, MA: Belknap Press.

Schott, R.M. (2013) 'Resilience, normativity and vulnerability', *Resilience*, 1(3): 210–18.

Seeman, N. and Luciani, P. (2011) *XXL: Obesity and the Limits of Shame*, Toronto: University of Toronto Press.

Settersten, R.A., Jr (2003) *Invitation to the Life Course: toward New Understandings of Later Life*, Amityville, NY: Baywood.

Settersten, R. and Ray, B.E. (2010) *Not Quite Adults: Why 20-Somethings Are Choosing a Slower Path to Adulthood, and Why It's Good for Everyone*, New York: Bantam Books.

Sheehy, G. (1974) *Passages: Predictable Crises of Adult Life*, New York: Dutton.

Shuttleworth, F.K. (1938) *The Adolescent Period: a Graphic and Pictorial Atlas*, Washington, DC: Society for Research in Child Development, National Research Council.

Small, H. (2007) *The Long Life*, Oxford: Oxford University Press.

Sokolovsky, J. (ed) (2009) *The Cultural Context of Aging: Worldwide Perspectives* (3rd edn), Westport, CT: Praeger.

Standing, G. (2011) *The Precariat: the New Dangerous Class*, London: Bloomsbury Academic.

Swinnen, A. and Schweda, M. (eds) (2015) *Popularizing Dementia: Public Expressions and Representations of Forgetfulness*, Bielefeld: Transcript.

Tanner, J.M. (1962) *Growth at Adolescence* (2nd edn), Oxford: Blackwell Scientific.

Tanner, J.M. and Whitehouse, R.H. (1982) *Atlas of Children's Growth*, New York: Academic Press.

Thornton, D.J. (2011) *Brain Culture: Neuroscience and Popular Media*, New Brunswick, NJ: Rutgers University Press.

Tyler, I. (2008) '"Chav mum chav scum": class disgust in contemporary Britain', *Feminist Media Studies*, 8(1): 17–34.

Werner, E.E. (2013) 'What can we learn about resilience from large-scale longitudinal studies?', in S. Goldstein and R.B. Brooks (eds), *Handbook of Resilience in Children* (2nd edn), New York: Springer, pp 87–102.

Werner, E.E. and Smith, R.S. (1977) *Kauai's Children Come of Age*, Honolulu: University Press of Hawaii.

Werner, E.E. and Smith, R.S. (1982) *Vulnerable but Invincible: a Longitudinal Study of Resilient Children and Youth*, New York: McGraw-Hill.

Werner, E.E. and Smith, R.S. (1992) *Overcoming the Odds: High Risk Children from Birth to Adulthood*, Ithaca: Cornell University Press.

Werner, E.E., and Smith R.S. (2001) *Journeys from Childhood to Midlife: Risk, Resilience, and Recovery*, Ithaca: Cornell University Press.

Whitehouse, P.J. and George, D. (2008) *The Myth of Alzheimer's: What You Aren't Being Told about Today's Most Dreaded Diagnosis*, New York: St. Martin's Press.

Wild, K., Wiles, J.L. and Allen, R.E.S. (2013) 'Resilience: thoughts on the value of the concept for critical gerontology', *Ageing & Society*, 33(1): 137–58.

Williams, S.J., Higgs, P. and Katz, S. (2012) 'Neuroculture, active ageing and the "older brain": problems, promises and prospects', *Sociology of Health & Illness*, 34(1): 64–78.

Wilson, J.A. and Yochim, E.C. (2017) *Mothering through Precarity: Women's Work and Digital Media*, Durham, NC: Duke University Press.

Wilson, R.A. (1966) *Feminine Forever: the Amazing New Breakthrough in the Sex Life of Women*, New York: Evans.

Woodward, K. (2009) *Statistical Panic: Cultural Politics and Poetics of the Emotions*, Durham, NC: Durham University Press.

Zeilig, H. (2014) 'Dementia as a cultural metaphor', *The Gerontologist*, 54(2): 258–67.

PART II
Precarity across situations

4

Rereading frailty through a lens of precarity: an explication of politics and the human condition of vulnerability

Amanda Grenier

Introduction

Over the last 15 years, frailty has emerged as one of the most powerful constructs in gerontology, geriatrics and health care delivery.[1] Authors from biomedicine have highlighted the clinical importance of the concept (Fried et al, 2001; Rockwood et al, 1994; Rockwood and Mitnitski, 2007), with researchers in the social sciences calling attention to its powerful position in establishing the foundations for medical expertise and disciplining older bodies according to function and risk (Grenier, 2007; Katz, 2011; Pickard, 2014). The concept of frailty appears in countless calls from medical interest groups (Morley et al, 2013; Turner and Clegg, 2014), and is used to frame a number of international research priorities such as the Canadian Frailty Network,[2] as well as national care priorities such as that of the National Health Service in the UK (Vernon, 2016; Young, 2014).[3] The concept of frailty is also now central to service eligibility across a range of settings and international contexts,[4] and has appeared in advocacy campaigns such as that of the charity AGE UK. Over time, the use of the concept of frailty has expanded across community and hospital settings, international policy, and local governments, with a growing basket of tools, measures and training to guide assessment and intervention.

The dominant portrayal and response to frailty is deeply rooted in biomedical knowledge, professional health expertise, and institutional or organizational practices such as hospital care, rehabilitation settings and home care. Yet, this view tends to mask that frailty is both experienced by older people (with the lens of frailty ever widening to the 'pre-frail'), and is historically situated in a wider political context of neo-liberal priorities and managed care. Contemporary features such as population ageing, longevity and the neo-liberalization of care thus represent an important landscape against (and through) which frailty is experienced, and responses are configured and enacted. That is, the concept of frailty is not without meaning or context; it is a human experience, a representation of the need for care and a response (or multiple responses) to this need. The experiences that are often labelled and classified as 'frail' are thus both part of the human condition and deeply political.

This chapter suggests that the lens of precarity can be used to inform discussions of the risks and insecurities experienced by older people, and in doing so, convey complex understandings of need in late life, and build approaches that are more in line with older people's experiences. The chapter begins by outlining key lines of thinking with regards to frailty, including problems that emerge from a social and cultural perspective. Next, it sketches emerging work on precarity with regard to ageing, pointing to two angles that can be used to reconsider 'frailty' in late life. First, it engages with the politics of frailty, through detailed attention to the political context of care. Second, it turns to consider the relationship between vulnerability as part of the human condition, and the constitution, and response, to 'frail' subjects. It follows this by outlining the contributions that can be made through an analysis of precarity, and concludes with suggestions for theoretical and methodological development.

Problems and limits of responses to frailty

Dominant approaches conceptualize frailty as an individual biomedical issue that can be observed and measured through functional limitation as the basis for service eligibility and/or specialized intervention (or not). Leading geriatricians have drawn attention to the 'burden of frailty' (Canadian Frailty Network, n.d.) identifying it as 'the most problematic expression of population ageing' (O'Shea, 2017). Two models of thought characterize the debate in medical approaches to frailty. The first is a phenotype model, whereby frailty is considered a distinct syndrome characterized by poor physical performance across a range of domains including unintentional weight loss, weakness/grip strength, slow walking speed, and/or low levels of physical activity (Fried et al, 2001). The second is an accumulation of deficits model, whereby frailty is the cumulative effect of stressors and deficits in multiple domains that accumulate over time, and place people at risk for adverse outcomes (Rockwood et al, 1994; Rockwood and Mitnitski, 2007). While these sets of literature differ on the root causes and the potential to include the social dimensions of experience, both treat frailty as the purview of biomedical and health care specialists, and the best means to prioritize resources and design responses for older people.

Although rarely brought to light, especially in the context of standard configurations of frailty, experiences and responses to need in later life are also interconnected with social, cultural, economic and political priorities. Frailty is experienced in and through the body, as both older people's insights and biomedical indications have established. It is also socially located, with the challenges attributed to frailty experienced across a range of environments and settings including the home, public transit, neighbourhoods and communities (Grenier, 2005). For example, older people may experience falls, experience reduced mobility and/or weakness, and have visible and observable signs that within health care settings would be used to classify someone as 'frail'. They may also experience a range of disadvantages that result in health and social disparities. These attributes, often discussed as frailty, operate to mark impairment, loss and decline, and take on meaning related to impairment and/or mortality (such as fear and anxiety). The cultural critic Margaret Morganroth Gullette (1997) refers to the tendency to depict experiences of ageing according to impairment and loss as part of a 'decline narrative', and sociologists of ageing Gilleard and Higgs (2010, p 137) refer to the 'fourth age', often associated with frailty, as a 'social imaginary', imbued with ideas of old age as 'horrific, disgusting and tainted by mortality'.

Frailty, however, is not only a marker of illness, decline or a period of the life course where one is 'closer to death'. Frailty is also a set of discourses and practices that have emerged in tandem with contemporary ideas of autonomy and individual responsibility, including that of 'success' (Lloyd, 2004; 2015). Frailty and success are mutually reinforcing sides of a binary, with frailty employed in alignment with individual risk in order to encourage, bolster, and reinforce independence and autonomy as attributes of success (Grenier, 2012; Katz, 2011). It is also very much situated in the medicalized interpretations of ageing, and as an able-bodied construct, with impairment and function classified according to deficient models (that is, scales measuring deficit in function, rather than the ability to complete a task with or without assistance). Yet, unlike 'successful ageing', now widely critiqued for its exclusionary implications (Dillaway and Byrnes, 2009), frailty continues to gain momentum across international contexts, and at all levels of practice, with less critical attention to the historical development, associated oversights and political implications.

Frailty emerged in the context of managed care in the United States in the late 1980s, through the powerful practices of medical and other health care professionals, including most notably a focus on individual risk measured through standard assessments of bodily function (Kaufman, 1994a; 1994b; Kaufman and Becker, 1996). The concept of frailty, and accompanying practices, were shaped by and operate within a care context characterized by neoliberal priorities of reduced public spending, residual benefits, the retrenchment of public services, and the reliance on family and/or kin care (see Armstrong and Armstrong, 2003; Armstrong and Braedley, 2013; Grenier et al, 2017a; 2017b). Understandings and approaches to frailty thus simultaneously carry with them representations of the 'social imaginary of decline', the prioritization and application of individualized biomedical and functional risk, and residual approaches to care that are enacted in neoliberal conditions such as austerity. However, the dominant approaches to frailty remain relatively unaffected (or unaware) of these critiques, thereby sustaining discontinuity between the experience of need, the context within which need and frailty operates, and the individual biomedical and technological interpretations and responses to older people who are 'frail'. Yet, as cultural debates over resources shift from notions of chronological age to measures of biomedical deficit, with practice eligibility following suit, frailty becomes a contested terrain.

Insights from older people highlight the experience of vulnerability that lies beneath the configuration of the concept of frailty. A range of work across the social sciences draws attention to the distinction between the classification of frailty and life course experience – that is, the distinction between 'being' and 'feeling' frail (Grenier, 2006). Older women interviewed by Kaufman, Becker, Grenier and Nicholson, for example, made a clear distinction between classifications of frailty and their experiences by rejecting the construct of frailty as a defining feature of their lives (Grenier, 2007; Kaufman and Becker, 1996; Nicholson et al, 2012). Instead, they highlighted that frailty came from the outside: it was, in the words of one of the older women who participated in Grenier's (2007) research, 'something that others say about you', and a condition that seems to provoke a sense of judgement or pity. Older women also highlighted that frailty was not necessarily about age and impairment (although they acknowledge that losses happen more frequently as one progresses farther along the life course). Instead, they focused on the human experiences of frailty, the moments of feeling vulnerable, insecure and uncertain.

Insights from older women who were frail acutely convey two aspects about frailty that are obscured by the dominant discourse and practices, but which are at the forefront of precarity. Older people's interpretations are deeply reflective of the vulnerability that is brought on by changes to the body over time, to loss, and to their own mortality and that of their families and friends (Gadow, 1983; 1996; Kaufman and Becker, 1996; Lloyd, 2004; Lloyd et al, 2014; Lustbader, 2000; Taylor, 1992). They are also cognizant of how needs come to alter their habits, daily lives and experiences (Grenier, 2005; 2006; 2007; 2008; Kaufman, 1994a; 1994b; Kaufman and Becker, 1996; Nicholson et al, 2012; Pickard, 2009). Interviews with older people are replete with discussions of what they need (including meals, shopping, assistance, conversation and interaction), what they can afford (or not), who helps them (such as friends, neighbours, families, and workers), and the disjunctures between their needs and available supports. These discussions play out in a number of ways. While some older people minimize or understate their needs, and some express their frustration with being let down by a social contract that promised to provide, others speak about not wanting to be a nuisance, thereby simultaneously embedding their experiences in the context of personal vulnerability, and a larger cultural discourse that links population ageing with burden (Grenier, 2007; see also Gee and Gutman, 2000). The point being made here is that older people's understandings of frailty are inseparable from the need for care: they are acutely aware of the human experience of vulnerability that is linked to the need for care, and the politics of assessing available social resources, be they personal, familial, social or public.

The concept of precarity as a lens of analysis

The concept of precarity draws attention to insecurities in the context of global economic and social change, including unwanted risks, and the costly hazards of contemporary life that result from globalization, neoliberalization and declining social protection (Grenier and Phillipson, 2018). Although relatively new as applied to ageing and late life, the concept has been used across a range of fields, primarily with regard to shifting conditions and the labour market, and in other works, the constructions of subjectivities and lives. Waite (2009, p 412) details precarity as 'life worlds characterized by uncertainty and insecurity', implying 'both a condition and a possible rallying point for resistance', and Millar (2017) outlines three ways of thinking about precarity, including as a condition, as a category and as an experience that includes political action. Both Waite (2009) and Millar (2017) point to the contextual readings of precarity as a relationship between lives or life worlds, social relations, and shifting conditions that produce insecurity and as such may warrant negotiation or resistance.

The interdisciplinary application of the concept of precarity to ageing and late life has drawn attention to the potential relevance of this term by connecting two disparate sets of scholarship on precarity (see Grenier et al, 2017a; 2017b).[4] The first, rooted in political science and labour studies, often attributed to the work of Standing (2011), draws attention to social relations, and in particular, how structural inequalities are reinforced through differential options and choices about work and care in later life. While Standing (2011) focuses on precarious work conditions and the subsequent social and economic inequalities, his work can be extended to late life, in particular through groups who are poorly served by traditional programmes like pension schemes (such as immigrants, casual employees, women and people with disabilities), as well as to disadvantages and inequalities that may extend into and past retirement, especially as older people begin to need care.

The second understanding of precarity considered in relation to late life, emanating from cultural studies and philosophy, and made known through the work of Judith Butler (2009), is chiefly concerned with the construction of subjects and questions of 'what it means to have a life' and 'when life is grievable'. Here, Butler's reading emphasizes the importance of cultural frameworks, coupled with the political and shared nature of such conditions and readings. Butler's (2009) argument is that we all experience precariousness at different points in our lives, that interdependence is a feature of the human condition and that precariousness is political. According to Butler (2009, p 25), precarity is a 'politically induced condition in which certain populations suffer from failing social and economic networks of support and become differentially exposed to injury, violence, and death'. Her analysis draws attention to how mutually held frameworks create and sustain particular responses, and can be used to shed light on the politics of ageing. Drawing on Butler's reading of precarity offers new insights on processes whereby older people become devalued through cultural scripts about dependency and decline, and on how this shared reading legitimates responses that leave older people suffering from unequal access to material goods, and the absence of public forms of care and support. Her approach can be employed to raise questions about care in later life, and points to how the construction of a devalued ageing may, in the context of declining social protection, place older people at greater risk of responses such as ill treatment or neglect.

The argument that is being pursued in this chapter is that the concept of precarity can move the conversation from that of frailty as an individual configuration of biomedical and functional risk written on the body to an acknowledgement of the shared vulnerabilities and shifting risks and insecurities in late life. Namely, how the experiences often attributed to frailty and that result in a need for care are experienced and responded to within a particular social, cultural, economic and political context. The suggestion is that frailty, viewed through a lens of precarity, reveals the existing shortcomings and problems that are inherent within the classification and responses to frailty. As a result, researchers may begin to witness how frailty is imbued with both the unevenness of 'reaching late life' and a relatively universal experience of vulnerability for those that survive. While the aspects of Standing's (2011) analysis, concerned with the political context within which risk operates, can be used to carry out a critique of altered forms of insecurity and risk in contemporary conditions (particularly the result of labour conditions), it is the interpretation of Butler (2009), focused on vulnerability as a feature of the human condition, that provides the means for deeper exploration of the construction of the 'frail subject', and the implications of being deemed a 'life less valuable'. We turn now to consider these contributions in greater detail to shift the debate about frailty.

Precarious conditions and the political context of care

The concept of precarity draws attention to the impact that current economic priorities and neoliberal practices may have on older people who are in need of support and care. Extending insights to late life draws attention to the effects of precarious conditions that accumulate into late life, or may become more pronounced at the onset of the need for care. Stretching Standing's (2011) examples of migrant workers, temporary workers without benefits and temporary contract workers over time, can signal how the current context may set the conditions for a precarious late life, through, for example, reduced public supports, housing insecurity or pension coverage (see Chapter 5). Older people increasingly find themselves confronted by the effects of insecure work histories (sometimes directly related to care for others), combined with reduced forms of social protection and public safety nets. Yet, in the case of ageing and late life, it is both the effects of earlier trajectories (unemployment, migration, caring and so on) and the need for care that become the pivot for precarity in late life (see Chapters 6 and 8).

The precarious conditions related to ageing and late life become most apparent through unmet care needs – whether real (current) or imagined (future). Since the 1980s, public programmes have been dismantled across international contexts, driven by neoliberal priorities of increased private and for-profit care, and public services, housing and social care have been altered and reduced (see Chapters 9 and 10). Writing in the United States in the late 1990s, Estes et al (1993) documented the existence of 'no care zones', whereby capitalist economies and structures of public services created the conditions and spaces where care became unavailable or inaccessible. These 'zones of no care', as they were labelled, emerged in the context of managed care, marked by minimal or residual service provision (if any), a lack of access to care, a shortage of material resources, a reliance on family care and the purchase of care from the private market – the very conditions (and historical timing) of the development of the assessment of measures of frailty. These 'no care zones', or 'gaps in care' as they are otherwise known (see Daly and Armstrong, 2016), can be seen as the direct result of political and economic decisions to reduce care, cut public supports, and rely on family or kin care – common features of neoliberal practices and conditions of austerity.

The concept of precarity highlights how decisions made about frailty and care are thus political. While the implications of neoliberal priorities and practices are most obvious on marginalized groups who no longer have access to the services they require, an analysis carried out through the lens of precarity also reveals how political priorities and particular responses create 'care gaps', and thus how the concept and practices related to frailty operate to reduce and limit access to services and supports. In this reading, the effects and implications of models that encourage individual responsibility and private market 'choices' over shared public responsibility are beginning to emerge. Consider the case of families who compensate for deficiencies in care systems by hiring their own workers to accompany family members who live in long-term care. Daly and Armstrong's (2016) research on 'private companions' in Ontario, for example, highlights the impact of hiring independent workers in the context of public long-term care. Their work reveals how although the 'private companion' fills a 'care gap', such choices 'remove the pressure to better staff public care, and limit the collective responsibility of the state to bear the costs of such care' (Daly and Armstrong, 2016, p 14). These choices, rendered necessary in a political and economic system where few options exist, reinforce existing problems in care systems and create significant gaps for those without pre-existing access to care (marginalized groups). Yet, such experiences, which potentially increase the precariousness of the older person in need of care, their families and workers, are often overshadowed by practices of assessment and distributions of care. We turn now to explore vulnerability in order to better understand and situate responses to the 'frail subject'.

Vulnerability and the construction of devalued subjects

Needing care, assessed through moments of bodily impairment and change such as that marked by the classification of frailty, draw attention to the precariousness of late life. Laceuelle (2017), a humanist philosopher writing in age studies, refers to such moments as the 'existential vulnerability' of ageing: the experience itself of vulnerability, and the shared reality that we all have the potential to be vulnerable and frail. In this line of thinking, the need for care – historically discussed as dependence, and more recently approached through functional notions of risk and frailty – can be considered to mark a moment where one's life is, in the words of Butler (2009), 'increasingly placed in the hands of another', whether they be professionals or family/kin. As such, this moment creates a new and/or altered (in the case of people with existing impairments) dynamic with having one's needs met (or not), and can produce vulnerability for individuals and families, and within the context of care.

Yet, changes to systems of care over time, described in the previous section on the politics of care, have also altered the attention to subjectivity and vulnerability in late life. Where configurations of need were historically organized (and delivered) according to linked notions of dependence and 'deservedness' (see Fine and Glendinning, 2005; Means et al, 2008), contemporary models of care are organized by mutually reinforcing terms of individual responsibility, autonomy and frailty (see Fine, 2005; Katz, 2011; see also Chapter 8). The result of such changes is that the responses to needs in late life, viewed through the angle of frailty, are less attuned to experiences of vulnerability. Contemporary responses, heavily biomedical and/or functional in their approach, vary from insistence on complete independence, to residual (and minimal) provision of home care services, to the purchase of market-based care and non-response. In this situation, one not only becomes dependent or frail, and therefore unsuccessful, but the 'existential vulnerability' at the heart of frailty remains unrecognized, and the older person is rendered 'at the mercy of another' in a context where few care options exist. The contradiction, however, is that while cultural scripts recognize and respond to this vulnerability – primarily through anxieties and fears of impairment – few public, institutional and organizational responses focus on this vulnerability and/or the real implications for care.

Ideas of vulnerability (and dependence) are central to discussions of care, subjectivity and social responses. Butler's (2009) discussions of precarious conditions, for example, are grounded in shared vulnerability as part of the human condition. Butler et al (2016, p 16) highlight the relational aspects of vulnerability as 'a relation to a field of objects, forces, and passions that impinge upon or affect us in some way … a kind of relationship that belongs to that ambiguous region in which receptivity and responsiveness are not clearly separable from one another, and not distinguished as separate moments in a sequence'. Feminist scholars writing about care have long focused on the problematic binary distinctions between dependence and independence, and outlined the importance of vulnerability, interdependence, and relationality as integral to a moral imperative to care (see Fine, 2005; see also Chapter 8). For example, authors such as Tronto (1993; 2010) have drawn attention to the biological and social processes of care and advocated for an ethic of care, whereas authors such as Sevenhuijsen (1998; 2003) have linked the arguments on giving and receiving care to issues of citizenship.

Although Butler's (2009) work provides a convincing basis for the analysis of the relationship between vulnerability and the construction of subjects and response, it is often critiqued for its relative silence with regard to suggested responses. A number of scholars have attempted to address shortcomings through the development of models for just understandings and responses. For example, Martha Fineman (2008), a legal scholar writing in the United States, formulates a version of vulnerability that is embodied, relational, and thus a matter of public and state responsibility. Fineman (2008, p 1) argues that 'vulnerability is—and should be—universal and constant, inherent in the human condition'. She goes on to argue that 'vulnerability initially should be understood as arising from our embodiment, which carries with it the ever-present possibility of harm, injury, and misfortune from mildly adverse to catastrophically devastating events, whether accidental, intentional, or otherwise' (Fineman, 2008, p 9). It is from this moral and ethical position that Fineman (2008) articulates vulnerability as the foundation of a legal and public response to care, through public rules, laws and structures (see also Fineman, 2010a; 2010b). In other words, it is 'precisely the shared threat of risk and harm that are located in and on the body, as well as mediated through social relationships, that merit shared responsibility at the state level'. Fineman's (2008, p 1) conceptualization of the 'vulnerable subject' is thus aligned with an ethical position of protection from harm, an analysis of structured forms of domination and marginalization, and a rational basis for a 'a more responsive state and egalitarian society'.

Writing in the context of feminist disability studies (in the United States), Kafer (2013) also focuses on the relationship between the cultural construction of particular subjects and responses to need. Kafer (2013) argues that responses to impairment and vulnerability are intricately connected to ideas about 'what counts as a life', and cultural scripts that have rendered people with disability to 'less valuable lives'. Her discussion centres on vulnerability in relation to the cultural narrative of 'disability as tragedy' and the accompanying ideas of people with disabilities as 'sites of no future' (Kafer, 2013, p 8). In doing so, Kafer (2013) highlights the need to recognize vulnerability and account for embodiment in social relations, including how pain, for example, may alter the everyday lives of people with disabilities – a recognition that has long been avoided in disability studies. Such thinking is indeed relevant to older people, who are also devalued through the 'decline narrative' and ideas of impairment in ageing as an 'already realized potential' and/or a burden related to the rising costs of care (see Gee and Gutman, 2000; see also Woodward, 2015). Kafer (2013) suggests that vulnerability be recognized and combined with the idea of 'futurity' and a sustainable future, as a moral and political imperative (see Kafer, 2013; McRuer, 2006). For Kafer (2013), futurity represents a utopian attempt to define an alternative vision of future possibilities that counter the 'disability as tragedy' narrative, the idea of a life deemed unworthy, thereby offering the means to improve care. Although conceptual distinctions and suggested actions differ between theorists, both Fineman (2010a; 2010b) and Kafer (2013) share a focus on recognizing and responding to vulnerability as a relational, moral and ethical responsibility.

Reconsidered approach: the potential of precarity for relocating frailty

This section outlines how an analysis of frailty informed by attention to the structured and cultural readings of precarity leads to three insights with regard to contemporary experiences of need in later life. First, frailty is not an individual experience, but a shared experience of vulnerability marked by changes to the body and the need for care. Second, although frailty is a shared feature of the human condition, the risks associated with needing care are socially, culturally, economically and politically situated, and as such uneven, with some older people at greater risk for insecurities and unmet need than others. Third, frailty and the need for care as experienced in contemporary conditions can deepen vulnerability and signal a potential abandonment of disadvantaged populations who may not have the necessary resources (financial or other).

Frailty is a shared experience of vulnerability

Reading frailty through a lens of precarity reveals that frailty is not only a biomedical classification and/or configuration of individual bodies at risk. Experiences that are commonly associated with frailty are also a shared experience of vulnerability that is part of the human condition. It is an experience of uncertainty and insecurity related to change over time, experiences of multiple losses, reflections about mortality, and a need for assistance, support and care. Further, it is precisely the need for care that places an individual at greater risk, both for devaluation as a result of dependency and for sustained disadvantage and/or unmet need. That is, the need for care in later life brings about emotional and practical forms of vulnerability, as well as a potential powerlessness related to the question of whether one's needs will be met, and in ways that are deemed acceptable. Turning to precarity as a lens through which to reconsider frailty thus loosens the reins of individual biomedical and functional interpretations by relocating it as part of the human condition, and situating the experience within the broader societal context of responses to care.

Locating frailty as a shared feature of the human condition renders visible the social relations that are constructed and enacted around dependency and need. Ideas of vulnerability applied to frailty relocate the 'frail subject' from individualized interpretations and enactments of risk to shared experiences that are part of life, embodied, and interconnected with public priorities, social systems and responses. As such, precariousness and vulnerability serve to challenge the binary of frailty/success and the attribution of individual (and familial) fault for dependence and/or need. Rather than deny vulnerability and suffering, as is the case in dominant readings and practices that surround frailty, feminist readings of precariousness and vulnerability offer a relational platform for collective action, alternate visions for late life, and different arrangements for care. Such readings also draw attention to the link between embodied vulnerability, the socioeconomic conditions that render one precarious and the heightened insecurities that result from inaction or failing support. The illustrative power in an analytic lens of precarity is in recognizing that frailty and the need for support is composed of diverse life course trajectories and risks over time, shared moments of vulnerability and contextually situated needs. This leads to the second insight linked to the social constructions and contextual 'situatedness' of frailty and risk.

Risk is socially, culturally, economically and politically situated

A lens of precarity makes evident how risks and insecurities associated with frailty are created, situated and experienced in social, cultural, economic and political contexts. Further, the concept of precarity turns attention to the impact of structured conditions and disadvantage over time, and how risks and precarious conditions are uneven, impacting some more than others, and in different ways. For example, groups with a history of unstable attachment to the labour force, or who have been excluded from paid work, may 'grow old' with fewer material resources, and thus experience elevated risks for housing instability or unmet needs (such as an inability to afford basic necessities, medication, care and so forth). Perhaps unsurprisingly, older women, people with disabilities, the foreign-born (Grenier et al, 2017b), low-paid or migrant care workers (Daly and Armstrong, 2016), and older people who live alone (Portacolone et al, 2019) have been identified as having a greater potential to be affected by precarity as it accrues throughout the life course and into late life. In such contexts and locations, the intersections between racialized and gendered care labour, for example, can deepen vulnerability on global and local levels, as workers and families engage in care labour chains (Yeates, 2012). This can include how families without the required resources assumed to be in place by neoliberal care systems may 'step in to provide care' at great personal and financial cost, resulting in their own precarity that may build and deepen over time.

The lens of precarity as applied to the ideas and practices that surround frailty exposes how while such vulnerabilities are part of the human experience, certain locations or lives are more susceptible to risks and hazards, and particularly so in a context characterized by precarious work and declining social protections. The idea – that risks are both shared and particular – is not new, and is best expressed by Beck (1992, p 41), who argues that, 'while we live in a global risk society, some people are at greater risk than others' (see also Sassen,

2014).[5] Famously citing differences with regard to poverty, housing and the environment, Beck (1992) draws on the illustration of the poor living on former landfill sites to highlight global, heightened and unequal risk. Such insights are easily extended to the case of care, whereby low income limits care options, in terms of the type of care one may afford and access, and the subsequent risks of unmet need.

The result of this analysis of frailty through the lens of the concept of precarity provides an awareness of the inequalities that are created and sustained for older people who need care and are deemed 'frail'. Although such an exploration could also have been carried out through the concept of risk, this notion, while offering a similar and relevant angle for analysis, has had less impact where critiques of frailty are concerned. This is in part because risk, like frailty, is also misunderstood as individual, biomedical and functional, rather than resulting from structures and social relations across international contexts and amid social conditions. In this case, the suggestion is that the concept of precarity helps to expose the dominance of individual configurations of risk, and to render visible how frailty is socially and culturally situated, as well as created and sustained through political and economic decisions about care and other forms of support to older people in need. Building on this, the chapter now turns to the third insight on how the politics of frailty may deepen experiences of vulnerability in the contemporary context.

Social conditions and political systems are deepening vulnerability

Adopting a lens of precarity draws attention to how altered social conditions and political systems can foster responses that deepen insecurities, risks and vulnerabilities among older people. In particular, it highlights how attention to frailty has gained momentum in the context of market models of care (that is, where care needs to be purchased) and political systems that prioritize residual public services characterized by reductions in programming, public spending, and a reliance on family and kin care. A lens of precarity renders visible the extent to which frailty operates as a taken-for-granted practice based on an acceptance of individual and biomedical/functional interpretations, thus masking the historical emergence (and situatedness) of frailty and its power relations. That is, it draws attention to how assessments of frailty are conducted with the sole purpose of discriminating between needs and targeting service responses, and are thus intricately involved in sustaining residual models of care that reduce access to services and silence alternate possibilities (see Grenier, 2007; Kaufman, 1994a;

Kaufman and Becker, 1996). As such, dominant responses to frailty in fact become complicit in creating and sustaining conditions of risk and insecurity. The problem that emerges in the context of population ageing is that greater numbers of older people, and thus greater numbers of people who may require care, may find themselves in precarious situations in the context of ever-shrinking social protections and expanding zones of 'no care'.

An analysis of precarity can therefore be used to reposition frailty in the context of medical practices, neoliberal priorities, and conditions of austerity that worsen vulnerabilities through declining social protection and political choices about care. This includes how risks may mount over time, not only as a result of reduced services, but because the lack of services sustain unmet need and disadvantage. An emerging concern that becomes visible through considering precarity in relation to frailty is the extent to which older people who need care and other forms of support are being left with unmet needs, abandoned by the public and the state. Whereas the focus on structural aspects of precarity reveals care gaps created through neoliberal policies and the shift away from shared collective responsibility, the focus on cultural aspects reveals how such responses are bolstered through the devaluation of age, impairment and decline often depicted through the social imaginary of the 'fourth age' (see Gilleard and Higgs, 2010).

Yet, it is here that the linkage between structural and cultural interpretations of precarity hold the most promise in understanding frailty from an interdisciplinary perspective. It is not merely that social conditions have changed, and that there is an ongoing devaluation of dependency, but that these are intricately linked with the cultural devaluation of the 'frail subject' situated in a particular social, cultural, economic and political context that deems older subjects in need of care as less worthy of a shared public response. And further, that the available or expected responses are individual responsibility, medical models of treatment, and residual care provided either by family/ kin or the purchase of care from the market. This analysis of frailty from the angle of precarity thus points to how social conditions, the constructions of subjects and political decisions about care serve to deepen vulnerability and sustain suffering, and may be used (either explicitly or implicitly) to justify the abandonment of older people in moments of need. It is here that Butler's (2009) attention to 'what counts as a life', and political decisions about devalued lives, become crucial to understand the precarity experienced in late life and in the context of austerity.

Conclusion

The argument of this chapter was that the concept of precarity provides a useful means to unhinge configurations of frailty from biomedical and individual interpretations of risk, and to expose an alternate storyline whereby the insecurities and risks associated with frailty, and the subsequent responses, are part of the human condition, the result of changing structures and political and economic systems. What becomes apparent through this analysis is that the stakes are high with regard to frailty because older people are caught in moments of existential vulnerability, experiencing needs in a context where few supports are available, and where the public emphasis seems to be moving away from care as a shared social responsibility. In establishing this, the analysis presented in this chapter sidesteps the current debate on frailty in order to consider another possibility: that responses to frailty have emerged at the intersections of biomedical specialization, neoliberal care systems, cultural imperatives of individual responsibility and the devaluation of decline, and amid longevity and population ageing.

This chapter has made the case for rethinking frailty through precarity, thereby altering the analytic frame to the historical, sociocultural, economic and political conditions within which it has emerged and operates. It has explored precarity as a means to reconsider frailty, and future possibilities for care, by drawing attention to the experiences of vulnerability and the political practices that surround frailty. It has also suggested that the risks and insecurities experienced in relation to the need for care, through what is often considered frailty, are particular because they tend to occur in later life, in the context of smaller support networks, amid disadvantages that have accrued over time, and after exit from the labour force (which reduces income and purchasing power). In this light, the analysis has reiterated the point that care becomes a crucial turning point for amplifying risks and insecurities that are produced over the life course and are experienced in the context of declining social commitments and austerity.

This chapter has drawn on precarity as a lens through which to illustrate how late life, and in particular the experiences and situations that are often configured as frailty, contain the vulnerabilities of the human condition, the accumulation of structured inequalities and the sociocultural assumptions of failure that are associated with social locations of needing care. Drawing attention to precarity and vulnerability as such thus underscores the need to slow down the speed at which research and practices organized around frailty are hurtling, reconsider frailty as a shared vulnerability that is part of the human condition, and revise approaches to care so that they foster the conditions for a sustainable life. The concept of precarity and ideas of precariousness have drawn attention to the aspects of human suffering and the problems that occur when needs are overlooked or remain unmet – in particular, how those with fewer personal or family resources may be at greater risk in the current neoliberal contexts of care.

Yet, while this chapter has engaged in a critique of frailty, carried out through the lens of precarity, it has not addressed the issue of how to best reconfigure responses. The suggestion is not to replace the language of frailty with that of precarity. Although this would undoubtedly alter the analysis from the medical to the social, and include the systemic, cultural and personal, it fails to address the larger political issues and existential aspects that accompany vulnerability and the need for care in late life. Instead, the suggestion is that an analysis of precarity be paired with principles such as justice and/or responsibility that provide the basis for an acceptable and liveable life, and open the possibilities for resistance and action (see also Grenier and Phillipson, 2018 and Chapter 10). This entails the consideration of moral imperative and ethical position with regard to care and late life, and the development of responses that are just and fair. Directions could include, for example, asking whether responses to need in late life foster the conditions for flourishing and/or a sustainable life. Part of this responsibility also contains the realization that such conditions will not emerge on their own; they must instead be created and nurtured through social commitment and political will (see Chapter 11).

Notes

[1] Google Scholar reveals that the article by Fried et al (2001) was cited 9,968 times as of 27 September 2018.

[2] For further information on the Canadian Frailty Network see www.cfn-nce.ca.

[3] The initial statement of intent concerning future directions in national ageing policy and NHS commissioning, given by Dr Martin Vernon, National Clinical Director for Integration and the Frail Elderly (NHS England), states, 'As the new NCD for Older People I intend to pursue all available opportunities for preventative, collaborative care offered by identification of pre- and moderate frailty…'. See Vernon 2016, https://www.england.nhs.uk/blog/martin-vernon/ [Accessed 25 August 2019].

⁴ A number of Canadian provinces have drawn attention to Falls and introduced Fall Prevention Programs at the ministry level. The Ministry of Health in the provinces of British Columbia and Ontario are cases in point (see: https://www2.gov.bc.ca/gov/content/family-social-supports/seniors/health-safety/disease-and-injury-care-and-prevention/fall-prevention [Accessed 25 August 2019] and https://www.ontario.ca/page/exercise-and-falls-prevention-programs [Accessed 25 August 2019].

⁵ The linkage of structural and cultural arguments need not be considered contradictory. Drawing on insights from an analysis of political and economic systems and a sociocultural analysis makes sense in the case of applied disciplines such as gerontology, in which the questions at hand have real impacts on the lives of older people. Critical approaches to the study of ageing have historically drawn on insights from both political economy and more interpretive dimensions as a means to understand ageing from a social and cultural perspective (see Baars et al, 2013; Twigg and Martin, 2015).

⁶ The quote here is: 'the proletariat of the global risk society settles', and 'there is a systematic attraction between extreme poverty and extreme risk' (Beck, 1992, p 41).

References

Armstrong, P. and Armstrong, H. (2003) *Wasting Away: the Undermining of Canadian Health Care*, Toronto: Oxford University Press.

Armstrong, P. and Braedley, S. (eds) (2013) *Troubling Care: Critical Perspectives on Research and Practices*, Toronto: Canadian Scholars' Press.

Baars, J., Dohmen, J., Grenier, A. and Phillipson, C. (eds) (2013) *Ageing, Meaning and Social Structure: Connecting Critical and Humanistic Gerontology*, Bristol: Policy Press.

Beck, U. (1992) *Risk Society: towards a New Modernity*, translated by M. Ritter, London: Sage.

Butler, J. (2009) *Frames of War: When Is Life Grievable?*, London: Verso.

Butler, J., Gambetti, Z. and Sabsay, L. (eds) (2016) *Vulnerability in Resistance*, Durham, NC: Duke University Press.

Canadian Frailty Network, (n.d.) Frailty Matters: A Growing Health System Challenge. https://www.cfn-nce.ca/frailty-matters/ [Accessed 25 August 2019].

Daly, T. and Armstrong, P. (2016) 'Liminal and invisible long-term care labour: precarity in the face of austerity', *Journal of Industrial Relations*, 58(4): 473–90.

Dillaway, H.E. and Byrnes, M. (2009) 'Reconsidering successful aging: a call for renewed and expanded academic critiques and conceptualizations', *Journal of Applied Gerontology*, 28(6): 702–22.

Estes, C.L., Swan, J.H. and Associates (1993) 'No care zone and social policy', in *The Long Term Care Crisis: Elders Trapped in the No-Care Zone*, Newbury Park, CA: Sage, pp 258–71.

Fine, M. (2005) 'Individualization, risk and the body: sociology and care', *Journal of Sociology*, 41(3): 247–66.

Fine, M. and Glendinning, C. (2005) 'Dependence, independence or inter-dependence? Revisiting the concepts of "care" and "dependency"', *Ageing & Society*, 25(4): 601–21.

Fineman, M.A. (2008) 'The vulnerable subject: anchoring equality in the human condition', *Yale Journal of Law & Feminism* [online], 20(1), available from: https://digitalcommons.law.yale.edu/yjlf/vol20/iss1/2 [Accessed 10 August 2019].

Fineman, M.A. (2010a) 'The vulnerable subject: anchoring equality in the human condition', in M.A. Fineman (ed.) *Transcending the Boundaries of Law: Generations of Feminism and Legal Theory*, Abingdon: Routledge-Cavendish, pp 177–91.

Fineman, M.A. (2010b) 'The vulnerable subject and the responsive state', *Emory Law Journal* [online], 60(2): 251, available from: https://ssrn.com/abstract=1694740 [Accessed 10 August 2019].

Fried, L.P., Tangen, C.M., Walston, J., Newman, A.B., Hirsch, C., Gottdiener, J., Seeman, T., Tracy, R., Kop, W.J., Burke, G. and McBurnie, M.A. (2001) 'Frailty in older adults: evidence for a phenotype', *Journals of Gerontology Series A: Biological Sciences & Medical Sciences*, 56(3): M146–57.

Gadow, S. (1983) 'Frailty and strength: the dialectic in aging', *The Gerontologist*, 23(2): 144–7.

Gadow, S. (1996) 'Aging as death rehearsal: the oppressiveness of reason', *Journal of Clinical Ethics*, 7(1): 35–40.

Gee, E.M. and Gutman, G.M. (eds) (2000) *The Overselling of Population Aging: Apocalyptic Demography, Intergenerational Challenges, and Social Policy*, Oxford: Oxford University Press.

Gilleard, C. and Higgs, P. (2010) 'Aging without agency: theorizing the fourth age', *Aging & Mental Health*, 14(2): 121–8.

Grenier, A.M. (2005) 'The contextual and social locations of older women's experiences of disability and decline', *Journal of Aging Studies*, 19(2): 131–46.

Grenier, A. (2006) 'The distinction between being and feeling frail: exploring emotional experiences in health and social care', *Journal of Social Work Practice*, 20(3): 299–313.

Grenier, A. (2007) 'Constructions of frailty in the English language, care practice and the lived experience', *Ageing & Society*, 27(3): 425–45.

Grenier, A. (2008) 'Recognizing and responding to loss and "rupture" in older women's accounts', *Journal of Social Work Practice*, 22(2): 195–209.

Grenier, A. (2012) *Transitions and the Lifecourse: Challenging the Constructions of 'Growing Old'*, Bristol: Policy Press.

Grenier, A. and Phillipson, C. (2018) 'Precarious aging: insecurity and risk in late life,' *Hastings Center Report*, 48(5): S15–18.

Grenier, A., Lloyd, L. and Phillipson, C. (2017a) 'Precarity in late life: rethinking dementia as a "frailed" old age', *Sociology of Health & Illness*, 39(2): 318–30.

Grenier, A., Phillipson, C., Laliberte Rudman, D., Hatzifilalithis, S., Kobayashi, K. and Marier, P. (2017b) 'Precarity in late life: understanding new forms of risk and insecurity', *Journal of Aging Studies*, 43: 9–14.

Gullette, M.M. (1997) *Declining to Decline: Cultural Combat and the Politics of the Midlife*, Charlottesville: University Press of Virginia.

Kafer, A. (2013) *Feminist, Queer, Crip*, Bloomington: Indiana University Press.

Katz, S. (2011) 'Hold on! Falling, embodiment, and the materiality of old age', in M.J. Casper and P. Currah (eds) *Corpus: an Interdisciplinary Reader on Bodies and Knowledge*, New York: Palgrave Macmillan, pp 187–205.

Kaufman, S.R. (1994a) 'Old age, disease, and the discourse on risk: geriatric assessment in U.S. health care', *Medical Anthropology Quarterly*, 8(4): 430–47.

Kaufman, S.R. (1994b) 'The social construction of frailty: an anthropological perspective', *Journal of Aging Studies*, 8(1): 45–58.

Kaufman, S., and Becker, G. (1996) 'Frailty, risk, and choice: cultural discourses and the question of responsibility', in M. Smyer, K.W. Schaie and M.B. Kapp (eds) *Older Adults' Decision-Making and the Law*, New York: Springer, pp 48–71.

Laceulle, H. (2017) 'Virtuous aging and existential vulnerability', *Journal of Aging Studies*, 43: 1–8.

Lloyd, L. (2004) 'Mortality and morality: ageing and the ethics of care', *Ageing & Society*, 24(2): 235–56.

Lloyd, L. (2015) 'The fourth age', in J. Twigg and W. Martin (eds) *Routledge Handbook of Cultural Gerontology*, London: Routledge, pp 261–8.

Lloyd, L., Calnan, M., Cameron, A., Seymour, J. and Smith, R. (2014) 'Identity in the fourth age: perseverance, adaptation and maintaining dignity', *Ageing and Society*, 34(1): 1–19.

Lustbader, W. (2000) 'Thoughts on the meaning of frailty', *Generations*, 23(4): 21–4.

McRuer, R. (2006) *Crip Theory: Cultural Signs of Queerness and Disability*, New York: New York University Press.

Means, R., Richards, S. and Smith, R. (2008) *Community Care: Policy and Practice* (4th edn), Basingstoke: Palgrave Macmillan.

Millar, K.M. (2017) 'Toward a critical politics of precarity', *Sociology Compass*, 11(6): e12483.

Morley, J.E., Vellas, B., Van Kan, G.A., Anker, S.D., Bauer, J.M., Bernabei, R., Cesari, M., Chumlea, W.C., Doehner, W., Evans, J., Fried, L.P., Guralnik, J.M., Katz, P.R., Malmstrom, T.K., McCarter, R.J., Gutierrez Robledo, L.M., Rockwood, K., von Haehling, S., Vandewoude, M.F. and Walston, J. (2013) 'Frailty consensus: a call to action', *Journal of the American Medical Directors Association*, 14(6): 392–7.

Nicholson, C., Meyer, J., Flatley, M., Holman, C. and Lowton, K. (2012) 'Living on the margin: understanding the experience of living and dying with frailty in old age', *Social Science & Medicine*, 75(8): 1426–32.

O'Shea, D. (2017) 'Frailty is the most problematic expression of population ageing', *British Geriatrics Society Blog*, 21 April, available from: https://britishgeriatricssociety.wordpress.com/2017/04/21/frailty-is-the-most-problematic-expression-of-population-ageing/ [Accessed 10 August 2019].

Pickard, S. (2009) 'Governing old age: the "case managed" older person', *Sociology*, 43(1): 67–84.

Pickard, S. (2014) 'Frail bodies: geriatric medicine and the constitution of the fourth age', *Sociology of Health & Illness*, 36(4): 549–63.

Portacolone, E., Rubinstein, R.L., Covinsky, K.E., Halpern, J. and Johnson, J.K. (2019) 'The precarity of older adults living alone with cognitive impairment', *The Gerontologist*, 59(2): 271–80).

Rockwood, K. and Mitnitski, A. (2007) 'Frailty in relation to the accumulation of deficits', *Journals of Gerontology Series A: Biological Sciences & Medical Sciences*, 62(7): 722–7.

Rockwood, K., Fox, R.A., Stolee, P., Robertson, D. and Beattie, B.L. (1994) 'Frailty in elderly people: an evolving concept', *Canadian Medical Association Journal*, 150(4): 489–95.

Sassen, S. (2014). *Expulsions: Brutality and Complexity in the Global Economy*, Cambridge, MA: Belknap Press.

Sevenhuijsen, S. (1998) *Citizenship and the Ethics of Care: Feminist Considerations on Justice, Morality and Politics*, translated by L. Savage, London: Routledge.

Sevenhuijsen, S. (2003) 'The place of care: the relevance of the feminist ethic of care for social policy', *Feminist Theory*, 4(2): 179–97.

Standing, G. (2011) *The Precariat: the New Dangerous Class*, London: Bloomsbury Academic.

Taylor, B.C. (1992) 'Elderly identity in conversation: producing frailty', *Communication Research*, 19(4): 493–515.

Tronto, J.C. (1993) *Moral Boundaries: a Political Argument for an Ethic of Care*, London: Psychology Press.

Tronto, J.C. (2010) 'Creating caring institutions: politics, plurality, and purpose', *Ethics and Social Welfare*, 4(2): 158–71.

Turner, G. and Clegg, A. (2014) 'Best practice guidelines for the management of frailty: a British Geriatrics Society, Age UK and Royal College of General Practitioners report', *Age and Ageing*, 43(6): 744–7.

Twigg, J. and Martin, W. (2015) 'The challenge of cultural gerontology', *The Gerontologist*, 55(3): 353–9.

Vernon, M. (2016) 'Our ageing population presents the NHS with its greatest challenge', https://www.england.nhs.uk/blog/martin-vernon/ [Accessed 25 August 2019].

Waite, L. (2009) 'A place and space for a critical geography of precarity?', *Geography Compass*, 3(1): 412–33.

Woodward, K. (2015) 'Feeling frail and national statistical panic: Joan Didion in *Blue Nights* and the American economy at risk', *Age, Culture, Humanities*, 2: 347–67.

Yeates, N. (2012) 'Global care chains: a state-of-the-art review and future directions in care transnationalization research', *Global Networks*, 12(2): 135–54.

Young, J. (2014) 'We must recognise frailty as a long term condition', *NHS England Blog*, 7 May, available from: https://www.england.nhs.uk/blog/john-young/ [Accessed 10 August 2019].

5

Older workers and ontological precarity: between precarious employment, precarious welfare and precarious households

David Lain, Laura Airey,
Wendy Loretto and Sarah Vickerstaff

Introduction

There has been a substantial increase in research dealing with the various forms of what has been termed 'precarious employment' (Arnold and Bongiovi, 2013; Campbell and Price, 2016; Kalleberg, 2018; Prosser, 2016; Vosko, 2010). Guy Standing's book *The Precariat* (2011) drew attention to what he saw as the precarious employment situation of older people (among other population groups), arguing that inadequate pension provision had led many to take new insecure jobs in later life. Standing conceptualized precarity as a labour outcome, related to individuals being *in* precarious employment, rather than older workers *feeling* precarious in a psychological sense. He argued (2011, p 59) that while some may be dissatisfied with being in precarious jobs (so-called 'groaners'), others might be perfectly happy with this situation ('grinners').

This chapter contributes to debates on precarity among older workers in two ways. First, it develops the concept of 'ontological precarity' as a means of describing the individual experience of anxiety arising from the everyday experience of precarious work. This builds on the work of scholars such as Millar (2017) and Worth (2016), who focus on precarity as a *lived experience* rather than solely as a labour outcome. Second, it develops a new theoretical framework for understanding ontological precarity, which extends the scope of enquiry beyond individuals' labour market position in order to take account of their broader circumstances (Campbell and Burgess, 2018).

We argue that for a significant proportion of older workers, the financial pressure to work for longer, combined with limited alternative employment prospects, gives rise to a heightened sense of precarity. To understand this, it is crucial to locate older workers' experiences of precarity within the context of a shifting 'welfare state' landscape; this includes rising State Pension ages and attempts to extend working lives (Grenier et al, 2017; Lain and Loretto, 2016). It is also important to take into account the fact that pressures to work longer are related to a decline in the financial support within households, a key change in recent years being the rise in the number of older people living alone (Office for National Statistics, 2017).

The theoretical model presented in this chapter identifies three intersecting 'domains' of precarity: precarious employment, precarious welfare states and precarious households. We suggest that older workers' sense of ontological precarity stems from feeling 'trapped' by the varying interactions of precarity in these three domains.

By 'precarious employment', we refer not only to various dimensions of job insecurity but also to an individual's perception that, for them, the prospect of working up to or beyond traditional retirement age is unsustainable, due to declining physical health or increased caring responsibilities. Meanwhile, 'precarious welfare states' and/or 'precarious households' may offer insufficient alternative financial support. Our approach to understanding precarity among older workers is underpinned by a life course perspective. Older workers' circumstances in later working life are shaped by personal life events and wider social processes over the life course, and the process of cumulative (dis)advantage means that inequalities widen as people age (Dannefer, 2003). Individuals' household and employment trajectories change over time in ways that are often highly gendered. For example, women may be particularly disadvantaged by the outcomes of divorce, separation and widowhood (Vickerstaff and Loretto, 2017). In this broader context, even older workers in relatively 'secure' employment may feel that their situation is precarious.

The chapter starts by developing what we mean by the term 'ontological precarity' and then proposes our theoretical model. Following this, we present case studies of three female UK hospitality workers; this illustrates how ontological precarity arises from varying interactions between precarious employment circumstances, a precarious welfare state and precarious households. The chapter concludes by discussing the policy implications and how our framework could be used for future research.

Conceptualizing ontological precarity among older workers

The concept of precarity has taken root within academic literature at the same time as neoliberalism and globalization have come to dominate economic and social regimes (Arnold and Bongiovi, 2013; Grenier et al, 2017; see further Chapters 1 and 10). Waite (2009) makes the point that there are a number of different meanings associated with the term 'precarity' but that they all convey a sense of uncertainty and insecurity. We would argue that such insecurity is *subjectively experienced* by individuals in the form of affective states such as increased anxiety (Lewchuck, 2017). This is partly anticipatory: anxiety is grounded in a set of current circumstances but also concerned with what may happen in future (Molé, 2010).

In this chapter, the term 'ontological precarity' is used to describe the state of anxiety experienced by individuals when they perceive their circumstances to be precarious. This differs from Standing's (2011) conceptualization of precarity, whereby an individual member of the precariat may not necessarily view their own circumstances as precarious in a negative sense. The relationship between subjective experience and objective reality is therefore crucial to this understanding of precarity. As Worth (2016, p 603) notes, 'objective uses of precarity do not tell the whole story as affective experiences of insecurity have a significant impact on a worker's choices and experiences of the labour market'. Perceptions of security are therefore crucial, because they guide behaviour and attitudes. It may be the case that an individual *feels* precarious even when their position seems to be relatively secure from an 'objective' standpoint. However, more generally the 'objective world' is likely to exert a strong influence on feelings of precarity. We therefore take the position that examination of both the 'objective' conditions structuring older workers' lives *and* individuals' subjective interpretations of their situations will lead to deeper insights into the lived experience of precarity among older workers.

Further, the extent to which an individual is in a precarious position cannot simply be reduced to their labour market status; wider circumstances, social relations and structural conditions are also highly relevant (Campbell and Price, 2016; Grenier et al, 2017; Strauss, 2017). As Campbell and Burgess (2018, p 61) argue, it is necessary to examine 'the way in which social forces outside the workplace mediate individual experiences of precariousness in employment'. For example, with regard to financial circumstances, a wealthy management consultant may have a series of temporary employment contracts; they would not, however, be considered to be in a precarious position in any meaningful sense. Reflecting these points, Millar (2017, p 5) asserts that precarity is 'both a socio-economic condition and an ontological experience.... It aims to capture the relationship between precarious labour and precarious life'.

To understand precarity as a lived experience among older workers, we therefore argue that it is necessary to consider not only individuals' job situations (precarious employment), but also the wider influences of precarious households and precarious welfare states. Broadly speaking, evidence suggests that the support older people have traditionally relied on from the welfare state and from their families or households has significantly declined in recent years (Phillipson, 2013). As a result, while older generations' living standards have generally improved in the UK, there are significant and growing inequalities between groups (for a broad comparative discussion, see OECD, 2017). This reduction in state/family support intensifies the sense of job-related precarity that many older people feel.

The next section examines the domains of precarious employment, precarious welfare states and precarious households, before considering the interaction between these domains.

Theorizing the three domains of ontological precarity

Precarious employment

Since the financial crash of 2007–08, work has arguably become less secure for many workers in the UK. Many of the jobs replacing those lost during the crash have been part-time, low-skilled and/or in self-employment. It is commonly assumed that many individuals involuntarily took these forms of employment because they lacked alternative options (Klair, 2016). Average wage levels declined during much of this period, making it harder to obtain a decent, secure income (Romei, 2017). In addition, following the election in the UK of a Conservative-led coalition government in 2010, the public sector has also been hit by severe funding cuts and job losses associated with austerity (Cunningham et al, 2016; Van Wanrooy et al, 2013). Given that this sector has historically had comparatively high levels of job security, this has meant that there are now relatively few 'safe places' in the UK labour market. In this context, older people appear to view their prospects of finding new work as limited, in part due to employer ageism (Loretto et al, 2017; Porcellato et al, 2010; Smith,

2000). Indeed, US research analysis suggests that unemployed older job-seekers find it significantly harder to get another job than their younger counterparts (Johnson and Mommaerts, 2010).

Even older workers in apparently secure work may feel precarious for a range of reasons. For example, some may they feel that they cannot sustain working at the levels expected in the workplace today. Work intensification – the expectation that workers will do more work per hour – has increased across a range of developed countries (Burchell et al, 2005; Green, 2006). US evidence suggests that work has also become increasingly stressful (Johnson et al, 2011). Physically demanding work continues to be a reality for many older workers, with almost a third of those aged 50 and over employed in jobs defined as physically arduous (Lain, 2016). At the same time, there is evidence in the UK that 'more than three quarters of the population do not have disability-free life expectancy as long as 68' (Marmot et al, 2010, p 17). Taken together, older workers may experience the influence of these factors as 'employment precarity' – in other words, they may view their job as potentially unsustainable, but perceive limited alternative prospects for employment.

Precarious welfare states

The anxieties experienced by older workers may be heightened if the individual has limited options for drawing on alternative non-wage incomes, such as pensions. Traditionally, the purpose of the welfare state is to 'de-commodify' individuals' reliance on the market for survival (Esping-Andersen, 1990). When governments instigate significant increases in State Pension age, with no compensatory mechanisms for supporting those who exit work early, the financial pressures to continue working increase dramatically (Lain, 2016). In 2010, individuals in the UK were able to receive their State Pension at age 60, and men at age 65. Since then State Pension age has risen dramatically for women, such that male and female pension ages are now equal at 65. Many older women therefore expected a State Pension at age 60 but found themselves having to continue in employment. The prominent Women Against State Pension Inequality campaign highlights concerns that women must now wait longer for a State Pension when they had based their plans (and expectations) on retirement at a much younger age (Vickerstaff and Loretto, 2017).

In addition to the changes for women, State Pension ages for both men and women will rise to 66 in 2020, 68 in 2028, and is expected to rise still further following regular reviews. It is important to note that there will be no option to take a reduced pension early, and 'Pension Credit' will no longer be available before State Pension age (Lain, 2016). Eligibility criteria have been tightened for Employment Support Allowance (for those unable to work due to ill health), and it is only worth around half the value of Pension Credit. The lack of a safety net to support those older workers involuntarily exited from work (via redundancy, ill health or caring responsibilities) is therefore likely to result in anxiety among older workers, in the context of jobs that they view as precarious.

Precarious households

UK policy for much of the 20th century was based on the premise of a 'modified male breadwinner model' (O'Connor et al, 1999), under which women commonly worked part-time and their careers were secondary to those of their husbands. As a result, the household circumstances of women determined their financial position in later life to a significant degree. While working patterns of women have continued to reflect this model, households have become increasingly precarious and uncertain in respect of sources of income (OECD, 2011). In 2014–15, only 53 per cent of women and 57 per cent of men aged 50–59 were married and with their first husband/wife (Banks et al, 2016); these were the individuals who were best off financially. By contrast, divorced and widowed older people were more likely to be in the lowest wealth quintiles. In general, older women are likely to have been particularly disadvantaged by divorce: their labour market participation throughout their lives is likely to have been limited by gendered family caring responsibilities, and they may not have a partner with whom to pool resources in later life (Blackburn et al, 2016; Ginn, 2003).

Our contention is that to fully understand precarity among older workers, we need to recognize that some individuals are in precarious employment, live in households that have had precarious trajectories, and are negatively affected by the precariousness of the welfare state.

Bringing together precarious employment, welfare states and households

While precariousness in each of these three domains may engender a sense of ontological precarity, it is when individuals experience precariousness in multiple domains of their lives that it is most severe. Indeed, precariousness in one domain may have limited impact on an individual's sense of ontological precarity if they are buffered by relatively secure circumstances in the other two domains. Individuals in precarious jobs, for example, may not feel a sense of precarity if they have access to generous welfare state support or a supportive household situation. It is therefore the interactions between different forms of precarity that are most significant. Conceptually, we may view individuals as being 'stuck between' different forms of precarity; the interactions between these are illustrated in Figure 5.1 and are outlined in turn.

When older workers are 'between precarious employment and welfare states', they may view their job and wider employment prospects as unsustainable or insecure, and they perceive little alternative support available from the welfare state. In these instances, the households in which they live have *not* undergone precarious trajectories over time. This may mean, for example, that marriages/partnerships have remained intact and any existing mortgages are paid off or near completion. However, because the welfare state is of importance to these individuals, it follows that their household situation cannot entirely compensate for precarity in relation to jobs and welfare.

In contrast to the previous group, older workers who are 'between precarious welfare states and households' do not view their jobs as unsustainable in the long term. However, their precarious household circumstances and their lack of access to publicly provided welfare create anxiety about the future. They feel stuck, or perhaps trapped,

Figure 5.1: Mapping the interactions between precarious employment, welfare states and households

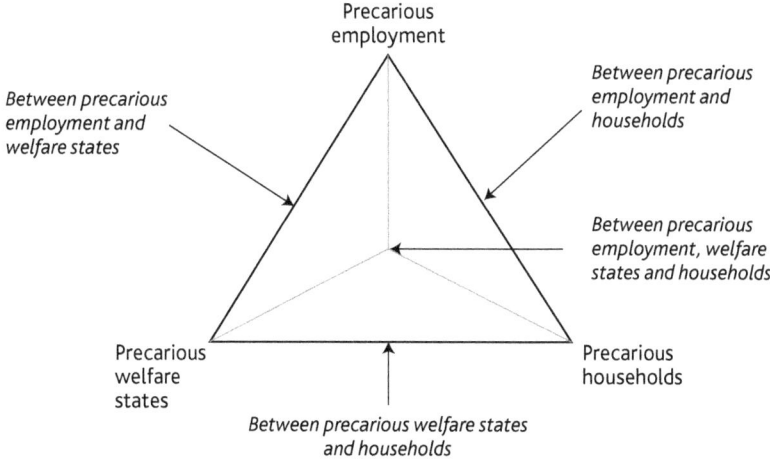

in their jobs without knowing how and if they will be able to retire. In some instances, this will include women whose expected retirement trajectory was thrown off-course financially by divorce or widowhood.

The third category relates to people who are 'between precarious employment and households'. These individuals have jobs that they view as unsustainable or insecure, and this insecurity is reinforced by precarious household circumstances. For these individuals, the welfare state is relatively unimportant, which suggests that they may have a reasonable level of income and have higher expectations about living standards, or that they have outgoings that exceed what can realistically be expected from the welfare state. This might include individuals who have high incomes but have suffered the financial consequences of divorce, and are left with large outstanding mortgage debts. Alternatively, this could include individuals who have remarried and taken on significant financial responsibilities for step-children. This is a relatively marginal category, because the State Pension is in fact a potentially important component of retirement income for most older individuals (Pensions Policy Institute, 2017).

Finally, older individuals could be 'between precarious employment, welfare states and households'. This category is more common than the previous one, because most individuals who have precarious jobs and households are also likely to be potentially dependent on the welfare state as well. These individuals are likely to have the most heightened sense of precarity. Their jobs are viewed as insecure or unsustainable, and yet because of circumstances such as divorce and widowhood they have limited financial support from others in the household. Added to this, the welfare state more often than not fails to provide essential security to their lives. Many will be divorced women who now have to wait much longer than previously expected for a State Pension; when they do receive a State Pension it may not be adequate for their household circumstances.

The next section of this chapter explores the notion of interacting domains of precarity, examining the situation of three female UK hospitality workers who were interviewed as part of a wider research project.

Methods

The analysis presented in this chapter is drawn from a study of transitions from work to retirement within five organizations in the UK. In the context of government policies designed to encourage the extension of working life, the research examined how key stakeholders within each organization managed the opportunities and challenges associated with later-life working. Data were collected from human resources managers, line managers, occupational health managers and employees aged 50 or over, via a mix of in-depth interviews, focus groups and documentary evidence. This case study methodology enabled construction of a 'comprehensive description of the setting' within each organization (Marshall, 1999, p 30).

In this chapter we focus on one of the five case study organizations: 'Hospitality', a catering and cleaning business unit of a large educational establishment. Unusually for the sector, jobs within Hospitality were relatively secure, in the sense that individuals were generally free from the threat of dismissal. This case study was therefore chosen because it illustrates how older workers might experience ontological precarity even when their jobs are not insecure in the sense envisaged by Standing (2011). Instead, workers often felt their jobs were *unsustainable* due to the physically arduous nature of employment, work intensification and health problems, and yet they often saw little financial option but to continue working.

Semi-structured interviews were conducted with 22 employees aged 50 or over in blue-collar, white-collar and managerial positions. Demographic information about the interviewees is presented in Table 5.1. The majority of the interviewees in this case study had jobs that involved manual labour, and most of them had worked in this or a similar sector for most of their working lives. In general, these interviewees did not have occupational pensions that would provide a financial cushion in retirement. A substantial proportion of employees in the group reported chronic health complaints that are

Table 5.1: Demographic information of the interviewees

		All	Women	Men
Marital status	Single	1	1	0
	Married	13	6	7
	Cohabiting	4	3	1
	Divorced	4	4	0
Self-reported health status	Good	8	4	4
	Fair	9	6	3
	Poor	4	3	1
	Don't know	1	1	0
Type of job role	Blue collar	16	6	6
	White collar	3	3	0
	Managerial	3	5	2
	Total	22	14	8

common among manual workers over the age of 50, such as arthritis and diabetes.

Interviews covered a range of topics in order to explore employees' views and experiences of their current jobs, and their plans for retirement. At the outset, interviewers collected biographical information about interviewees' work and family histories; this provided crucial contextual data about the dynamics of interviewees' household circumstances over the course of their lives. Employees were then asked to describe their current day-to-day work, and whether their feelings about their job had changed at all over time. Other topics covered in the interviews included: factors that would influence interviewees' decisions about the timing and nature of their retirement; views on government policies to extend working lives, such as the abolition of the Default Retirement Age and the rise in State Pension age; financial matters such as pension savings and retirement income; employer treatment of older workers within the organization; and how retirement was managed within the organization.

All interviews were recorded and transcribed. Data storage, coding and analysis were supported by the use of NVivo 10. Team members collaborated to develop a data coding framework, based upon both the interview topic guide and emergent themes derived from preliminary close reading of interview transcripts. All interviews were coded in NVivo using this framework, which allowed for a rigorous and theoretically underpinned approach to data analysis.

In this chapter we focus on the accounts of three female employees in the Hospitality case study, whom we have given the pseudonyms Thelma, Pearl and Angela. These particular women were selected because the forms of precarity that they experienced differed in terms of the interaction between precarious employment, precarious welfare states and precarious households (see Figure 5.2). Women were chosen over men because they were more likely to articulate a sense of ontological precarity (although it should be recognized that many men, too, were anxious about the future). Women were arguably more likely to feel a sense of precarity because, unlike men at this point, they were experiencing rapidly rising State Pension ages (having spent much of their careers expecting to retire at 60). The negative financial consequences of divorce were also keenly felt by significant numbers of these women. We therefore adopt a life course approach to illustrate the ways in which these women's current circumstances have been shaped by their family and employment experiences at earlier stages in their lives. The themes that emerged from the interviews with Thelma, Pearl and Angela were broadly consistent with findings from the wider data set for Hospitality.

Figure 5.2: Positioning individuals between precarious employment, welfare states and households

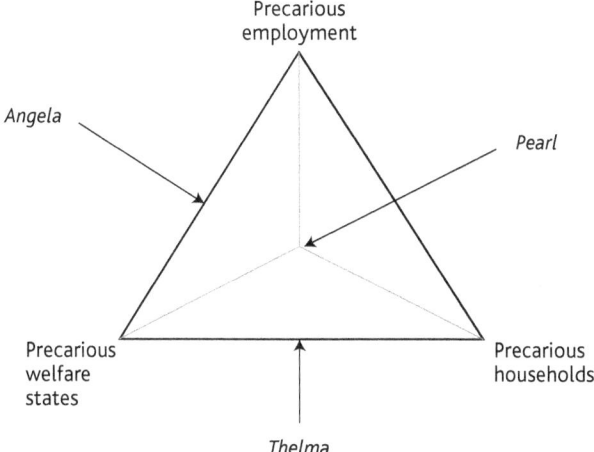

Findings

Thelma: between a precarious household and the precarious welfare state

Thelma, aged 64, is divorced and self-defines as being in good health. She has worked for Hospitality for 15 years in a full-time permanent white-collar job. Her domestic situation is a major driver of her thoughts about retirement. She lost access to her husband's pension on divorce and lives in rented accommodation. She feels that she cannot afford to retire as the size of the State Pension means she will have insufficient income without her salary. For Thelma, precarity arises from both the household and the welfare state domains.

Thelma's account of her current employment situation, her family circumstances and her anticipated retirement reveals a sense of ontological precarity engendered by interactions between a precarious household and a precarious welfare state. It is important to note that for Thelma, feeling precarious was *not* rooted in her job circumstances. Indeed, she spoke about her working conditions in positive terms: "I've got a secure job. I'm happy with my pay, which is unusual these days it seems, most people are not, but it certainly seems fine to me. The working conditions are excellent. The people I work with are lovely."

Despite her stable job, Thelma perceived herself to be very financially insecure, and her narrative was suffused with anxiety about her current and future finances. Thelma's account of financial insecurity in later working life is a powerful example of the ways in which divorce may lead to long-term financial disadvantage for women in particular. In common with many women of her generation, Thelma had given up paid employment upon her marriage, and had undertaken unpaid domestic labour at home. Upon divorce, Thelma was required to re-enter the labour market for the first time in 30 years. Further, she did not have the financial resources to remain in owner-occupied housing, and consequently moved into social rented accommodation. Her story illustrates the potential financial vulnerability of married women who do not have recourse to independently earned income, savings and pensions in the event of marital breakdown. At the time of interview, Thelma explicitly linked her divorce to her current state of financial insecurity and her need to remain in paid employment beyond State Pension age. Specifically, divorce had engendered precarity of housing tenure. Whereas Thelma had previously expected to own a home outright by this stage in her life, she now faced significant ongoing housing costs in the social rented sector. This made the prospect of retirement untenable: "If I didn't have rent to pay, I'd be a position of it being much easier, I think, to be able to say I'm going to retire."

The argument here is that Thelma's sense of ontological precarity was not simply a consequence of precarious household circumstances, but was also linked to the precarious welfare state. At the time of interview, Thelma had been claiming a State Pension for four years. This was clearly insufficient to cover her living costs, given that she anticipated needing to work indefinitely. Unsurprisingly, Thelma's outlook on retirement was bleak:

> 'I often do think will I retire ever … will I be able to retire?… I keep doing sums and looking at figures and thinking I want to do things and if I retire I won't be able to do anything 'cause I won't have any, I'll have just about enough income to survive.'

If individuals feel under pressure to continue in paid employment because the State Pension is inadequate to ensure a decent standard of living, then the welfare state may itself be thought of as 'precarious'. Rather than acting as a buffer against precarious household circumstances, the minimal income provided via the State Pension actually reinforces this precarity.

A life course lens renders visible the chain of events and circumstances that may contribute to a sense of ontological precarity in later working life, even when an individual's job is ostensibly secure. Thelma's story demonstrates how precarity in later working life may stem from disruption to household circumstances at an earlier life course stage. Individuals who are caught between an inadequate State Pension (precarious welfare state) and the continued need to pay for housing (precarious household circumstances) may face financial pressure to continue working indefinitely when they might otherwise have expected to retire.

Angela: between precarious employment and a precarious welfare state

Angela, aged 57, is married and self-defines as being in poor health. She has worked for Hospitality for six years; she works 30 hours a week on a permanent contract as a cleaner. She feels that her health problems will make it very difficult to continue working until State Pension age (67 in her case). The workload has increased and she finds it increasingly difficult to manage the work, but her husband is also in low-paid work so maintaining household income is dependent upon her wage. For Angela, precarity arises from both the employment and the welfare state domains.

Angela's account offers a vivid portrayal of ontological precarity arising from the experience of being caught between the precarious welfare state and a precarious employment situation. On the surface, Angela's employment situation might be considered to be as stable as Thelma's: both were employed in permanent jobs in the same organization. However, their subjective experiences of work stood in stark contrast to each other. Thelma felt secure in her job, whereas for Angela work was highly precarious. This job precarity was bound up with Angela's fear that she might lose her job if she disclosed to her employer the fact that she suffered from osteoporosis. Despite experiencing severe pain every day, which made it difficult for her to manage her work tasks, Angela went to considerable efforts to conceal her health condition from her line manager. She perceived her employer to be unsympathetic and unresponsive, as illustrated by the following quotation:

> 'If I went and said to them, you know, "Oh, I'm finding it really difficult," they normally say, "Well, obviously if you can't do the job, you need to leave, then". That's their answer…. It's not, "Well, let's see what we can do to help you," it's not like that at all.'

The physical demands of the job had intensified in recent months and Angela reported that managers were resistant to acknowledging employees' complaints about being overloaded: "There is a very lot of pressure. And even when you go to management and say 'Look, this isn't possible, we cannot do it with three members of staff or two members of staff,' 'I don't care, just go and get it done'. That's what you get."

For Angela, another aspect of job precarity was uncertainty about how long she would be physically able to continue doing her job. This was compounded by low expectations of being able to find alternative, less physically demanding work elsewhere; she perceived employers to be ageist and reluctant to recruit older workers:

> 'I was applying for 20, maybe 30, jobs on a daily basis, and this was the only one I got. And it was basically down to my age. I'm not a stupid person, I wasn't under-qualified for a lot of them, but they look at your age and they go, "Well, we're only going to get five years out of her".'

The employment-related precarity experienced by Angela interacted with and was reinforced by precarity in the domain of the welfare state. In contrast to Thelma, for whom precarity in the welfare state related to the low level of State Pension income, it was the rise in State Pension age that had led to great insecurity for Angela. Angela's overall household income was relatively low, and she felt under great financial pressure to work until State Pension age. The fact that she would not be eligible to receive a pension until the age of 67 was a major blow to her hopes of exiting the labour market at 60. In light of her health problems, Angela was very doubtful that she would actually be physically capable of working until her late sixties. Her account of her life suggested that she felt trapped, compelled to remain in work for longer than she would choose, or indeed felt physically able, due to the lack of alternative income sources before she reached State Pension age: "I know I've got to carry on working till the day I drop, basically, and there's nothing I can do about it."

Unlike Thelma, who linked her sense of precarity to her family circumstances, Angela did not give the impression that she perceived her household circumstances to be precarious; she was married and lived in owner-occupied housing, albeit on a low income. Rather, Angela's narrative indicates that her anxieties stemmed predominantly from the challenges of maintaining her job while struggling with debilitating health problems – without recourse to state support in the event that her health problems forced her out of work.

Angela's story brings into focus the precarious position of many older workers with health problems. The welfare state is arguably a precarious domain for older workers in poor health as it offers little in the way of a safety net for older workers in poor health who are below SPA. For example, Employment Support Allowance does not provide sufficient income to enable labour market exit in many cases. Indeed, older workers with health problems now face increased financial pressure to remain in employment for longer, due to rises in State Pension age. Employment may also represent a domain of precarity for older workers with health problems, if employers do not implement supportive policies and practices designed to help employees manage health problems while remaining in employment.

Pearl: between a precarious household, precarious employment and a precarious welfare state

Pearl, aged 61, is divorced and self-defines as being in fair health. She has worked for Hospitality for 6 years in a full-time permanent white-collar job. Her health and finances are major influences on how she thinks about retirement. The workload has intensified in recent years, and she worries about the impact on her health and whether she will be able to carry on doing her work at the current pace. She anticipates working until she is 70 because she needs the income from employment. For Pearl, precarity arises from the employment, household and welfare state domains.

Pearl's narrative offers insights into how precarity in the three domains of the welfare state, employment and household might intersect and interact over the life course, shaping individual experiences of ontological precarity.

Like Thelma and Angela, Pearl was in the position of having to work for much longer than she had originally anticipated in order to stay afloat financially. Rather than retire at 60 as she had previously envisaged, Pearl now viewed 70 as a more realistic retirement age. Like Thelma, Pearl's household circumstances had followed a precarious trajectory. Divorce had left her financially vulnerable after several years out of the labour market to care for her children. As she had been dependent on her husband's income and pension savings during their marriage, divorce had far-reaching implications for Pearl's ability to ensure an adequate income in retirement; at 61 she had minimal occupational pension savings of her own. Pearl's situation differed from that of Thelma in one key respect: housing tenure. Pearl had managed to remain in owner-occupied housing after her divorce, and she talked about the possibility of releasing financial resources by downsizing once her children had left home. However, this did not appear to alleviate Pearl's sense of financial insecurity and she still anticipated needing to work until she was 70.

In common with Thelma, the precarity associated with Pearl's household circumstances was reinforced by precarity associated with the welfare state. Pearl had to wait until she was 67 to claim her State Pension, and she calculated that this pension income would be inadequate to enable her to retire. In the following quotation, Pearl links the financial pressures to remain in paid employment to both her disrupted family trajectory (precarious household) and the lack of financial security offered by the State Pension (welfare state precarity):

> 'I mean, if I'd still been married, I would have been quite happy to retire at 60, because financially we would have been fine, because the pension that my husband was paying into would have covered both of us. On his leaving, I got left with nothing, so I've had to work and start paying into a pension here. So financially I'm not in a position to retire. Even when I get to 67, I still don't know how financially I would be able to manage. So I would say I would work as long as I could possibly work.'

The precarity in Pearl's life that arose from the intersections between precarious household circumstances and the precarious welfare state was further reinforced by precarity in the domain of employment. Like Angela, Pearl had a chronic health condition. Having adequate rest was vital in enabling her to sustain employment. However, her work had intensified over time and her shifts had recently been extended from eight to ten hours. Pearl claimed that management had portrayed the extra two hours of work as optional overtime, yet employees felt under pressure to work these additional hours. Unlike Angela, Pearl had disclosed her health problem to her line manager and had managed to gain exemption from working the extra two hours through liaison with Occupational Health: "Somebody comes from another college at 8pm and finishes my two hour shift, which makes me feel guilty. But, you know, it's better than me saying, 'Yes, I'll do it', and then, you know, not being well."

Although Pearl's job was apparently secure, she was anxious about whether her employer would continue to accommodate her health problems in the long term. She did not make reference to any employer policies designed to support her as she sought to manage her health at work. Rather, she felt that she had been "lucky" because her line manager had a family member with the same health condition, which meant that this manager was sympathetic to Pearl's situation. Thus, Pearl perceived the support available to her as being contingent upon individual managers, rather than it being a right enshrined in employer policy. Pearl was likely to be moved to a different area of Hospitality in future years, and she was worried that in future, line managers might not take her health condition into account when arranging her working hours: "Say, for instance, they make it compulsory that we all did till 10pm during conference time, I might have to think about giving up at 67, because I just don't think I could do it."

Thus, in a similar way to Angela, Pearl was caught between the financial pressure to work until 70, alongside the fear that an unsupportive employer response to her health problems might force her out of the labour market before then. Pearl shared Angela's perceptions of ageist attitudes among employers, which presented a barrier to her seeking other employment: "As you get older, it is a lot harder to find a job. So I think, whereas if I was in my twenties and I was unhappy, I would go and find something else you know … at my age, not so easy."

In summary, exploring Pearl's account in detail provides an opportunity to understand how subjective experiences of precarity among older workers may have their roots in multiple intersecting life domains. Our analysis has highlighted the similarities between Pearl's story and those of Thelma and Angela. We suggest that the key themes running through these women's accounts are indicative of trends affecting many older female workers. In the context of a precarious welfare state, those workers who have experienced a precarious trajectory in respect of the household and welfare state, and whose employment situation is also precarious, may unsurprisingly experience considerable anxiety regarding the timing and nature of exit from the labour market, and their anticipated standard of living in retirement. As Pearl commented, "It's a bit of a dark road, really".

Discussion

The case studies presented here illuminate a variety of ways in which interactions between three separate domains of precarity (employment, household and welfare state) may result in older workers experiencing anxiety about their current and future circumstances – a state that we have termed 'ontological precarity'. On the surface, the three women in the case studies were objectively secure, in the sense that they had permanent (albeit relatively low-paid) jobs. However, the ontological precarity articulated by these women reflected their sense that they were trapped in circumstances that they had not chosen. The financial insecurity engendered by precarious household circumstances and a precarious welfare state meant that they had effectively lost control over the end of their working lives, in terms of being able to choose the timing of their retirement. The combination of rises in State Pension age, the minimal income provided by the State Pension, and low levels of organizational and personal pension savings meant that the women in our case studies had to work for far longer than they had originally anticipated or would have chosen if they had been more financially secure. For two of the three women, uncertainty around their employer's response to their chronic health problems reinforced their sense of precarity: they were caught between the financial pressure to continue working indefinitely, while at the same time feeling uncertain about how long they would be physically able to work.

Our analysis has demonstrated that precarity cannot be considered solely as a labour condition, nor as an individual characteristic. Rather, ontological precarity is constituted at the intersections between specific sociopolitical conditions, employment contexts and individual life course trajectories. The case studies expose the dynamic interplay between structural conditions and individual circumstances over time; precarity in later working life is intimately connected to prior life events (events which themselves occurred within particular sociocultural contexts). The case study approach adopted in this chapter thus contributes to an enriched understanding of subjective experiences of precarity in later working life by situating individuals' accounts of their current employment within the broader economic and social context.

While we have identified three domains of precarity, we recognize that other relevant contexts, structural conditions, social processes and life events may contribute to the experience of ontological precarity among older workers. Future research could explore whether and how ontological precarity has been influenced by the recent widespread shifts in organizational and private pension provision from Defined Benefits (DB) schemes to Defined Contribution (DC) schemes. The adoption of DC schemes means that individuals are now more exposed to financial risk because retirement income is no longer guaranteed but instead is dependent on the performance of pension funds (Foster, 2018; Ginn, 2013).

There are other policy areas that are not necessarily age-related, but which may impact upon the labour market participation of older workers and influence the extent to which they experience ontological precarity. For example, UK policies concerning care for children, elderly people and disabled people shape the context within which older workers face increasing pressure not only to provide unpaid, informal care for grandchildren, elderly parents and other dependants, but also to extend their own working lives (Ginn, 2013; Vickerstaff and Loretto, 2017). The nature of older workers' experiences of negotiating unpaid caregiving and paid employment represents a point of intersection between the domains of work, family and the state that we would expect to have implications in terms of older workers' experience of ontological precarity; this is a topic worthy of further research.

The concept of ontological precarity could be elaborated and developed through further empirical work. We have focused here on the experiences of older female workers in relatively low-paying jobs. Given that gender roles and relationships structure labour market participation and unpaid caring roles over the life course, it would be useful to examine how older men's experiences of ontological precarity in later working life differ from those of women. For example, it would be interesting to explore the perceptions of men who have been the sole earner in a household over a long period, and the responsibilities and anxieties that they may feel. Finally, cross-national studies could investigate the ways in which ontological precarity are played out in different institutional contexts.

Conclusion

In this chapter we have developed a framework for understanding ontological precarity as a lived experience affecting older workers, which involves heightened feelings of anxiety and insecurity. We argue that ontological precarity involves older workers feeling 'trapped' by the interaction of precariousness in different life domains. 'Precarious employment' circumstances mean that continuing in paid work is viewed as unsustainable due to job cuts/work reorganization, work intensification or the difficulties of performing physically demanding work while suffering from chronic health problems. Linked to this is the sense that there are limited suitable alternative job opportunities in the wider labour market for older people; empirical evidence indicates that they find it much harder than younger workers to secure new jobs. Until recently, any anxieties older workers felt about this could be lessened by the fact that they were entitled to age-related benefits from age 60 ('Pension Credit' and/or a State Pension in the case of women). However, because of the second factor identified here – 'precarious welfare states' – individuals must now wait much longer in order to receive income via the State Pension, causing significant anxiety. For financial reasons, many individuals now need to work for much longer than they would have done in the past, and yet they worry that because of health problems and/or the nature of the work they will find it increasingly difficult or even impossible to continue in employment. Even when in fairly secure employment, individuals may experience psychological distress if they cannot envisage a time at which they will be financially stable enough to retire.

In addition to these worries, a third issue affects older workers: increasingly 'precarious households'. The impact of precarious household circumstances is highly gendered. In the past, women could generally rely on their husbands' pensions and savings if they were no longer able to continue working. Divorce, separation and new partnerships may pose financial risks for men and women. However, the negative impact of such changes are more likely to be experienced by women, as their careers and pension contribution records are often limited by their unpaid family caring responsibilities (Ginn, 2003).

The women discussed in this chapter exemplified how these domains of precarity may interact in different ways. Thelma, for example, had what looked like quite secure employment, but precarious household circumstances (divorce) and a lack of financial support from the welfare state meant that she felt indefinitely trapped in employment at the age of 64. Angela, on the other hand, had quite stable household circumstances, albeit with a low income; however, pension reforms meant that she would have to work much longer than previously expected in a job viewed as unsustainable from a health perspective. Finally, Pearl suffered from heightened precarity emanating from all three domains: employment precarity as a result of work intensification; financial difficulties as a result of divorce; and an inadequate welfare state from which to draw alternative forms of income. In this chapter, we have focused on women, partly because the backdrop of rising female State Pension ages highlights the sense of precarity experienced by this group. However, in future we envisage that this framework could be used to broaden out the study of precarity to older men, given that men may typically feel different pressures to work longer if, for example, they see themselves as the traditional 'main breadwinner'.

From a policy perspective, it is clear from this research that it is insufficient to focus solely on the issue of precarious employment. Labour market reforms, such as abolishing mandatory retirement, will do little to address many of the causes of unsustainable employment in older age. Further, such reforms do not take into account the precarious nature of the welfare state and many households. The situation facing these Hospitality workers is likely to be far from unusual. The incidence of chronic health conditions and declining physical ability increases with age, particularly among individuals in lower socioeconomic groups (Marmot et al, 2010). This is a particular problem given that benefit reforms have restricted pathways out of the labour market due to ill health (Vickerstaff and Loretto, 2017). Likewise, rises in State Pension age affect everybody, and DB occupational pensions – which in the past provided a degree of financial security in order age – are now rare in the private sector (Lain, 2016).

The UK government seems to accept that, as State Pension age rises, full-time work may not be sustainable for many older people. In this context, the government has promoted flexible/part-time work as a key means for extending working lives, and older workers have been granted the 'right' to request flexible working. However, flexible work is not a panacea for this problem. First, many employers seem reluctant to provide it (Loretto and Vickerstaff, 2015). Second, without access to additional sources of income – such as a pension – many of those in low-paid physically demanding work cannot afford to reduce their working time. Third, even with reductions in working time, it is morally questionable whether we should expect individuals with health problems to continue working until they 'drop', especially when their health problems have been built up from doing many years of physically demanding work. We therefore need to urgently consider how we can provide a proper safety net for older workers, so that ontological precarity is no longer a feature of later working life.

References

Arnold, D. and Bongiovi, J.R. (2013) 'Precarious, informalizing, and flexible work: transforming concepts and understandings', *American Behavioral Scientist*, 57(3): 289–308.

Banks, J., Batty, G.D., Begum, N., Demakakos, P., de Oliveira, C., Head, J., Hussey, D., Lassale, C., Littleford, C., Matthews, K., Nazroo, J., Oldfield, Z., Oskala, A., Steptoe, A. and Zaninotto, P. (2016) *The Dynamics of Ageing: Evidence from the English Longitudinal Study of Ageing, 2002–15 (Wave 7)*, London: Institute for Fiscal Studies [online], available from: https://www.ifs.org.uk/publications/8696 [Accessed 13 August 2019].

Blackburn, R.M., Jarman, J. and Racko, G. (2016) 'Understanding gender inequality in employment and retirement', *Contemporary Social Science*, 11(2/3): 238–52.

Burchell, B., Ladipo, D. and Wilkinson, F. (eds) (2005) *Job Insecurity and Work Intensification*, London: Routledge.

Campbell, I. and Price, R. (2016) 'Precarious work and precarious workers: towards an improved conceptualisation', *Economic and Labour Relations Review*, 27(3): 314–32.

Campbell, I. and Burgess, J. (2018) 'Patchy progress? Two decades of research on precariousness and precarious work in Australia', *Labour & Industry*, 28(1): 48–67.

Cunningham, I., Baines, D., Shields, J. and Lewchuck, W. (2016) 'Austerity policies, "precarity" and the nonprofit workforce: a comparative study of UK and Canada', *Journal of Industrial Relations*, 58(4): 455–72.

Dannefer, D. (2003) 'Cumulative advantage/disadvantage and the life course: cross-fertilizing age and social science theory', *Journals of Gerontology Series B: Psychological Sciences & Social Sciences*, 58(6): S327–37.

Esping-Andersen, G. (1990) *The Three Worlds of Welfare Capitalism*, Princeton: Princeton University Press.

Foster, L. (2018) 'Active ageing, pensions and retirement in the UK', *Journal of Population Ageing*, 11(2): 117–32.

Ginn, J. (2003) *Gender, Pensions and the Lifecourse: How Pensions Need to Adapt to Changing Family Forms*, Bristol: Policy Press.

Ginn, J. (2013) 'Austerity and inequality: exploring the impact of cuts in the UK by gender and age', *Research on Ageing and Social Policy*, 1(1): 28–53.

Green, F. (2006) *Demanding Work: the Paradox of Job Quality in the Affluent Economy*, Princeton: Princeton University Press.

Grenier, A., Phillipson, C., Laliberte Rudman, D., Hatzifilalithis, S., Kobayashi, K. and Marier, P. (2017) 'Precarity in late life: understanding new forms of risk and insecurity', *Journal of Aging Studies*, 43: 9–14.

Johnson, R.W. and Mommaerts, C. (2010) *Age Differences in Job Displacement, Job Search, and Reemployment*, Boston, MA: Boston College Center for Retirement Research [online], available from: https://crr.bc.edu/working-papers/age-differences-in-job-displacement-job-search-and-reemployment/ [Accessed 13 August 2019].

Johnson, R.W., Mermin, G.B. and Resseger, M. (2011) 'Job demands and work ability at older ages', *Journal of Aging & Social Policy*, 23(2): 101–18.

Kalleberg, A.L. (2018) *Precarious Lives: Job Insecurity and Well-Being in Rich Democracies*, Cambridge: Polity.

Klair, A. (2016) 'Employment is at record levels – so what's the problem?', *Touchstone* [Blog] 8 April, available from: https://touchstoneblog.org.uk/2016/04/employment-record-levels-whats-problem/ [Accessed 17 July 2017].

Lain, D. (2016) *Reconstructing Retirement: Work and Welfare in the UK and USA*, Bristol: Policy Press.

Lain, D. and Loretto, W. (2016) 'Managing employees beyond age 65: from the margins to the mainstream?', *Employee Relations*, 38(5): 646–64.

Lewchuk, W. (2017) 'Precarious jobs: where are they, and how do they affect well-being?' *Economic and Labour Relations Review*, 28(3): 402–19.

Loretto, W. and Vickerstaff, S. (2015) 'Gender, age and flexible working in later life', *Work, Employment and Society*, 29(2): 233–49.

Loretto, W., Airey, L. and Yarrow, E. (2017) *Older People and Employment in Scotland: Equality, Poverty and Social Security*, Edinburgh: Scottish Government [online], available from: https://www2.gov.scot/Resource/0052/00523780.pdf [Accessed 17 July 2017].

Marmot, M.G., Allen, J., Goldblatt, P., Boyce, T., McNeish, D., Grady, M. and Geddes, I. (2010) *Fair Society, Healthy Lives: Strategic Review of Health Inequalities in England Post-2010*, London: The Marmot Review [online], available from: http://nccdh.ca/resources/entry/fair-society-healthy-lives [Accessed 13 August 2019].

Marshall, V.W. (1999) 'Reasoning with case studies: issues of an aging workforce', *Journal of Aging Studies*, 13(4): 377–89.

Millar, K.M. (2017) 'Toward a critical politics of precarity', *Sociology Compass*, 11(6): e12483.

Molé, N.J. (2010) 'Precarious subjects: anticipating neoliberalism in northern Italy's workplace', *American Anthropologist*, 112(1): 38–53.

O'Connor, J.S., Orloff, A.S. and Shaver, S. (1999) *States, Markets, Families: Gender, Liberalism and Social Policy in Australia, Canada, Great Britain and the United States*, Cambridge: Cambridge University Press.

OECD (2011) *Doing Better for Families*, Paris: OECD Publishing.

OECD (2017) *Preventing Ageing Unequally*, Paris: OECD Publishing.

Office for National Statistics (2017) *Statistical Bulletin: Families and Households: 2017*, London: Office for National Statistics [online], available from: https://www.ons.gov.uk/peoplepopulationandcommunity/birthsdeathsandmarriages/families/bulletins/familiesandhouseholds/2017 [Accessed 26 July 2017].

Pensions Policy Institute (2017) *Dependency on the State Pension Through Retirement*. London: Pensions Policy Institute [online], available from: https://www.pensionspolicyinstitute.org.uk/media/1372/201801-bn104-how-much-do-people-depend-on-state-pension-throughout-the-retirement-process.pdf [Accessed 23 August 2018]Office

Phillipson, C. (2013) *Ageing*, Cambridge: Polity.

Porcellato, L., Carmichael, F., Hulme, C., Ingham, B. and Prashar, A. (2010) 'Giving older workers a voice: constraints on the employment of older people in the North West of England', *Work, Employment and Society*, 24(1): 85–103.

Prosser, T. (2016) 'Dualization or liberalization? Investigating precarious work in eight European countries', *Work, Employment and Society*, 30(6): 949–65.

Romei, V. (2017) 'How wages fell in the UK while the economy grew', *Financial Times*, 2 March.

Smith, T.W. (2000) *A Cross-National Comparison on Attitudes towards Work by Age and Labor Force Status*, Paris: OECD Publishing.

Standing, G. (2011) *The Precariat: the Dangerous New Class*, London: Bloomsbury Academic.

Strauss, K. (2018) 'Labour geography 1: towards a geography of precarity', *Progress in Human Geography*, 42(4): 622–30.

Van Wanrooy, B., Bewley, H., Bryson, A., Forth, J., Freeth, S., Stokes, L. and Wood, S. (2013) *Employment Relations in the Shadow of Recession: Findings from the 2011 Workplace Employment Relations Study*, London: Palgrave Macmillan.

Vickerstaff, S. and Loretto, W. (2017) 'The United Kingdom – a new moral imperative: live longer, work longer', in A. Ní Léime, D. Street, S. Vickerstaff, C. Krekula and W. Loretto (eds) *Gender, Ageing and Extended Working Life: Cross-National Perspectives*, Bristol: Policy Press, pp 175–91.

Vosko, L.F. (2010) *Managing the Margins: Gender, Citizenship, and the International Regulation of Precarious Employment*, Oxford: Oxford University Press.

Waite, L. (2009) 'A place and space for a critical geography of precarity?', *Geography Compass*, 3(1): 412–33.

Worth, N. (2016) 'Feeling precarious: millennial women and work', *Environment and Planning D: Society and Space*, 34(4): 601–16.

6

Precarity, migration and ageing

Karen Kobayashi and
Mushira Mohsin Khan

Introduction

The profile of older adults in the Global North is rapidly diversifying, with increasing proportions of foreign-born ageing populations in large immigrant-receiving countries like Canada and the United Kingdom. In Canada, for example, 30 per cent of those aged 65 years and over are foreign-born (Ng et al, 2012). Yet, despite this demographic significance of the foreign-born older adult population, very little research has been conducted on the complex and varied experiences of risk and insecurity vis-a-vis ageing and life course events such as international migration. It is, therefore, timely to critically examine the markers of immigration, race and ethnicity, and cultural beliefs and practices, as they intersect with poverty and socioeconomic inequality among immigrant older adults. This is particularly the case given that these intersections are likely to manifest in experiences of invisibility, marginalization and social exclusion.

This chapter presents a nuanced analysis of precarity, risk and vulnerability as it relates to ageing and migration. It begins with a story of migration that sets the context for the chapter. It then provides an outline of precarity in relation to migration, and a brief overview of the key economic and psychosocial/cultural markers of precarity in older immigrants. Next, it highlights the 'politics of precarity' that are inherent in the larger political economy of immigration and the relative invisibility of racialized immigrant older adults in health and social care policies, and, drawing on these, returns to a discussion of precarity among older immigrant adults. Examples of media stories about, and interviews with, older immigrants are provided throughout the chapter as a means to ground our analysis in everyday examples. The chapter concludes with a discussion of the challenges to understanding precarity in the context of migration, and provides suggestions for future research.

A story of migration: setting the context

> Keith Bi is a forty-seven-year-old Chinese immigrant and the owner of Coffee Corner, a café located in the windowless basement below the office of Citizenship and Immigration Canada. Bi immigrated from the city of Xi'an, China, on a working visa after being told by one of his relatives who lives in Halifax that Canada is a good place to live. He was told he wouldn't have to deal with the complicated social relationships that occur in China; relationships are more straight-forward in Canada. And he could even open his own business.
>
> He decided to come to Canada first, and then hopefully bring his wife and son in the future. Six years later, Bi, estranged from his wife and son, has realized that opening a new chapter in life is never easy. The first time he tried to launch a restaurant it fell flat, he says due to a poor choice of partners. And although his second attempt is also struggling, he will never give up. He gets up at 5:30 a.m. before the sun rises and leaves after 6 p.m. on most nights. He doesn't sit down until noon. Since the café is in a basement, the only time he gets to see the sun on a winter weekday is when he goes outside to have a smoke. He throws on his ten-year-old leather jacket and strolls down the hallway, joking that smoking for him is like an injection, to motivate himself.
>
> (Excerpt from Xu, 2017)[1]

Bi's story effectively captures the social risk, vulnerability and precarity that are deeply embedded in the immigrant experience. It renders problematic narratives around migration: the stories of the successful rebuilding of lives in a 'foreign land'; the inspirational accounts of human agency in response to social, political and economic imperatives; and the journeys bravely undertaken in the quest for a 'better life'. It also serves as a reminder of the insecurity, unpredictability and fragmented life situations that often accompany the process of migration and settlement, particularly for those who immigrate in mid- or later life.

Recent reports from Canada indicate that a growing proportion of immigrant older adults live in a heightened state of precarity characterized by low income and health disparities. In 2012, the highest chronic low-income rates were observed among immigrants over the age of 65: 30 per cent among all immigrant older adults, and as high as 50 per cent among more recent immigrants (with less than 10 years in Canada) (Picot and Lu, 2017). Further research suggests that compared to non-immigrants, older immigrants are twice as likely to reside in multigenerational households with their adult children (see, for example, Battams, 2013; De Valk and Schans, 2008; Ng et al, 2007), a living arrangement marked by complex cultural, social and practical considerations (Khan and Kobayashi, 2017; Khan, 2018). In addition, predispositions to certain diseases exist among particular ethnic groups. For example, immigrant populations from South Asia, one of the fastest-growing population subgroups in North America, experience higher rates of diabetes mellitus and heart disease (Gupta et al, 2006; Raymond et al, 2009). The diversity in health status found among older immigrants is nonetheless better understood as the outcome of different life course trajectories that are influenced only minimally by biology, genetics or behaviours. Rather, it is sociocultural determinants that produce health inequalities in precarious populations and account for 75 per cent of the influences on health (Mikkonen and Raphael, 2010). To a large extent, the differential impact of interactions of these factors across groups of older adults depends on their social location in Canadian society (Neysmith and Reitsma-Street, 2005).

The health and well-being of older immigrants, then, requires focused attention, particularly given the increasing ethnocultural diversity of the population in the Global North. Statistics Canada's 2016 census data predict 'future cohorts of older Canadians to be more ethnoculturally diverse, as a larger portion of them could be born outside of Canada' (see Figure 6.1). Yet, little research exists on the intersections of migration, ageing, risk and insecurity in this group.

Of the existing studies, a significant number have focused on the impact of political and legal exigencies on the social integration and/or labour market participation of immigrant older adults (see, for example, Grubel, 2005; Koehn et al, 2010; McLaren, 2006). But a more comprehensive understanding of vulnerability and social risk among older immigrants, as Grenier et al (2017) have also pointed out, necessitates that closer attention also be paid to the fragmented lived experiences of those outside the labour force, such as recently-arrived older immigrants. To this end, the conceptual framework of precarity is useful in that it brings into sharp focus the creation of marginal identities and 'the devaluation of particular lives' (Grenier et al, 2017, p 322) that are often tied to life course transitions like migration. The chapter now turns to the concept of precarity and to outlining the markers of precarity in relation to migration.

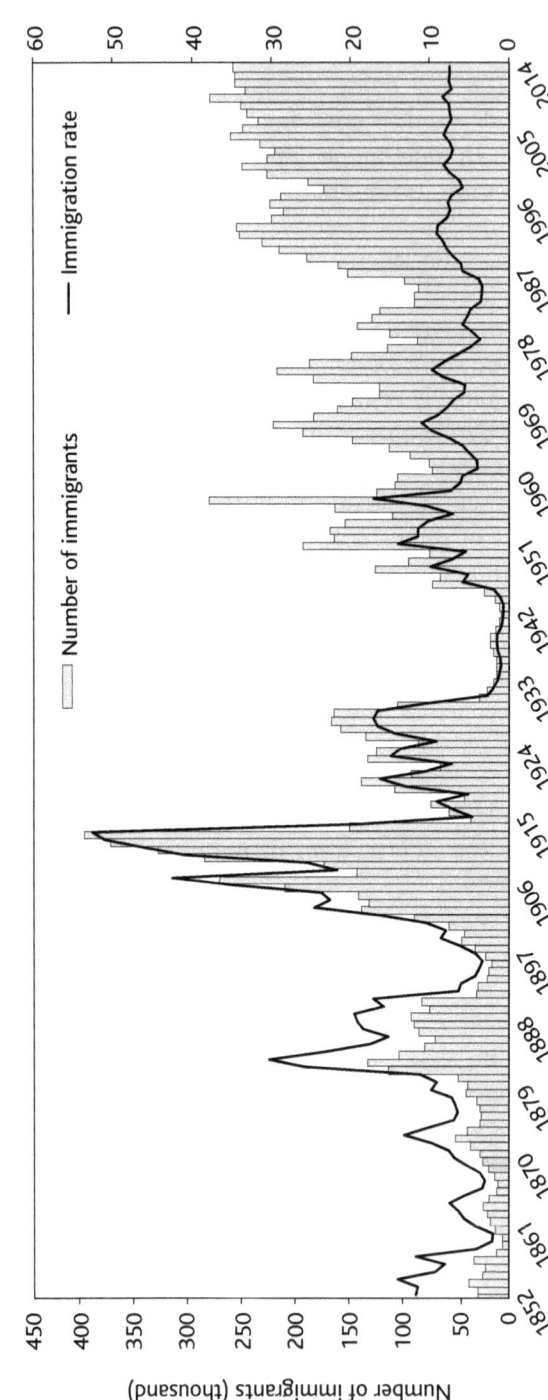

Figure 6.1: Number of immigrants and immigration rate (1852–2014)

Notes: A study conducted for the Statistics Canada's Insights on Canadian Society series focused on several cohorts of current and future seniors. The cohorts comprised individuals born in 1937–41, 1957–61, 1967–71 and 1997–2001. One of the key findings was that immigration was a catalyst for the population increase observed in the 1937 and 1941 cohorts. The authors concluded that the population level was 36 per cent higher due to immigration (Houle and Maheux, 2016).

Sources: Immigration, Refugees and Citizenship Canada (Facts and Figures 2014); Statistics Canada, Demography Division, Population Estimates Program

Migration and precarity

Ettlinger (2007, p 319) equates precarity with the uncertainty and unpredictability inherent in the 'microspaces of everyday lives'. Likewise, Judith Butler (2006, p 25) proposes a more expansive definition of precarity that connotes a 'politically induced condition in which certain populations suffer from failing social and economic networks of support and become differentially exposed to injury, violence, and death'. Paret and Gleeson (2016) have called for an analysis of precarity that underscores the significance of broader political and economic shifts as they mediate and shape, on the one hand, relationships between individuals and groups, and on the other, capital and the state. They argue that precarity is a multi-dimensional concept that provides a sharper 'analytical point of departure' (Paret and Gleeson, 2016, p 285) for understanding everyday experiences of vulnerability, exclusion from public services and state protections, institutional discrimination, and social isolation in migrants' lives. Conceptualized as such, precarity serves as a useful link between the micro and the macro. Indeed, in the context of migration, it offers not only a lens to capture the complex range of experiences and uncertainty that shape the everyday lives of immigrant older adults, but a means to foreground these experiences within a broader sociopolitical setting.

The markers of precarity among immigrant older adults

The following section identifies and discusses the key markers of precarity that exist among immigrant older adults. It focuses on two types of markers: economic markers, and those broadly grouped together as psychosocial and cultural markers. In the case of the latter, the markers are further broken down into six aspects, including abuse and stigma, loss of status and role, immigrant status, life course events, language, and health literacy. Each of the two types of markers begins with illustrations derived from a range of sources to render the experiences of precarity among older immigrant adults visible, and to situate these within a larger institutional, social and cultural context.

Economic markers of precarity

> Mr. Wang and his wife immigrated to Canada to re-unite with their son and his family seven years ago. In Canada, they contributed

their retirement savings towards purchasing a house for their son. Initially, they actively participated in everyday household activities like caring for their grandchildren, cooking, cleaning, and grocery shopping. But over time, as their grandchildren grew up and became more independent and self-sufficient, and with their own declining health, the Wangs' relationship with their son and daughter-in-law began to rapidly deteriorate. With limited financial resources at their disposal, the Wangs have no choice but to continue to live with their son's family, often confined to their cold, tiny room in the basement of the house.

(Authors' interview with front-line worker)

Older adults, particularly those who immigrated later in life to reunite with their adult children, like the Wangs, are perhaps one of the most vulnerable subgroups of immigrants. In one US-based study, O'Neil and Tienda (2010) found that late-age immigrants face considerable economic disadvantages as a result of exclusion from public benefits such as old age security pensions. A Canadian study by Curtis et al (2017) highlighted gaps in the social safety net by exploring disparities in Old Age Security (OAS) uptake based on immigration status: recent immigrants were less likely to utilize OAS benefits, largely due to length of residency, but also due, in part, to limited language proficiency and visible minority status. Such disadvantages and patterns of service use can result in economic insecurity and/or financial dependence, especially in situations of sponsorship. Added to this, findings by Nam et al (2015), for example, found that those who immigrated to the United States when they were aged 55 years or older exhibited low levels of financial knowledge and asset ownership. Further, older immigrants who live in poverty may also encounter specific economic barriers to the adoption of health-promoting behaviours, such as those related to good nutrition and physical activity, thereby adversely affecting their health over time (Rusch et al, 2015).

Economic markers of precarity may be particularly acute in cases of sponsorship and/or family reunification. Although family reunification has long been a cornerstone of North American immigration policy, there is inadequate government support available for sponsored family members. Sponsored older adults (like parents), for example, have limited access to available health and social services such as social security benefits and health insurance programmes such as Medicaid upon arrival in the US (Castañeda et al, 2015). Likewise, in Canada, sponsored older relatives do not have adequate access to available social assistance benefits like OAS, and sponsors must agree to financially support their dependents for a period of 20 years.[2] At the same time, families are often unable to provide for their members due to resource constraints, and not all older immigrants have children in North America to take care of their needs (Koehn et al, 2011), factors that may lead to increased experiences of precarity. As such, financial dependence on sponsors (often for decades), coupled with underutilization of and/or ineligibility for many publicly funded assistance programmes, may result in situations where many immigrant older adults get caught in what Standing (2011) refers to as the 'precarity trap' (see further Chapter 5). Manifestations of precarity among vulnerable older immigrants, however, are shaped not only by their material circumstances, but also by a range of psychosocial and cultural factors, which unfavourably affect their emotional well-being. These are identified and discussed in the following section of this chapter.

Psychosocial and cultural markers of precarity

> A 76-year old woman was sponsored by her daughter and son-in-law from Sri Lanka in 1995 to cook and clean the couple's house and babysit their two children.
>
> The Toronto woman was not allowed to talk on the phone or have visitors. Her savings were seized. The son-in-law, an alcoholic, once pushed her so hard she fell on her back. She was then taken in by a distant relative.
>
> 'I didn't want to leave the house because I was very attached to my grandchildren,' the woman said through a Tamil interpreter. 'They said they would send me to a nursing home so I wouldn't see them again.'
>
> She said she never contacted authorities because she felt ashamed and afraid.
>
> (Excerpt from Keung, 2010)

> Mr. Singh, a widower, grew up in a boisterous Indian household with 14 family members. In Fremont, California, he moved in with his son's family and devoted himself to his grandchildren, picking them up from school and ferrying them to soccer practice. Then his son and daughter-in-law decided 'they wanted their privacy,' said Mr. Singh, an undertone of sadness in his voice. He reluctantly concluded he should move out. When he leaves the Hub, a mall near his home where several older adults like him gather five

days a week to fend off the well of loneliness and isolation, dead leaves swirling around its fake cobblestones. Mr. Singh drives to the rented room in a house he found on Craigslist. His could be a dorm room, except for the arthritis heat wraps packed neatly in plastic bins.

(Excerpt from Brown, 2009)

'It is like I am not here ... I don't matter anymore. I am of no use. I live a life of no value anymore. Even the place where I once had power, inside my home, in my family, I now feel that I have none.'

(Authors' interview with recently immigrated,
family-sponsored Punjabi male, 72 years)

Abuse and stigma

These excerpts effectively capture the vulnerable, marginalized and precarious lives of older immigrants. Indeed, research has underscored the salience of psychosocial markers such as stigma, social isolation and self-esteem as important determinants of health and well-being in ethnic populations (Hatzenbuehler et al, 2013; Phelan et al, 2010; Schvey et al, 2011). Elder abuse and neglect in ethnoculturally diverse communities, for example, often goes unreported due to the complex interplay of race, ethnicity, immigrant status, and cultural perceptions around stigma and shame (Lai et al, 2014). Roger et al (2015) found that apart from familial and cultural considerations, limited proficiency in mainstream languages, ageism, and the difficulty of identifying and 'naming' abuse may also contribute to low levels of reporting among older immigrant women.

Further, the precarious health status of older immigrants may be exacerbated by a range of psychosocial factors. Stigma may also intersect with health and well-being. For example, the stigma attached to cancer as an 'untreatable' disease may act as an additional barrier to accessing timely treatment among older immigrants (Choudhry, 1997). As Lai and Surood (2013) have also noted, older visible minority patients are more likely to deny health problems because of the stigma related to disease and illness, particularly mental health issues such as dementia (McCleary et al, 2013). The 'visible stigma' (Goffman, 1963; 2009) associated with the colour of one's skin, accented or limited proficiency in 'mainstream' languages, and wearing religious attire like the *hijab* and *abaya*, have also been noted to culminate in worsening feelings of marginalization, disempowerment and distress among racialized immigrants (Padilla and Perez, 2003).

Loss of status and role

Racialized older immigrant women may also experience a number of adverse consequences such as poverty, discrimination, low social status and vulnerability to interpersonal violence (Hyman et al, 2006), and are, not surprisingly, at greater risk of unfavourable mental health outcomes (Astbury, 2001). Further, 'loss of role', or role reversal, may result in poor self-esteem in older immigrants such as the mothers-in-law in Koehn and Bains' (2012) study on Punjabi older adults in Vancouver, Canada. The participants in this study experienced ambivalence and confusion about the evolving nature of their relationship with their acculturated daughters-in-law and grandchildren, a finding supported by Blair (2012) in his study on immigrant older men in California.

Immigrant status

Life course transitions such as immigration and the stressors associated with settling down in an unfamiliar country may adversely affect the health of immigrants over time (Castañeda et al, 2015). Research has suggested that upon arrival, immigrants typically have better health as measured by age-standardized mortality rates than their native-born counterparts, a phenomenon that has been referred to in the literature as the 'healthy immigrant effect' (HIE) in Canada (Dunn and Dyck, 2000; Ng and Omariba, 2014; Vissandjee et al, 2004) or the 'Latino paradox' in the US (Castañeda et al, 2015; Nazroo, 2003). This can be attributed largely to the selective nature of international migration, whereby healthy individuals may consider themselves better positioned to successfully negotiate the challenges of settlement and adaptation to an unfamiliar environment, and therefore self-select for migration (Jasso, 2003). Immigration policies of the receiving country, such as the mandatory health exam for Canadian immigrants, may also act as a 'second filter' for these individuals, thereby ensuring that only the healthiest immigrants are admitted into the country (Urquia et al, 2015).

The health advantage of new immigrants, however, tends to lessen over time (Ng and Omariba, 2014), and those who immigrate in later life (65 years and older) tend to report poorer overall health in comparison to native-born older adults (Gee et al, 2004). Further, health status declines, as indicated by higher morbidity of chronic disease (Newbold, 2005) or increased body mass index (McDonald and Kennedy, 2005) among longer-term immigrants, are often associated with changes in behaviour following migration (Dean and Wilson, 2010; Newbold, 2005). More recently, Vang et al (2017) found that the healthy immigrant advantage does indeed vary across and within each stage of the life course and according to different health outcomes. The effect appears to be strongest during adulthood but less so during childhood/adolescence and late life. But even in adulthood, some discrepancies between different immigrant subgroups persist depending on the type of health measure used. For example, there is greater variation for self-rated health, but less variation for mental health, disability/functional limitations, risk behaviours and chronic conditions.

Life course events

Some of these differences in health and well-being can be understood by placing them within the frame of lifelong habits and behaviours. To illustrate, gender segregation, patriarchal protection, and/or preparation for marriage and family life in their early years in their birth country may prevent older immigrant women from accessing available health and social support services that do not align with internalized traditional and cultural health-seeking norms (Weerasinghe and Numer, 2011). Moreover, becoming less active is often regarded as a normal part of ageing in some ethnic communities, an attitude that may be compounded by a fatalistic approach towards health and illness (Horne and Tierney, 2012). These factors, combined with limited linguistic proficiency and/or literacy, may render precarious the health and well-being of older immigrants (Weerasinghe and Numer, 2011).

Language

Limited language proficiency is another salient marker of precarity. The lack of English (and/or French in the Canadian context) language skills, compounded by scant availability of interpreting services, particularly those with expertise in cultural interpretation, and the poor quality of clinical interactions due to language barriers, may result in limited use of available health and social care services (Spence and Koehn, 2010). Linguistic capability may also affect the ability of immigrants to become effective advocates for their needs. For example, research in the US found that despite the availability of information-seeking avenues such as health information hotlines in California, immigrant older adults may be unable to coherently express their health-related needs over the telephone due to limited language proficiency, often resulting in a communication breakdown between the patient and the provider (Blair, 2012). Similarly, Ng et al (2003), in their study on immunization rates among Hispanic adults, determined that participants were more likely to be receptive to health messages from Spanish-speaking *promotoras* (promoters) than to messages from those who spoke only English.

Health literacy

With regard to health literacy, that is, the capacity to make informed and appropriate decisions about their health, immigrants in general score significantly below the national average, both in Canada (Canadian Council on Learning, 2008) and in the United States (Soto et al, 2015). Low levels of health literacy along with inadequate linguistic capability may result in limited uptake of health-related resources and present significant challenges to chronic disease management in older adults. For example, some participants in Poureslami et al's (2012) Canadian study on the prevalence of asthma in immigrant older adults falsely regarded asthma as a communicable disease. Likewise, in a study based in the United States, Choi and Smith (2004) found that immigrant older adults with chronic conditions often have limited knowledge/information or misinformation about their condition, resulting in a lack of trust in the formal health care system.

Social isolation and loneliness

Another key marker of precarity in older immigrants is social isolation. Immigrant older adults from non-European countries are at increased risk of social isolation and loneliness compared to their European-born counterparts, partly because of language and cultural barriers that may make forging new connections more difficult in the receiving country, and/or separation from lifelong networks of family and friends (De Jong Gierveld et al, 2015). In addition, older adults often encounter challenges such as the cold North American weather, transportation issues and administrative barriers upon arrival, factors that may add to their social isolation and loneliness (Lai and Surood, 2013). The process of migration may thus result in feelings of helplessness and marginalization, particularly for those who immigrate later in life.

The women in Dastjerdi and Mardukhi's (2015) qualitative study on social isolation in older Iranian immigrant women in Canada, for example, were deeply affected by what they perceived as 'losing control over their lives and familiar connections' after migration (Dastjerdi and Mardukhi, 2015, p 83). Likewise, in a study conducted in the United States, Mukherjee and Diwan (2016) concluded that the quality of social relationships and strength of social networks was positively associated with quality of life and sense of well-being in late-life immigrants from India. Sponsored older immigrant adults may also be socially isolated under the weight of domestic responsibilities such as caring for their grandchildren and a 'collective ethos' that mandates that ageing parents 'subordinate their needs to those of other [younger] family members' (Treas and Mazumdar, 2002, p 243). Further, acculturation – the process by which culturally diverse groups become more homogeneous through changes in identity, values and beliefs (Greenland and Brown, 2005) – may bring logistical challenges and psychological barriers to well-being, adding to the precarious life situation of older immigrants.

Acculturation

Acculturative stress, induced by social isolation and the stressors associated with migration and cross-cultural adjustment, may also lead to depression in less acculturated older immigrants (González et al, 2001). More recently, Sun et al (2018) noted that the effect of low acculturation on mental health is significantly reduced when older adults have adequate social support and close ties with family members. In research on older Iranian immigrants in Canada, Moztarzadeh and O'Rourke (2015) identified links between acculturation and mental health. The authors found that involuntary migration and loss of occupational status were associated with low levels of acculturation and reduced life satisfaction. This finding is significant and warrants further interrogation. For many late-life immigrants, the decision to migrate may stem from complex culturally-mandated expectations around ageing, caregiving and filial responsibility. Many older immigrants, like the Wangs in the vignette presented at the beginning of the chapter, leave behind financially secure and comfortable lives in their home countries in order to reunite with their adult children in the receiving country. This disruption in their life course trajectory, coupled with stringent sponsorship and immigration rules, limited financial resources, dependence on their adult children for support and maintenance, social isolation and the loss of core social and generational networks, and low levels of integration into the receiving country, raise crucial questions around 'choice' and the voluntary nature of family reunification. Indeed, for many sponsored older immigrants, life course transitions like migration and ageing out-of-place may result in uncertainty, unpredictability and fragmented life situations.

Clearly, the markers of precarity among older immigrants are complex and intersect in several important ways. Here it should be pointed out that the previous discussion is not intended to undermine or discount the importance of human agency and initiative; indeed, a vast body of research suggests that racialized immigrant older adults often incorporate diverse and creative negotiation practices into their everyday lives as a means to make sense of their lived experiences in the receiving country (Guglani et al, 2000; Kim, 2009; Ng et al, 2005). Religious values, faith and cultural beliefs, for example, may act as effective everyday coping strategies, particularly for older immigrant women (Lee and Chan, 2009; Sin, 2015). Similarly, mindfulness (Ryan et al, 2018), 'keeping busy' with familial obligations and engagement in culturally-meaningful activities (Acharya and Northcott, 2007), density of social networks (Soto et al, 2015), strength of transnational ties (Zhou, 2015), and use of technology and social media (Khvorostianov et al, 2012) may all serve as 'buffers' to offset challenges associated with ageing in a new country. But as the discussion that follows demonstrates, experiences of precarity among immigrant older adults are often embedded within debilitating institutional and structural contexts that may considerably limit the exercise of individual agency.

The 'politics of precarity'

> There are many challenges for immigrant seniors to stay healthy. Many come with their children, at an older age. They are cut off from the support network in their old country.... I am lucky I can communicate in English. Language is the biggest barrier for these seniors. They are not familiar with the system here and must depend on other people who can speak English to help them.
> (Una Choi, who immigrated to Canada in 1982 with her family and four children; excerpt from Keung, 2017)

The following section turns to the politics of precarity. It outlines three political aspects of precarity that researchers should consider when attempting to understand the lives and experiences of immigrant older adults. These include systemic racism and discrimination, immigration policy and health care systems. Following these, the chapter returns to a discussion of precarity and precariousness among older immigrant adults.

Systemic racism and discrimination

Hyman (2009) has outlined that discrimination negatively affects health in direct and indirect ways. For example, metabolic and immune systems may weaken over time due to the stress associated with experiences of interpersonal and/or institutional discrimination among racialized immigrants, and as a result, individuals may resort to unhealthy coping strategies and behaviours (Noh et al, 1999). Indirectly, discrimination may influence health through other social determinants of health, such as socioeconomic status, by limiting educational and/or job opportunities (Krieger et al, 2003). Factors such as racism and discrimination, immigrant status, language barriers and lack of 'North American work experience' may also result in fatigue, economic exploitation and engagement in risky behaviours on the job (Facey, 2003). Further, experiences of discrimination may extend to problems in access within health services and institutional settings. For example, longer waiting times in order to receive primary care for urgent, non-emergency conditions (Bierman et al, 2012) may lead to structured subordination and the creation of social conditions wherein powerful and privileged groups advance their interests at the cost of the vulnerable and marginalized.

For ethnic older adults, the process of racialization significantly impacts health and quality of life. The social categories of ethnicity and immigrant status and the corresponding social production of ethnic and immigrant identities interact with other fundamental determinants of health such as gender and age to impact an individual's ability to access the key social resources necessary for health promotion and maintenance (Benoit and Shumka, 2009). In practical terms, racism affects health through systemic and individual level occurrences of discrimination, marginalization and susceptibility to poverty, to name a few.

Yet, there is a tendency for research on immigrant older adults to reproduce the essentializing and othering that occurs in society. Othering practices often remain invisible to those who perpetrate them, but may include, for example, ahistorical and abstracted overgeneralizations applied to specific individuals to explain their behaviour (Johnson et al, 2004). Typically, these explanations invoke the socially constructed notions of ethnicity, immigrant status, culture or even gender as a means of creating distinctions between 'us' and 'them'. Othering fails to recognize the complex interactions between different categories or sources of social inequality and how these constructions are based on a range of biases. This form of inadvertent discrimination often originates or is supported by policies and institutional structures intended to be equal and equitable, but which are actually designed in accordance with white, native-born, middle-class values (Brotman, 2003). Together, these experiences of institutionalized discrimination can be considered to reflect a range of 'cumulative disadvantages' (Dannefer, 2003) that contribute to precarity in later life for immigrant older adults.

Immigration policy

It is well documented that immigration policy is a key macro-level determinant of health and well-being; just and humane immigration policies are considered a necessity to support and maintain the health of individuals (Novak et al, 2017). To illustrate, Canada's 'merit' or points-based system of immigration privileges individuals with advanced skills with a view to drive its economy. However, highly qualified recently landed immigrants, despite possessing significant levels of cultural capital, are often subject to considerable setback and stress when they are forced to work in low-paying jobs in order to acquire the mandatory Canadian work experience (Saraswati, 2000). Relatedly, the neoliberal political ideology of fiscal conservatism, the discourse on cost containment and the retrenchment of the welfare state over the past several decades have resulted in significant reductions to federal funding of health and social service programmes in both the US and Canada (Coburn, 2004). These cutbacks likely have a disadvantageous impact on available settlement services for immigrants, and alongside previously discussed trends, may render particular groups such as sponsored older adults particularly vulnerable. Indeed, in response to all of these challenges, the release of high-stress hormone levels may have a negative effect on several body systems, such as the cardiovascular, reproductive and immune systems (Novak et al, 2017), leading to unfavourable health outcomes in later life.

Health care system

In its list of key social determinants of health, the World Health Organization's Commission on the Social Determinants of Health included, for the very first time, health care systems as critical determinants of health. Health care systems influence the type and quality of health care available to individuals in several important ways, with poorly performing health systems leading to inequities in the distribution of health services and unfair burden of health care costs

(World Health Organization, 2008). In the United States, which does not have a system of universal health care, and where market forces determine the costs of health care delivery and access, immigrants generally have lower rates of insurance coverage compared to native-born populations (Liebert and Ameringer, 2013; Siddiqi et al, 2009). Given the high costs associated with health services, immigrants are less likely to visit a physician for either primary (Lucas et al, 2003) or preventive (Xu and Borders, 2008) care, thereby negatively affecting their health and quality of life in the long term. The 2008 Affordable Care Act (ACA), passed under the stewardship of President Barack Obama, attempted to address health inequities by expanding health care benefits to include millions of uninsured Americans; specifically, it prevented health insurance companies from denying insurance to individuals on the basis of pre-existing conditions (Weiss and Lonnquist, 2017). Further, several new health insurance benefits were provided, including coverage for adult children under their parents' plan up until the age of 26, and compulsory coverage for preventive services, such as childhood immunizations, cancer screenings and contraceptives (Weiss and Lonnquist, 2017). Although critics highlighted the high costs associated with the plan, and related challenges of such measures (see Chapter 9) it was nonetheless an important step towards advancing health equity. Unfortunately, with the resurgence of fiscal conservatism and the debate around repealing and replacing the ACA, universal health coverage for Americans remains a distant and elusive possibility.

Conversely, access to health care is enshrined as a basic human right under the 1984 Canada Health Act, and the availability of universal health insurance (Medicare) is a matter of national pride for Canadians (Armstrong et al, 2001). Yet, overwhelming evidence from advanced capitalist societies indicates that national measures of morbidity and mortality are (at least) as dependent upon prevailing social conditions as they are upon the size of the health care system (Armstrong et al, 2001). Given this, although the Canada Health Act strives to ensure the equitable distribution of health services, it is hardly surprising that health inequities stubbornly persist, with marginalized and vulnerable populations often at the receiving end of the negative effects of neoliberal public policies and programmes (Coburn, 2004). For example, large immigrant-receiving provinces such as British Columbia and Ontario impose a mandatory three-month waiting period for access to provincial health care plans for recently landed immigrants (Government of Canada, 2017). Consequently, newly arrived immigrants are either forced to purchase expensive private health insurance, pay for services out of their own pocket, or delay seeking treatment until after they obtain access to their provincial health care plan (Asanin and Wilson, 2008). For sponsored older adults, financial dependence on their sponsors is exacerbated by the difficulties experienced in finding a family physician with culturally sensitive skills, let alone one that speaks their language (Asanin and Wilson, 2008), leading to vulnerability and insecurity.

Precariousness, discourses of burden and processes of dehumanization

Addressing precisely the sorts of vulnerabilities outlined earlier, we turn to the writings of Judith Butler as a means to reconsider precarity among older immigrant adults. In *Frames of War*, Butler (2016) asks us to consider the ontology of precarity, that is, the conditions that make a life precarious: 'What is a life?' she wonders. For Butler, all human beings live in a state of precariousness, and yet, some lives are valued more than others, resulting in a heightened state of precarity for those whose lives are perceived as less valuable, less worthy of recognition. The precarity of immigrant older adults, particularly those who are racialized, is not only evident in the insecurity, uncertainty and unpredictability embedded in their everyday lives, but, as the previous discussion demonstrates, is also reflected in their relative 'invisibility' in health and social care programmes and policies. In what is an interesting paradox, then, while immigrant older adults are largely invisible in public policy, in recent years, they have acquired a new visibility in public discourse.

Current heightened debates on immigration in North America and the discourse around immigrants as either a 'burden on the public purse' or a threat to national security exemplify the power of language in the creation of 'troubling' and excluded – or, in the words of Butler (2006), 'dehumanized' – bodies. This process of dehumanization, Butler argues, is enacted and reinforced through social and political institutions, powerful media portrayals, and established norms and values that deem certain lives more precarious, more deserving of attention than others. It encourages the creation of marginal identities that render certain individuals not worthy of recognition. To the disadvantage of marginalized and vulnerable immigrant older adults, this discourse masks the multiple axes of inequality that define their everyday lived experiences. Indeed, labelling them 'problematic' allows the state to disavow the fundamental interdependence of human life, the assumption of ethical responsibility, and thereby the creation of socially just and equitable policies (Butler, 2006). Highlighting the pitfalls of such victim blaming, Bacchi (2000) argues that 'issues get represented in ways that mystify power relations and often create individuals responsible for their own 'failures', drawing attention away from the structures that create unequal outcomes. The focus on 'the ways issues get represented' produces a focus on language and on 'discourse' (Baachi, 2000, p 46).

Likewise, Beiser (2005) denounces an emphasis on 'sick' and 'healthy' immigrants as misguided, and asks instead what policymakers are doing to ensure the ongoing health of immigrants. In particular, he argues, there is a need to adopt a model that examines 'salient resettlement stressors that act alone or interact with predisposition in order to create health risk, and the personal and social resources that reduce risk and promote well-being' (Beiser, 2005, p 30). Clearly, understanding the diverse experiences of ageing both across and within North America's numerous immigrant groups requires complex theoretical and methodological approaches that move beyond a focus on immigrant status and age to explore the effects of other interlocking markers of precarity in studying the lives of older adults.

The call for such research notwithstanding, the recent surge of populist nationalism, particularly in the United States and some European countries, and the risky political discourse around immigrants has added to their precarious life situations.

Conclusion

> 'When I asked Mr. Ahmad [72-year-old man] [pseudonym] have you planned for your funeral, he just looked at me. I knew what he was thinking. So I said, "how can I perform your last rites? You are a Muslim, I don't know your religion. How will I do it?" He replied, "when I die, just throw me somewhere".'
>
> (Authors' interview with front-line worker)

Significant changes in the demographic composition, and in particular, the increasing diversification of the population by immigrant status and age in countries like Canada, the United States and the United Kingdom have been the impetus for the development in theory and research on migration and ageing since the mid-1980s. Indeed, a large proportion of the research in this area comes from these increasingly multicultural countries, work that has focused for the most part on outcomes in the health and social support domains (see further Torres, 2019). Yet, the current body of research is limited where knowledge on life courses of risk and insecurity through migration are concerned. Mr Ahmad's story serves as a poignant example of the risk, vulnerability and insecurity that defines the lives of many older immigrants. Chronically ill, isolated, impoverished, with limited linguistic proficiency, his social worker is his fictive kin, his 'only living relative'. Having immigrated to Canada 20 years ago, Mr Ahmad barely managed to get by working odd jobs at restaurants. Like countless other immigrant older adults, today he lives his life precariously perched on the edge of exigency, a product of failed economic and social support networks.

Precarity, as a concept, has received considerable scholarly attention over the past few decades, particularly as it relates to economic vulnerability and risk, as well as with regard to migration (albeit often among younger people). This chapter has expanded upon the definition of precarity and provided a discussion of salient economic as well as psychosocial and cultural markers of precarity in older immigrants. It has highlighted the politics of precarity and underscored the need to identify and acknowledge the everyday experiences of immigrant older adults in the construction of just and equitable health and social care policies. Drawing together the insights from existing research, supplemented by public stories and interviews with stakeholders, it concludes with a discussion of the avenues to explore, and the challenges to understanding precarity in the context of migration and among older immigrant adults.

Precarity, migration and ageing

First, in terms of conceptualization, precarity needs to be understood as a complex, multidimensional construct with intersecting economic, psychosocial and cultural markers (see Chapter 7). The applicability of precarity to the study of migration and ageing has much promise, insofar as it underscores the importance of understanding the differential impacts that markers of social inequality have on the health and social support outcomes of immigrant older adults. In order to adequately address health and social inequities in such populations, however, the analysis must move beyond predictors like immigration status and age to explore the intersections of these locations, alongside several markers of difference (gender, ethnicity, class, marital status, geographic place of residence and sexual orientation, to name a few). This includes attention to how differences intersect, and are inherent in the production of health and social support among immigrant older adult populations. To this end, the theoretical framework of intersectionality offers a useful lens through which to consider the simultaneous interactions between multiple dimensions of social identity (gender, age, immigrant status, ethnicity and so on) that are contextualized within broader systems of power, domination and oppression (such as sexism, ageism and racism) (Hankivsky et al, 2009). These intersections play out at each of the micro, meso, and macro levels – that is, relative to identities and interactions with others in different sociocultural contexts, and at the broader societal level wherein values are entrenched within and across a range of policies (Spence et al, 2009).

Second, precarity needs to take quantitative as well as qualitative measures of the experiences into account. For example, economic precarity in immigrants is easy to capture using metrics such as the Low Income Cut-Off. However, the psychosocial aspects of precarity related to quality of life, loneliness, social isolation, experiences of discrimination and the influence of life course events are more difficult to measure. Yet, these experiences intersect to impact the health and well-being of older immigrant adults. Indeed, ethno-gerontologists such as Sandra Torres (2019) have maintained that there is enormous merit in expanding our 'gerontological imagination' to incorporate lived experiences that are salient to the migratory life course. The suggestion, therefore, is for researchers to explore new ways of understanding precarity across a range of situations, and to consider adopting a mixed methods approach to precarity in immigrant older adults in order to acquire a holistic understanding of the phenomenon (see Chapter 7).

Third, findings from this area suggest that older immigrants from particular regions, such as South Asian or East Asian source countries like India or China, may experience changes in health status as lifestyle behaviours change at an accelerated rate after immigration. The rate at which such behaviours converge to the norm within host countries such as Canada will of course vary according to a number of factors related to assimilation and acculturation processes, including age at immigration, country of birth, level of adherence to traditional (country of birth) value and belief systems, place of residence (urban versus rural), and degree of institutional completeness of the older adult's ethnocultural group in the place of residence. Researchers must understand and take into account how processes of risk and vulnerability among racialized older immigrants are inherently marked by experiences of discrimination at the micro, meso, and macro level from pre- to post-immigration (Koehn et al, 2011).

Further, an examination of the intersections of gender and sponsored immigrant status reveals a number of implications for other determinants of health such as living arrangements, class, and access to health and social care. For example, women who are sponsored by their adult children to provide care for grandchildren are economically dependent for 20 years and at risk of being isolated due to a combination of caregiving responsibilities, lack of English language skills and/or limited experience with Canadian social institutions, and problems accessing subsidized transportation. In many cases, older adults are unable to access health and/or social care without the assistance of time-constrained adult children who must provide interpretation and transportation, and as a result they have little to no means of communicating issues of abuse or neglect to anyone outside their families. Researchers thus need to pay increased attention to the multidimensional nature of immigrant status so as to acknowledge how different types of immigration impact access to resources, and their implications for health care and social support. In the end, these and other related factors should be considered in the construction of any comprehensive Canadian health and social care policy and programme planning initiatives for immigrant older adults in mid-life – a rapidly growing age group.

Precarity and migration: policy recommendations

Finally, several recommendations for policy emerge from the analysis of precarity in later life and migration. First, as highlighted earlier, health and social care policymakers must continue to address key issues related to the growing diversity according to immigrant status in their populations – in particular, the differential health and social care needs of immigrant adults by gender and age group. For example, as Kobayashi and Prus (2012) point out, recent immigrant visible minority men in mid-life, and to a lesser extent their later-life female counterparts, may have fewer needs for services and programmes in the early years of their residency in Canada, while certain new immigrant subgroups, namely older men and mid-life visible-minority women, may have increased need for services due to poor health status. This increased need is likely to continue for these women as they age in Canada. In response to this reality, it is important that policies and programmes be developed at both the federal and the provincial level – particularly in Ontario, Quebec and British Columbia, provinces in which the majority of immigrants choose to reside – that (a) target mid-life immigrant and certain subgroups of older immigrant women as they age over time; and (b) respond to the needs of an older immigrant male population from the outset.[3]

Immigration and related policies and regulations ranging from pensions to housing bylaws also require scrutiny with respect to their implications for the health and well-being of older adults (Koehn et al, 2010). Of central importance is the recommendation that was adopted by the Special Senate Committee on Aging in 2009 that the dependency period for sponsored parents be reduced to three years in line with sponsored spouses. This would enable older dependents to avoid the pitfalls of the deleterious power differential and the associated 'precarity trap' that sponsorship often engenders. In critiquing the World Health Organization for paying insufficient attention to the power relations that shape social determinants of health, Navarro (2009, p 440) states that 'it is not inequalities that kill people … it is those who are responsible for those inequalities that kill people'.

Over time, research on immigration and ageing has continued to reflect the increasing ethnocultural diversification of the older adult population globally. And as social researchers increasingly facilitate the mobilization of this knowledge with key stakeholders, including policymakers, health care practitioners, front line workers, family members and the older adults themselves, we are likely to see continued growth and the uptake of important work in this area. It is possible to set a strong foundation for future research on immigration and ageing across the globe by including the experiences of a broader group of older immigrants, individuals in their informal and formal support networks, and those who have the power to empower these individuals through the establishment of culturally relevant policies and programmes. To support this endeavour, the conceptual framework of precarity serves as a promising lens to document the insecurity, risk, vulnerability and marginalization inherent in the everyday lives of ageing immigrants, and also to identify the broader structures of power and oppression that foster and sustain precarious and fragmented lives.

Notes

[1] Quotes are excerpted from public sources. The data for this project was collected by the first author as part of a SSHRC funded programme on Precarity and Aging.

[2] In Canada, for example, the Minimum Necessary Income (MNI) for a family of four must exceed CAN$59,426 for the preceding three-year period in order to be eligible to apply for parent and grandparent sponsorship (Government of Canada, 2018). Additionally, as a rule, sponsored older relatives do not have access to available social assistance benefits, and sponsors must agree to financially support their dependents for a period of twenty years (ten years for Quebec).

3   The fact that 'evidence of strong positive selection effects for immigrants from all regions of origin in terms of education' (Kennedy et al, 2006) was found across all four countries in a study seeking to explain the HIE – despite differences in demographic composition and policy frameworks in the immigration and health care domains – supported the cross-national application of Kobayashi and Prus' (2012) findings and their policy implications.

References

Acharya, M.P. and Northcott, H.C. (2007) 'Mental distress and the coping strategies of elderly Indian immigrant women', *Transcultural Psychiatry*, 44(4): 614–36.

Armstrong, P., Armstrong, H. and Coburn, D. (eds) (2001) *Unhealthy Times: Political Economy Perspectives on Health and Care in Canada*, Don Mills: Oxford University Press.

Asanin, J. and Wilson, K. (2008) '"I spent nine years looking for a doctor": exploring access to health care among immigrants in Mississauga, Ontario, Canada', *Social Science & Medicine*, 66(6): 1271–83.

Astbury, J. (2001) *Gender Disparities in Mental Health: Background Report for World Health Assembly Roundtables*, Geneva: World Health Organization.

Bacchi, C. (2000) 'Policy as discourse: what does it mean? Where does it get us?', *Discourse*, 21(1): 45–57.

Battams, N. (2013) 'In it together: multigenerational living in Canada', *Transition*, 43(3): 11–13.

Beiser, M. (2005) 'The health of immigrants and refugees in Canada', *Canadian Journal of Public Health* 96(supplement 2): S30–44.

Benoit, C. and Shumka, L. (2009) *Gendering the Health Determinants Framework: Why Girls' and Women's Health Matters*, Vancouver: Women's Health Research Network [online], available from: http://bccewh.bc.ca/2014/02/gendering-the-health-determinants-framework-why-girls-and-womens-health-matters/ [Accessed 13 August 2019].

Bierman, A.S. (2012) 'Averting an impending storm: can we reengineer health systems to meet the needs of aging populations?', *PLOS Medicine*, 9(7): e1001267.

Blair, T.R.W. (2012) '"Community ambassadors" for South Asian elder immigrants: late-life acculturation and the roles of community health workers', *Social Science & Medicine*, 75(10): 1769–77.

Brotman, S. (2003) 'The primacy of family in elder care discourse: home care services to older ethnic women in Canada', *Journal of Gerontological Social Work*, 38(3): 19–52.

Brown, P.L. (2009) 'Invisible immigrants, old and left with "nobody to talk to"', *New York Times* https://www.nytimes.com/2009/08/31/us/31elder.html [Accessed 11 August 2019].

Butler, J. (2006) *Precarious Life: the Powers of Mourning and Violence*, London: Verso.

Butler, J. (2016) *Frames of War: When Is Life Grievable?*, London: Verso.

Canadian Council On Learning (2008) *Health Literacy in Canada: a Healthy Understanding*, Ottawa: Canadian Council on Learning [online], available from: http://www.en.copian.ca/library/research/ccl/health/health.pdf [Accessed 11 August 2019].

Castañeda, H., Holmes, S.M., Madrigal, D.S., Young, M.-E.D., Beyeler, N. and Quesada, J. (2015) 'Immigration as a social determinant of health', *Annual Review of Public Health*, 36: 375–92.

Choi, N.G. and Smith, J. (2004) 'Reaching out to racial/ethnic minority older persons for elderly nutrition programs', *Journal of Nutrition for the Elderly*, 24(1): 89–104.

Choudhry, U.K. (1997) 'Traditional practices of women from India: pregnancy, childbirth, and newborn care', *Journal of Obstetric, Gynecologic & Neonatal Nursing*, 26(5): 533–9.

Coburn, D. (2004) 'Beyond the income inequality hypothesis: class, neo-liberalism, and health inequalities', *Social Science & Medicine*, 58(1): 41–56.

Curtis, J., Dong, W., Lightman, N. and Parbst, M. (2017) 'Race, language, or length of residency? Explaining unequal uptake of government pensions in Canada', *Journal of Aging & Social Policy*, 29(4): 332–51.

Dannefer, D. (2003) 'Cumulative advantage/disadvantage and the life course: cross-fertilizing age and social science theory, *The Journals of Gerontology: Series B*, 58(6): S327–S337, https://doi.org/10.1093/geronb/58.6.S327

Dastjerdi, M. and Mardukhi, A. (2015) 'Social factors affecting the well-being and mental health of elderly Iranian immigrant women in Canada', in N. Khanlou and F.B. Pilkington (eds) *Women's Mental Health*, Cham: Springer, pp 83–95.

Dean, J.A. and Wilson, K. (2010) '"My health has improved because I always have everything I need here…": a qualitative exploration of health improvement and decline among immigrants', *Social Science & Medicine*, 70(8): 1219–28.

De Jong Gierveld, J., Van Der Pas, S. and Keating, N. (2015) 'Loneliness of older immigrant groups in Canada: effects of ethnic-cultural background', *Journal of Cross-Cultural Gerontology*, 30(3): 251–68.

De Valk, H.A.G. and Schans, D. (2008) '"They ought to do this for their parents": perceptions of filial obligations among immigrant and Dutch older people', *Ageing and Society*, 28(1): 49–66.

Dunn, J.R. and Dyck, I. (2000) 'Social determinants of health in Canada's immigrant population: results from the National Population Health Survey', *Social Science & Medicine*, 51(11): 1573–93.

Ettlinger, N. (2007) 'Precarity unbound', *Alternatives*, 32(3): 319–40.

Facey, M.E. (2003) 'The health effects of taxi driving: the case of visible minority drivers in Toronto', *Canadian Journal of Public Health*, 94(4): 254–7.

Gee, E.M., Kobayashi, K.M. and Prus, S.G. (2004) 'Examining the healthy immigrant effect in mid-to later life: findings from the Canadian Community Health Survey', *Canadian Journal on Aging* 23(supplement): S55–63.

Goffman, E. (1963). *Stigma: Notes on the Management of Spoiled Identity*. New York: Simon & Schuster.

Goffman, E. (2009) *Stigma: Notes on the Management of Spoiled Identity*, New York: Touchstone.

González, H.M., Haan, M.N. and Hinton, L. (2001) 'Acculturation and the prevalence of depression in older Mexican Americans: baseline results of the Sacramento Area Latino Study on Aging', *Journal of the American Geriatrics Society*, 49(7): 948–53.

Government of Canada (2017) 'Health care in Canada: Canada's universal health-care system', *Government of Canada* [online], available from: https://www.canada.ca/en/immigration-refugees-citizenship/services/new-immigrants/new-life-canada/health-care-card.html [Accessed 11 August 2019].

Government of Canada (2018) 'Guide 5772: application to sponsor parents and grandparents', *Government of Canada* [online], available from: https://www.canada.ca/en/immigration-refugees-citizenship/services/application/application-forms-guides/guide-5772-application-sponsor-parents-grandparents.html [Accessed 11 August 2019].

Greenland, K. and Brown, R. (2005) 'Acculturation and contact in Japanese students studying in the United Kingdom', *Journal of Social Psychology*, 145(4): 373–89.

Grenier, A., Lloyd, L. and Phillipson, C. (2017) 'Precarity in late life: rethinking dementia as a "frailed" old age', *Sociology of Health & Illness*, 39(2): 318–30.

Grubel, H. (2005) *Immigration and the Welfare State in Canada: Growing Conflicts, Constructive Solutions*, Vancouver: Fraser Institute.

Guglani, S., Coleman, P.G. and Sonuga-Barke, E.J. (2000) 'Mental health of elderly Asians in Britain: a comparison of Hindus from nuclear and extended families of differing cultural identities', *International Journal of Geriatric Psychiatry*, 15(11): 1046–53.

Gupta, M., Singh, N. and Verma, S. (2006) 'South Asians and cardiovascular risk: what clinicians should know', *Circulation*, 113(25): e924–9.

Hankivsky, O., Cormier, R. and de Merich, D. (2009) *Intersectionality: Moving Women's Health Research and Policy Forward*, Vancouver: Women's Health Research Network [online], available from: http://bccewh.bc.ca/2014/02/intersectionality-moving-womens-health-research-and-policy-forward/ [Accessed 13 August 2019].

Hatzenbuehler, M.L., Phelan, J.C. and Link, B.G. (2013) 'Stigma as a fundamental cause of population health inequalities', *American Journal of Public Health*, 103(5): 813–21.

Horne, M. and Tierney, S. (2012) 'What are the barriers and facilitators to exercise and physical activity uptake and adherence among South Asian older adults: a systematic review of qualitative studies', *Preventive Medicine*, 55(4): 276–84.

Houle, R. and Maheux, H. (2016). *150 Years of Immigration in Canada*. Ottawa: Statistics Canada, Analytical Studies Branch [online], available from: https://www150.statcan.gc.ca/n1/en/catalogue/11-630-X2016006 [Accessed 20 August 2019].

Hyman, I. (2009) *Racism as a Determinant of Immigrant Health*, Ottawa: Strategic Initiatives and Innovations Directorate of the Public Health Agency of Canada [online], available from: http://www.metropolis.net/pdfs/racism_policy_brief_e.pdf [Accessed 13 August 2019].

Hyman, I., Forte, T., du Mont, J., Romans, S. and Cohen, M.M. (2006) 'The association between length of stay in Canada and intimate partner violence among immigrant women', *American Journal of Public Health*, 96(4): 654–9.

Jasso, G. (2003) 'Migration, human development, and the life course', in J.T. Mortimer and M.J. Shanahan (eds) *Handbook of the Life Course*, Boston, MA: Springer, pp 331–64.

Johnson, J.L., Bottorff, J.L., Browne, A.J., Grewal, S., Hilton, B.A. and Clarke, H. (2004) 'Othering and being othered in the context of health care services', *Health Communication*, 16(2): 255–71.

Kennedy, S., McDonald, J.T. and Biddle, N. (2006) *The Healthy Immigrant Effect and Immigrant Selection: Evidence from Four Countries*, SEDAP.

Keung, N. (2010) 'Elder abuse among immigrants a growing concern', *Toronto Star*, 26 April, https://www.thestar.com/news/gta/2010/04/26/elder_abuse_among_immigrants_a_growing_concern.html [Accessed 11 August 2019].

Keung, N. (2017) '"Significant" health gaps found between Canadian and immigrant seniors', *Toronto Star*, https://www.thestar.com/news/immigration/2017/05/16/significant-health-gaps-found-between-canadian-and-immigrant-seniors.html [Accessed 11 August 2019].

Khan, M.M. (2018) 'Immigrant families and Canada's changing ethno-racial diversity', in A. Gazso and K. Kobayashi (eds) *Continuity and Innovation: Canadian Families in the New Millennium*, Toronto: Nelson, pp 113–28.

Khan, M.M. and Kobayashi, K. (2017) 'No one should be left behind: identifying appropriate health promotion practices for immigrants', in I. Rootman, A. Pederson, K.L. Frohlich and S. Dupéré (eds) *Health Promotion in Canada: New Perspectives on Theory, Practice, Policy, and Research* (4th edn), Toronto: Canadian Scholars, pp 203–19.

Khvorostianov, N., Elias, N. and Nimrod, G. (2012) '"Without it I am nothing": the internet in the lives of older immigrants', *New Media & Society*, 14(4): 583–99.

Kim, W. (2009) 'Drinking culture of elderly Korean immigrants in Canada: a focus group study', *Journal of Cross-Cultural Gerontology*, 24(4): 339.

Kobayashi, K.M. and Prus, S.G. (2012) 'Examining the gender, ethnicity, and age dimensions of the healthy immigrant effect: factors in the development of equitable health policy', *International Journal for Equity in Health*, 11: 8.

Koehn, S. and Bains, S. (2012) 'Punjabi seniors' wellness initiative: exploring the determinants of mental health', A poster presented at the Gerontological Society of America's 65th Annual Scientific Meeting, San Diego, CA, November 2012.

Koehn, S., Spencer, C. and Hwang, E. (2010) 'Promises, promises: cultural and legal dimensions of sponsorship for immigrant seniors', in D. Durst and M. MacLean (eds) *Diversity and Aging among Immigrant Seniors in Canada: Changing Faces and Greying Temples*, Calgary: Datselig, pp 79–102.

Koehn, S., Jarvis, P. and Kobayashi, K. (2011) *Taking Care of Chronic Disease: Realizing Approaches for Canada's Aging Ethnic Population: a Workshop: Final Report*, Vancouver: Immigrant Older Adults Care Accessibility Research Empowerment [online], available from: http://www.centreforhealthyaging.ca/documents/TakingCareofChronicDiseaseReport-FINAL.pdf [Accessed 13 August 2019].

Krieger, N., Chen, J.T., Waterman, P.D., Rehkopf, D.H. and Subramanian, S.V. (2003) 'Race/ethnicity, gender, and monitoring socioeconomic gradients in health: a comparison of area-based socioeconomic measures—the Public Health Disparities Geocoding Project', *American Journal of Public Health*, 93(10): 1655–71.

Lai, D.W.L. and Surood, S. (2013) 'Effect of service barriers on health status of aging South Asian immigrants in Calgary, Canada', *Health & Social Work*, 38(1): 41–50.

Lai, D.W.L., Daoust, G.D. and Li, L. (2014) 'Understanding elder abuse and neglect in aging Chinese immigrants in Canada', *Journal of Adult Protection*, 16(5): 322–34.

Lee, E.K. and Chan, K. (2009) 'Religious/spiritual and other adaptive coping strategies among Chinese American older immigrants', *Journal of Gerontological Social Work*, 52(5): 517–33.

Levy, C., Carter, S., Priloutskaya, G. and Gallegos, G. (2003) 'Critical elements in the design of culturally appropriate interventions intended to reduce health disparities: immunization rates among Hispanic seniors in New Mexico', *Journal of Health and Human Services Administration*, 26(2): 199–238.

Liebert, S. and Ameringer, C.F. (2013) 'The health care safety net and the Affordable Care Act: implications for Hispanic immigrants', *Public Administration Review*, 73(6): 810–20.

Lucas, J.W., Barr-Anderson, D.J. and Kington, R.S. (2003) 'Health status, health insurance, and health care utilization patterns of immigrant black men', *American Journal of Public Health*, 93(10): 1740–7.

McCleary, L., Persaud, M., Hum, S., Pimlott, N.J.G., Cohen, C.A., Koehn, S., Leung, K.K., Dalziel, W.B., Kozak, J., Emerson, V.F., Silvius, J.L., Garcia, L. and Drummond, N. (2013) 'Pathways to dementia diagnosis among South Asian Canadians', *Dementia*, 12(6): 769–89.

McDonald, J.T. and Kennedy, S. (2005) 'Is migration to Canada associated with unhealthy weight gain? Overweight and obesity among Canada's immigrants', *Social Science & Medicine*, 61(12): 2469–81.

McLaren, A.T. (2006) 'Immigration and parental sponsorship in Canada: implications for elderly women', *Canadian Issues*, 27(1): 34–7.

Mikkonen, J. and Raphael, D. (2010) *Social Determinants of Health: the Canadian Facts*, Toronto: York University School of Health Policy and Management.

Moztarzadeh, A. and O'Rourke, N. (2015) 'Psychological and sociocultural adaptation: acculturation, depressive symptoms, and life satisfaction among older Iranian immigrants in Canada', *Clinical Gerontologist*, 38(2): 114–30.

Mukherjee, A.J. and Diwan, S. (2016) 'Late life immigration and quality of life among Asian Indian older adults', *Journal of Cross-Cultural Gerontology*, 31(3): 237–53.

Nam, Y., Lee, E.J., Huang, J. and Kim, J. (2015) 'Financial capability, asset ownership, and later-age immigration: evidence from a sample of low-income older Asian immigrants', *Journal of Gerontological Social Work*, 58(2): 114–27.

Navarro, V. (2009) 'What we mean by social determinants of health', *Global Health Promotion*, 16(1): 5–16.

Nazroo, J.Y. (2003) 'The structuring of ethnic inequalities in health: economic position, racial discrimination, and racism', *American Journal of Public Health*, 93(2): 277–84.

Newbold, B. (2005) 'Health status and health care of immigrants in Canada: a longitudinal analysis', *Journal of Health Services Research & Policy*, 10(2): 77–83A.

Neysmith, S.M. and Reitsma-Street, M. (2005) '"Provisioning": conceptualizing the work of women for 21st century social policy', *Women's Studies International Forum*, 28(5): 381–91.

Ng, E. and Omariba, D.W.R. (2014) 'Immigration, generational status and health literacy in Canada', *Health Education Journal*, 73(6): 668–82.

Ng, E., Wilkins, R., Gendron, F. and Berthelot, J.M. (2005) *Dynamics of immigrants' health in Canada: evidence from the National Population Health Survey*, Ottawa: Statistics Canada.

Ng, R., Man, G., Shan, H. and Liu, L.W. (2007) *Learning to Be Good Citizens: Informal Learning and the Labour Market Experiences of Professional Chinese Immigrant Women: Final Research Report*, Toronto: CERIS – The Ontario Metropolis Centre.

Ng, E., Lai, D.W.L., Rudner, A.T. and Orpana, H. (2012) *What Do We Know about Immigrant Seniors Aging in Canada? A Demographic, Socio-Economic and Health Profile: CERIS Working Papers, 88–90*, Toronto: CERIS – The Ontario Metropolis Centre.

Noh, S., Beiser, M., Kaspar, V., Hou, F. and Rummens, J. (1999) 'Perceived racial discrimination, depression, and coping: a study of Southeast Asian refugees in Canada', *Journal of Health and Social Behavior*, 40(3): 193–207.

Novak, N.L., Geronimus, A.T. and Martinez-Cardoso, A.M. (2017) 'Change in birth outcomes among infants born to Latina mothers after a major immigration raid', *International Journal of Epidemiology*, 46(3): 839–49.

O'Neil, K. and Tienda, M. (2010) 'A tale of two counties: natives' opinions toward immigration in North Carolina', *International Migration Review*, 44(3): 728–61.

Padilla, A.M. and Perez, W. (2003) 'Acculturation, social identity, and social cognition: a new perspective', *Hispanic Journal of Behavioral Sciences*, 25(1): 35–55.

Paret, M. and Gleeson, S. (2016) 'Precarity and agency through a migration lens', *Citizenship Studies*, 20(3/4): 277–94.

Phelan, J.C., Link, B.G. and Tehranifar, P. (2010) 'Social conditions as fundamental causes of health inequalities: theory, evidence, and policy implications', *Journal of Health and Social Behavior*, 51(supplement 1): S28–40.

Picot, G. and Lu, Y. (2017) *Chronic Low Income among Immigrants in Canada and Its Communities*, Ottawa: Statistics Canada, Analytical Studies Branch [online], available from: https://www150.statcan.gc.ca/n1/pub/11f0019m/11f0019m2017397-eng.htm [Accessed 13 August 2019].

Poureslami, I., Nimmon, L., Doyle-Waters, M., Rootman, I., Schulzer, M., Kuramoto, L. and Fitzgerald, J.M. (2012) 'Effectiveness of educational interventions on asthma self-management in Punjabi and Chinese asthma patients: a randomized controlled trial', *Journal of Asthma*, 49(5): 542–51.

Raymond, N.T., Varadhan, L., Reynold, D.R., Bush, K., Sankaranarayanan, S., Bellary, S., Barnett, A.H., Kumar, S. and O'Hare, J.P. (2009) 'Higher prevalence of retinopathy in diabetic patients of South Asian ethnicity compared with white Europeans in the community: a cross-sectional study', *Diabetes Care*, 32(3): 410–15.

Roger, K.S., Brownridge, D.A. and Ursel, J. (2015) 'Theorizing low levels of reporting of abuse of older immigrant women', *Violence against Women*, 21(5): 632–51.

Rusch, D., Frazier, S.L. and Atkins, M. (2015) 'Building capacity within community-based organizations: new directions for mental health promotion for Latino immigrant families in urban poverty', *Administration and Policy in Mental Health and Mental Health Services Research*, 42(1): 1–5.

Ryan, D., Maurer, S., Lengua, L., Duran, B. and Ornelas, I.J. (2018) 'Amigas Latinas Motivando el Alma (ALMA): an evaluation of a mindfulness intervention to promote mental health among Latina immigrant mothers', *Journal of Behavioral Health Services & Research*, 45(2): 280–91.

Saraswati, J. (2000) 'Poverty and visible minority women in Canada', *Canadian Woman Studies*, 20(3): 49–53.

Schvey, N.A., Puhl, R.M. and Brownell, K.D. (2011) 'The impact of weight stigma on caloric consumption', *Obesity*, 19(10): 1957–62.

Siddiqi, A., Zuberi, D. and Nguyen, Q.C. (2009) 'The role of health insurance in explaining immigrant versus non-immigrant disparities in access to health care: comparing the United States to Canada', *Social Science & Medicine*, 69(10): 1452–9.

Sin, M.-K. (2015) 'A qualitative analysis of stress and coping in Korean immigrant women in middle-age and older-adulthood', *Issues in Mental Health Nursing*, 36(1): 52–9.

Soto Mas, F., Ji, M., Fuentes, B.O. and Tinajero, J. (2015) 'The health literacy and ESL study: a community-based intervention for Spanish-speaking adults', *Journal of Health Communication*, 20(4): 369–76.

Spence, J.C., Brawley, L.R., Craig, C.L., Plotnikoff, R.C., Tremblay, M.S., Bauman, A., Faulkner, G.E., Chad, K. and Clark, M.I. (2009) 'ParticipACTION: awareness of the participACTION campaign among Canadian adults: examining the knowledge gap hypothesis and a hierarchy-of-effects model', *International Journal of Behavioral Nutrition and Physical Activity*, 6: 85.

Spence, M. and Koehn, S. (2010) 'ICARE: immigrant older women – care accessibility research empowerment: researching mental health issues', *Visions*, 6(3): 17–19.

Standing, G. (2011) *The Precariat: the New Dangerous Class*, London: Bloomsbury Academic.

Sun, F., Gao, X., Gao, S., Li, Q. and Hodge, D.R. (2018) 'Depressive symptoms among older Chinese Americans: examining the role of acculturation and family dynamics', *Journals of Gerontology Series B: Psychological Sciences & Social Sciences*, 73(5): 870–9.

Torres, S. (2019) *Ethnicity and Old Age: Expanding Our Imagination*, Bristol: Policy Press.

Treas, J. and Mazumdar, S. (2002) 'Older people in America's immigrant families: dilemmas of dependence, integration, and isolation', *Journal of Aging Studies*, 16(3): 243–58.

Urquia, M.L., Berger, H. and Ray, J.G. (2015) 'Risk of adverse outcomes among infants of immigrant women according to birth-weight curves tailored to maternal world region of origin', *Canadian Medical Association Journal*, 187(1): E32–40.

Vang, Z.M., Sigouin, J., Flenon, A. and Gagnon, A. (2017) 'Are immigrants healthier than native-born Canadians? A systematic review of the healthy immigrant effect in Canada', *Ethnicity & Health*, 22(3): 209–41.

Vissandjee, B., Desmeules, M., Cao, Z., Abdool, S. and Kazanjian, A. (2004) 'Integrating ethnicity and migration as determinants of Canadian women's health', *BMC Women's Health*, 4(1): S32.

Weerasinghe, S. and Numer, M. (2011) 'A life-course exploration of the social, emotional and physical health behaviours of widowed South Asian immigrant women in Canada: implications for health and social programme planning', *International Journal of Migration, Health and Social Care*, 6(4): 42–56.

Weiss, G.L. and Lonnquist, L.E. (2017) *The Sociology of Health, Healing, and Illness* (9th edn), New York: Routledge.

World Health Organization (2008) *Closing the Gap in a Generation: Health Equity through Action on the Social Determinants of Health*, Geneva: WHO Press [online], available from: http://apps.who.int/iris/bitstream/handle/10665/69832/who_ier_csdh_08.1_eng.pdf;jsessionid=da391b7c9b321b40bac0777da12e1cf7?sequence=1 [Accessed 12 August 2019].

Xu, K.T. and Borders, T.F. (2008) 'Does being an immigrant make a difference in seeking physician services?', *Journal of Health Care for the Poor and Underserved*, 19(2): 380–90.

Xu, L. (2017) 'The loneliness of being an immigrant', *The Walrus*, 23 March, https://thewalrus.ca/the-loneliness-of-being-an-immigrant [Accessed 11 August 2019].

Zhou, Y.R. (2015) 'Time, space and care: rethinking transnational care from a temporal perspective', *Time & Society*, 24(2): 163–82.

7

A framework to identify precarity in the social sciences: insights from qualitative research

Elena Portacolone

Introduction

The concept of precarity, as noted in Chapter 1, emerged initially in the area of labour studies but has subsequently been applied to a wide range of issues and groups. The aim of this chapter is to advance research on this topic by proposing a framework for identifying and recognizing precarity based on qualitative research with older people. The chapter outlines the background to the author's initial interest in this topic, reviews relevant research literature and discusses two research studies exploring the lives of older adults living in precarious circumstances.

The chapter is divided into the following sections. First, the context for precarity is discussed from the vantage point of the author's background and broader theoretical influences. Second, the chapter reviews challenges associated with recognizing and measuring precarity. This discussion provides a framework for the chapter's primary objective of developing methods to identify precarity in qualitative data collection and analysis, with the ultimate goal of informing the development of a validated index of precarity. The chapter then turns to the methods used to detect precarity in two research studies in the field of ageing. Third, the chapter outlines and illustrates in-depth explanations of four specific markers of precarity. The chapter concludes with a discussion of the contribution made by the research studies as a means to inform future research and recommendations.

Personal and theoretical context

In the early 1990s, as a graduate student of political sciences at the University of Turin in Italy, I witnessed first-hand the increased use of *contratti a termine* (work contracts with an end date) or *contratti precari* (precarious contracts). I also observed resistance against this new form of employment, opposition that culminated (in 2002) in the murder of Marco Biagi, an Italian economics professor and main contributor to a law that permitted temporary employment, by the *Brigate Rosse* (Red Brigades) (Carroll, 2002). Social and political conflict was taking place across many European countries around that time, with the increase in precarious employment symptomatic of a political economy unable to guarantee its citizens secure jobs, decent pensions and affordable health coverage. In France, temporary workers christened themselves the 'precariat', combining 'precariousness' with 'proletariat' (Bodnar, 2006). As the term suggests, these workers denounced the injustice of flexible labour contracts stripped of the benefits associated with secure employment.

Social theorists, including Robert Castel, Ulrich Beck and Zygmunt Bauman, have identified new forms of risk and insecurity created by the retreat of the welfare state. Bauman (2007, p 10) argues that 'the ground on which our life prospects are presumed to rest is admittedly shaky', and identifies the rise of an 'age of uncertainty', where the influence of private capital and commodities at a global level is eroding the power of nation states. Castel (2003) underlines the social insecurity caused by the state's inability to gather sufficient resources to support citizens struggling due to illness, poverty or age. In a similar vein, Bauman (2007, p 2) takes the view that functions that were once exclusively state prerogatives have 'become a playground for the notoriously capricious and inherently unpredictable market forces and/ or are left to the private initiative and care of individuals'. Following on from this, he argues that the emphasis on private enterprise shifts 'the responsibility for resolving the quandaries generated by vexingly volatile and constantly changing circumstances ... onto the shoulders of individuals who are now expected to be "free choosers" and to bear in full the consequences of their choices' (Bauman, 2007, p 3). Beck (1992, p 93) draws the conclusion that 'people [are] suddenly confronting an abyss', a process driven by the chasm between vanishing public resources and the emphasis on the role of individual initiative. As a consequence, 'problems of the system are lessened politically and transformed into personal failure.... Social problems are increasingly perceived in terms of psychological dispositions, such as personal inadequacies, guilt feelings, anxieties, conflicts and neuroses' (Beck, 1992, p 100).

Exposure to the struggles of precarious workers, together with Biagi's assassination, led me to observe and identify the construct of precarity in my own research. The first 30 years of my life were spent in countries undergoing significant reductions in welfare provision. My familiarity with the work of Bauman, Castel and Beck in social theory, and Estes and Phillipson in the field of gerontology, as well as my residence in the United States starting in 2002, made me sensitive to the effects of changes in support for older people. In a subsequent qualitative study of older adults (Portacolone et al, 2019), my interest was extended through testing the hypothesis that having a cognitive impairment might exacerbate the precarity of older adults living alone in the United States (a study discussed in more detail later). This research also produced an interest in problems associated with the measurement of precarity, an issue discussed in the next section of this chapter.

Recognizing and measuring precarity

Theoretical constructs such as precarity, loneliness and stigma refer to phenomena that are real and that exist, independent of the awareness and interpretation of the researcher and study participant (Edwards and Bagozzi, 2000). Yet, such phenomena are often difficult to assess directly, requiring specific measures to understand their effects (DeVellis, 2017). Given the close relationship between policy, practice and older people's experiences of precarity, it is important to find ways to better understand, recognize and measure the kind of theoretical constructs discussed in this book. The argument here is that qualitative research studies may be especially effective in ultimately developing measures of precarity, with insights from this type of research pointing to key questions and results that can subsequently be refined through survey questions (Pope and Mays, 1995).

In order to advance understandings of precarity, it is critical to avoid ambiguities in the relationship between theoretical constructs (precarity, in this case) and the methods by which they are assessed or measured. A measure of a theoretical construct is an observed *score* gathered through self-report, interview and observation, or some other method. Duncan (1984, p 126) explains measurement as 'the assignment of numerals in such a way as to correspond to *different degrees of a quality* ... or property of some object or event [emphasis in original].' Here, the literature on construct validity distinguishes between reflective and formative measures. Reflective measures represent manifestations (or reflections) of constructs. For example, attending religious services may be a reflective measure of religiosity (Bhattacherjee, 2012). Conversely, formative measures are described as being comprised of indicators or constructs, such as a socioeconomic status index composed of education, occupation and income (Ganzeboom et al, 1992; MacKenzie et al, 2005).

This exercise of defining an index of precarity builds upon existing work in the field of employment. Lewchuk (2017) developed an Employment Precarity Index derived from responses to ten questions related to employment, including income variation, work schedule, type of employment and benefits. However, this index associates precarity only with employment type (ranging from 'secure' to 'stable' to 'vulnerable' to 'precarious'). My own research suggests that the precarity of older adults living alone stems from a combination of personal values usually influenced by prevailing ideologies (such as a desire to be independent), limited appropriate services (for example, affordable home care aides) and uncertainty concerning what do about the future. Past employment was not necessarily a key component of this generalized precarity, with some participants who had secure employment in the past leading a precarious life in old age.

The absence of an overall precarity measure or index that is inclusive of the needs and experiences of older people is thus a critical gap in research and practice. Without a common language, it is difficult for researchers to understand the nature of precarity and to elucidate the characteristics of precarious lives. Developing such a measure must also be regarded as essential for developing social policies that are able to alleviate the precarity faced by particular groups of older people. The next section of this chapter provides an overview of strategies used to identify precarity in qualitative data collection, based upon two research studies focusing on the relationship between precarity and ageing.

Precarity: studies of living alone in old age

This section of the chapter examines the construct of precarity as it emerged in data collection and analysis of two qualitative research studies on ageing (Portacolone, 2013; Portacolone et al, 2019). In the first, an investigation of older adults living alone (Portacolone, 2013), precarity emerged spontaneously in data analysis through the use of grounded theory. In the second, a study of older adults living alone with cognitive impairment (Portacolone et al, 2019), the analysis of data was refined to capture whether a specific condition (cognitive impairments such as Alzheimer's disease or mild cognitive impairment) exacerbated the precarity of living alone in old age.

The first study was a qualitative investigation of 47 older adults living alone, undertaken between 2011 and 2013 (Portacolone, 2013).

While one-third of older adults now live alone (Jamieson and Simpson, 2013), limited information is available about their experience of daily life. The goal of this investigation was to better understand the overall experience of living alone in old age through participants' narratives, combined with researcher's observations and self-reflection.

In the tradition of grounded theory, the research proceeded without a set theoretical framework to guide the analysis. Data were collected through ethnographic interviews (Spradley, 2016) and participant observation (Atkinson and Hammersley, 1994). The notion of precarity spontaneously emerged through the data analysis, using grounded theory (Charmaz, 2006; Glaser and Strauss, 2010). In particular, the construct of precarity best described a sense of insecurity and uncertainty, which stemmed from the multifactorial loss of resources across the micro, meso and macro levels (see further Silverstein and Giarrusso, 2011; Vandenberghe, 2007). This included the subjective realm of experience (micro level); the role of health care providers, institutions and social policies (meso level); and the ideologies (macro level) that emerged from participants' accounts of their lived experiences.

In this first study (Portacolone, 2013), precarity emerged as a product of the dynamics that were both visible and invisible to study participants. Although older adults living alone were acutely aware of receding resources at a micro level (for example, chronic conditions or the loss of a spouse), they were often unaware of diminishing resources on the meso (for example, strict eligibility rules for essential benefits, such as a public home care aide) or macro (for example, maintaining independence) levels. In other words, study participants rarely said that they experienced 'precarity', and typically did not question the social policies or the allocation of services according to given criteria, or compare these with policies adopted in other countries. Furthermore, study participants often considered their desire to remain independent for as long as possible to be natural, unaware that the trope of independence is an ideology that appears predominantly in Western societies (Cohen, 1998; Portacolone, 2011).

In sum, identifying precarity requires researchers to identify shrinking resources at the micro, meso and macro levels of analysis, to consider observations in the field, to hold and consider knowledge of social policies and prevailing ideologies, and to explore these in relation to participants' narratives. Participants' narratives often indicated depleted resources at a personal/micro level of analysis, such as chronic conditions or the loss of a spouse. Participants' narratives also pointed to salient values in their experience, such as wanting to be independent or remain in their home.

Narratives from older adults living alone also pointed to the effects of social policies. Field notes, including the researcher's observations, provided added depth to these narratives. For example, a participant might have said that they were extremely satisfied with their living arrangements and the services they received. Yet, the field notes might disclose that the participant lived in a freezing cold studio smelling of urine and a diet of mostly canned food. Finally, the researchers' knowledge of international social policies might give them awareness of a lack of policies that exist abroad to support individuals under circumstances similar to those of the study participants, policies whose absence further contributes to the participants' precarity.

The second study (Portacolone et al, 2019) focused on the experiences of 12 older adults living alone with cognitive impairment such as Alzheimer's disease or mild cognitive impairment (MCI), which is often a precursor to Alzheimer's disease (Brodaty et al, 2013). Participants for the study were referred by health care providers, and data were collected using ethnographic interviews (Spradley, 2016) and participant observation (Atkinson and Hammersley, 1994). Data analysis for the second study was conducted in two phases. First, inductive analysis was used (Elo and Kyngäs, 2008) to understand the overall experience of older adults living alone with cognitive impairment, which is an understudied and pressing topic, given that one-third of older adults with cognitive impairment live alone in North America (Amjad et al, 2016; Sibley et al, 2002). In this phase, we coded the data to identify themes that emerged from the data without a theoretical construct to guide us. Three themes were identified. Theme 1, 'awareness of cognitive impairment', described the distress and uncertainty that occurred when an individual was aware of having a cognitive impairment, a condition with a notably unpredictable course. Theme 2, 'self-management of the challenges caused by the cognitive impairment', drew attention to the tendency of participants to feel responsible for self-managing their cognitive impairment. Theme 3, 'lacking tailored services', described the pressures generated by a lack of appropriate services to support independent living for persons with cognitive impairment.

Given the results of our first research project on precarity (Portacolone, 2013), and the emergent themes from this second study, deductive analysis was then used (Elo and Kyngäs, 2008) to determine whether the construct of precarity was present in the material generated for each theme. In this phase, we also drew from the literature on the erosion of the welfare state and related 'age of uncertainty' as a context within which to understand the narratives (Bauman, 2007; Beck, 1992; Beck and Beck-Gernsheim, 2002).

This process resulted in the identification of four markers of precarity: (a) uncertainty; (b) limited appropriate services; (c) independence; and (d) cumulative pressures. These provided the initial sketch of a conceptual framework to identify precarity in the data. A primary analytic level (micro, meso, macro) was also assigned to each marker. Because of the permeability of each analytic level, the research team defined these analytic levels as 'primary', with the implication that each marker could be effectively observed under multiple levels of analysis. We then analysed whether these markers manifested in each of the three themes described earlier. According to our criteria, precarity was deemed present in a given theme if at least two of its markers could be identified, as discussed in detail in the article on the research results of this study (Portacolone et al, 2019). The following sections will describe each of the four markers of precarity in detail as manifest in the lives of the older people interviewed across the two studies.

Four markers of precarity

Marker 1: uncertainty

Based on the interviews with older adults living alone, precarity can be considered to evoke an intrinsic sense of uncertainty that results from coping with cumulative pressures while trying to preserve a sense of independence. Uncertainty often derives from limited resources at different levels of analysis. A common expression that indicates uncertainty is, "I don't know what to do." In the case of older adults in these studies, a generalized inability to solve a problem or deal with a particular situation may stem from limited financial resources and mobility, as well as limited appropriate and affordable services to allow the individual to continue living at home safely. As a result, researchers should pay particular attention to portions of text expressing uncertainty.

Examples that illustrate the first marker of precarity, uncertainty, included statements such as, "I can afford to stay paying rent through next year, and then I'm not sure, unless something happens, whether I can pay rent anymore. I don't know how long I can stay on my own." In another example, a woman with cognitive impairment said, "I have a hard time remembering now. I really hate that. That's tearing me apart. And I don't know what to do about that." One way to assess whether a sense of uncertainty is present in the data is to ask descriptive questions about the participant's situation, such as, "How do you see your future?" Researchers might also ask about immediate concerns; for example, "Is there anything that concerns you right now?"[1]

Most times, when participants described a sense of not knowing, they were expressing their uncertainty about a specific topic. In these cases, study participants should be asked to elaborate on statements such as, "I just don't know where I'm headed. That's preying on me a lot." This statement comes from Ms Left, a 79-year-old woman living alone with a diagnosis of Alzheimer's disease. A researcher could cue her to elaborate by asking, "Can you please tell me more about not knowing where you are headed?" With this strategy, her own words are used, which is a long-standing norm for establishing rapport with study participants (Spradley, 2016). A related note on such methods: it is important to *avoid* questions such as "Why?" or "What do you mean?" because they can be perceived as aggressive and they may compromise the rapport with study participants (Spradley, 2016), and therefore the richness of the collected data.

Uncertainty can also emerge in more subtle forms. For example, we identified uncertainty in the following excerpt of an interview with Ms Bates, a 71-year-old woman living alone with a diagnosis of MCI: "I'm like a crazy person. I'm checking [the calendar and watch] every time I know something is coming up." This quote expresses uncertainty coming from missing appointments in the context of living alone with cognitive impairment.

Some of the statements expressed by older people contained more than one marker of precarity. For example, Ms Left's use of the phrase "And I'm left not knowing what to do about myself," contains both the uncertainty marker and that of independence (to be discussed in further detail later). The uncertainty marker derives from this sense of not knowing. The independence marker comes from participants identifying themselves as solely responsible for their well-being, without mentioning other persons or organizations. Further, the mention of being "left" points to the isolation of the participant, who is trying to figure out how to manage herself in the context of living alone with a diagnosis of Alzheimer's disease. Finally, uncertainty was also seen to emerge in the interactions between study participants and researchers. In the research study on older adults living alone with cognitive impairment, participants often asked researchers for advice on what to do with their future, which pointed to the intrinsic uncertainty of their situation, as well as to the limited services available to support them, as the next section elaborates.

Marker 2: limited access to appropriate services

Experiences in a context of limited supports and services is also foundational to the construct of precarity. A number of interviews indicated that appropriate supports and services were too expensive, unavailable or hard to find. Here, the issues of access or use can be used as key identifiers of precarity. For example, a woman with Alzheimer's disease living alone questioned the appropriateness of the support that she received: "I call her [fiduciary, person managing finances] brittle.... She talks so fast and her body movements are so quick.... I'm always glad when she leaves." Another participant living alone with cognitive impairment complained about the lack of reminders for doctors' appointments: "Nobody would say to me, remember, you have a doctor appointment, you have to go."

Limited access to appropriate services fosters precarity because it reinforces the assumption that individuals should have primary responsibility for their own well-being. A robust body of literature (Bauman, 2007; Estes, 2001; Leonard, 1997), including other chapters in this volume, underline the close association between the erosion of the welfare state and the strengthening of individualistic perspectives (Beck and Beck-Gernsheim, 2002). Our interviews demonstrated the impact of the absence of services in a variety of ways. For example, Mr May, a 95-year-old participant, described the cost of hiring private home care aides with this statement: "The prices are astronomic. In short, thousands of dollars.... Everything in San Francisco has astronomic prices."

As we observed in many other participants, Mr May's precarity was also heightened by social policies that did not allow him to access public home care aides because he had savings. Similarly, Ms Baker, a 79-year-old woman with a diagnosis of Alzheimer's disease, after complaining about the poor quality of supports that she received, noted that "at this point it's like there's too many people, and I don't know who has the power to do what as far as my welfare.... Is there somebody that can come along and say 'You can't stay in your house anymore'?" We can see in this quote the relation between having limited appropriate services, not knowing how they are organized (implying uncertainty) and fearing relocation, all of which are identifiers of precarity.

To properly understand participants' understandings and perceptions, researchers must have a good sense of which services are appropriate and/or available (or not) for the population they are studying. This background knowledge is essential to inform in-depth conversations with study participants. For example, in the United States, subsidized home care aides who are well trained in dementia care are scarce, and inaccessible to most in-need individuals due to financial considerations. Home care aides, who themselves rarely receive rigorous training, are generally available only to extremely poor older adults through Medicaid, a public programme in the United States for eligible low-income individuals. On the other end of the spectrum, the agencies with an available workforce of private home care aides that might be well trained in dementia care charge fees that are too high for most older adults living alone with cognitive impairment to afford on a regular basis (Shih et al, 2014). This situation also fosters precarity (Portacolone et al, 2019), and understanding the dynamics of this interplay, expressed through the narratives of older people living alone, is therefore crucial to recognizing and measuring precarity.

A researcher with an in-depth understanding of the services available must also understand how to question participants about those services. Rather than using the term 'services', which is often perceived as too vague, it is better to ask questions related to specific types of provision. For example, one could start the interview with the statement, "Now I'd like to talk about any help that you pay for or receive for free." Specific follow-up questions could relate to health ("Do you get any help with any disabilities that you have?"), residential upkeep ("Do you get any help with maintaining your house? For example, with repairs or paying bills?"), food ("Do you get any help with food shopping and cooking?"), crucial mobility ("Do you get any help getting out of the house and seeing your doctor?") or transportation for entertainment ("Do you get any help getting out of the house to do things for fun?").

In attempting to understand and assess precarity, it is also important to ask study participants whether there are services that they would like to use, but that are not available to them. For example, older adults living alone with cognitive impairment sometimes mention that they would appreciate help with everyday tasks such as managing medical appointments and transportation. Mr Cooper, a 65-year-old man living alone with a diagnosis of Alzheimer's disease, explained, "What I should have, if the world was correct, I should have a patient advocate. And the patient advocate just does all the work for me." In his case, a patient advocate was a resource important for negotiating everyday activities, yet that resource was missing. This information helps us understand the elements that contribute to a sense of precarity.

Marker 3: importance of maintaining independence

The importance of being independent is often ingrained in older adults in the United States and Western societies. A former executive living alone explained, "I don't want or usually need to rely on anybody else to do something for me. There is virtually nothing I cannot do if I choose to do it, and I like that feeling of being very independent." Living alone and feeling independent often go hand in hand, a sentiment indicated by a woman living alone with Alzheimer's disease: "[Living alone] makes me feel, I feel in charge. I feel independent." A man under the same circumstances echoes her when he notes: "My sister puts restrictions, 'You should this, you should that. Why don't you do this? Why don't you do that?' Well no, why don't you just shut up and let me live my life?"

The tension in this marker stems from an individual wanting to be independent in a context where it becomes increasingly difficult to manage demands alone and where few supports exist (see Chapter 10). As Klinenberg (2012) noted in his investigation of living alone, 'the ordinary challenges of growing old … can become extraordinary hardships for someone who spends most of the time alone'. Older adults living alone often do not want to give out cues to family members or health care providers that it is becoming increasingly difficult to perform tasks, often for fear of being relocated. This creates a pressure in which the individual is reluctant to ask for help. As an outcome of not asking for help, the older adult performs a series of tasks alone or with limited assistance, which often contributes to a sense of precarity, and may worsen their level of unmet need.

In addition to their reluctance to ask for help, adults living alone often perceive themselves as isolated from others. Ms Left's quote, mentioned earlier, pointed to this isolation: "And I am left not knowing what to do about myself." The sense of "being left [alone]" indicates her isolation. Her narrative and the researcher's observations confirmed her isolation, as she spent most of her time alone, and her only family member (with whom she has a conflictual relationship) lived nearly two hours away. As a result of this, older adults often identify themselves as solely responsible for their own wellbeing.

Another participant, Ms Keiths, provided a powerful illustration of the need to be independent. Ms Keiths was a thin, stooped 85-year old woman, who lived by herself and had endured a stroke and a heart attack, as well as stomach and cataract surgery. She adamantly refused help to carry groceries up the 16 steps leading to her flat, and explained that every time someone helped her she felt that her "life force" was being drained out of her. Yet another example of the pressure generated from a reluctance to ask for help, as well as from a lack of affordable services, is evident in this quote from a 92-year-old woman living alone with a diagnosis of MCI, who could barely walk around her block alone: "I used to have a cleaning woman come twice a month, but it got too expensive.... *I don't really need any help. I can do it myself. It's good for me, too, to do exercise, to do my yardwork* [emphasis added]." Similarly, another woman in her nineties living alone with a diagnosis of MCI, in addition to other chronic conditions, explained, "If I need something I go to the store. *I don't ask anybody. I do it myself* [emphasis added]."

To determine if the construct of independence is present in the data, we can ask study participants questions such as, "What is important to you, right now?" Prompts to elicit description are also useful, such as, "Describe what you did yesterday." Evidence of the need to be independent also emerges in study participants' descriptions of the methods they use to cope with crises. For example, in the first research study several participants shared stories of sustaining injuries and then dealing with the injury as independently as possible. After she broke her foot on uneven pavement, a woman drove herself back to her home, celebrating her "grit".

A question that effectively solicits narratives on the subjective dimensions of experience is "How is your health?", with the researcher probing for specific events that may appear in the answers such as falls, surgeries or diagnoses. In these cases, it is important that the researcher take the time to understand the exact sequence of events related to the specific crisis, because this understanding can elucidate the motivations behind specific decisions (for example, the decision to drive home alone with a broken foot instead of accepting help from people nearby at the moment of the injury). To that end, ethnographic interviews are especially advantageous because they can be used to gather such granular and clarifying data, as discussed in the review by Spradley (2016).

Marker 4: cumulative pressures

Pressures that stem from a combination of uncertainty, limited appropriate services and longing for independence mark precarity. In particular, the multiple pressures coming from different factors in one's life produce precarity. For example, 80-year-old Ms Jones, a woman living alone with dementia, stated that, "It gets to be overwhelming trying to keep things straight," alluding in her case to pressures coming from her cognitive impairment, limited support, poverty, overdue bills, garbage to take out and weak legs. Other participants living alone with cognitive impairment talked about getting "burned out". The combined pressures of uncertainty, limited appropriate services and longing for independence are concerning because they amplify the negative effects of trying events or crises, such as receiving a diagnosis of cognitive impairment, dealing with chronic pain or losing a sibling – transitions that are recognized as leading to isolation and loneliness. The amplification comes from having to deal with yet "another" concern, despite limited resources. For example, Ms Bates, a woman living alone with cognitive impairment, explained,

> 'I write a ton of notes. I don't remember where I put them and so I have a hard time going back and finding them because I've written a ton of notes.... And the thing about notes, you can carry a little notebook that's like this. You fill the paper up right away. Then you have to have another notebook, and another little notebook, and another little notebook. And I don't want to walk around with a huge book to write all my notes.... But if I'm writing something [laughs] I fill the notebook up in twenty minutes. Well, not quite, but quickly. So it's exhausting. That's *another* exhausting thing.'

In this quote, Ms Bates expressed her exhaustion about having yet another thing to deal with, which was taking notes. To understand whether this statement marks precarity, we need to understand what the other "exhausting thing[s]" are in her everyday life. The cumulative pressures indicate precarity because over the course of four interviews, Ms Bates talked at length about her uncertainty about what to do, her drive to be independent and the limited appropriate services available to her. If such data were not available, then the researcher could elicit the details of the other "exhausting things" from the participant immediately. For example, the researcher might say, "I see [pause]. Can you please tell me what these other exhausting things are?"

One way to identify the types of cumulative pressures that exist is to ask study participants to talk about crises as well as everyday routines. Pressures can also emerge from asking participants to talk about current (that is, 'right now') concerns. In narratives, the researchers can focus on the cues about pressures that emerge at multiple levels. For example, consider the pressures revealed in the following statement from a woman living alone with cognitive impairment: "If they [solicitors] tried to call me, I would block them. I absolutely don't have the time. I'm too busy." It is then up to the researcher to investigate these pressures by asking pointed questions (for example, "Tell me, in what way are you too busy?"). The researcher might also wish to find out if the call from the solicitor provokes concern or worry, keeping in mind how factors such as being in arrears for rent or other outstanding legal issues present further risk for precarity.

In the pursuit of recognizing and measuring precarity, it is important not to force the data by asking specific pointed questions about precarity (for example, "Do you ever feel that you have a lot of pressures?"). Instead, we must step back and use open-ended questions that allow the data to speak for themselves. Further, to validate the data, it is critical to pay attention to evidence that appears at odds with the interview narrative (Miles and Huberman, 2014), that is, to cues indicating that study participants do not lead precarious lives because they have plenty of resources, their future is taken care of, they receive appropriate services and they are open to receiving help.

Conclusion

This chapter has examined the construct of precarity as it emerged in data collection and qualitative analysis in two research studies. The chapter offered a number of cues about how to 'ask questions' when conducting qualitative research with older people. Precarity emerged from four markers: uncertainty, limited appropriate services, independence and cumulative pressures. According to our criteria, spontaneously emerging themes had to contain at least two markers to indicate precarity.

As these markers suggest, studying older people in this way can contribute to understanding precarity by extending the analysis of the micro-subjective realm of study participants, to examine the influence of factors at an institutional-meso level of analysis and at a macro level of analysis. In doing so, this approach to precarity highlights the important role of health care providers, social policies, ideologies and the overall social system in increasing or alleviating the precarity of vulnerable populations – in this case, of older adults living alone with and without a diagnosed cognitive impairment.

Shifting the analytic focus of scientific and political communities to the roles of institutional and ideological factors in exacerbating the precarity of vulnerable populations is therefore critical to move analyses beyond the personal spheres of study participants. Studies solely concerned with personal subjectivities, such as studies of resilience (Pruchno and Carr, 2017), are limited as they often point to the individual as the source of both problems *and* solutions, often discounting the role of external factors (such as appropriate policies and services) in improving the study participants' situations. As a result, they reinforce the individualistic ideology (Beck and Beck-Gernsheim, 2002) that suggests individuals themselves, rather than the welfare state and the wider community, are responsible for their well-being as well as their resilience (see also Chapter 3).

Further, studies focusing on the micro level of analysis may assume the availability of services (Cooper et al, 2010; Vinson et al, 2014), without investigating their true availability. This practice is concerning because adverse health outcomes, such as those intertwined with precarity, are often facilitated by a lack of appropriate and available services. This interplay between needs and services is indeed a key finding of my research team's ongoing investigation into living alone with cognitive impairment in the United States (Portacolone, 2018; Portacolone et al, 2018; 2019), and has been corroborated by similar studies (Hill and Walton, 2013; Hinton et al, 2004; Ortiz and Fitten, 2000).

The research conducted with older adults living alone suggests that there is merit in applying the concept of precarity to issues relating to ageing and late life. While Bauman (2007), Beck (1992; Beck and Beck-Gernsheim, 2002) and Castel (2003) did not use the term 'precarity' in their work, they all pointed to different aspects of the phenomena that we have categorized as markers for risk and insecurity. This chapter contributes to developing the construct of precarity by organizing its various dimensions into markers and focusing on the effects that the dynamics discussed by these scholars have on older adults, with particular attention paid to those living alone with and without cognitive impairment.

The research reported in this chapter has broadened the concept of precarity, in its application to later life, by moving away from the dominant focus on the labour market and related issues (Bohle et al, 2010; Craciun et al, 2016). Our approach to studying precarity among older people encompasses the ripple effects of the retreat of the welfare state, the related emphasis on individual responsibilities and the pressures of ageing given limited community-based supports. The accumulated pressures take into account the increased strain that occurs at the intersection of these dynamics.

A better understanding of precarity in the academic community is therefore critical to the development of programmes and policies meant to relieve vulnerable populations from unnecessary and *socially constructed* pressures that occur at the intersections of the micro, meso and macro – or institutional and ideological – levels. The ability to identify precarity is essential in order to raise awareness of the reality that older adults are increasingly being stripped of access to institutions and supports that, in the previous century, sustained a more supported experience of old age (see further Chapter 10). This perspective is especially important if we consider that precarity derives from factors that might be taken for granted by study participants and researchers alike, such as the emphasis on independent living and individual responsibilities, as well as the design of social policies.

The suggestion made throughout this chapter is that a researcher's eyes must be trained to spot precarity in participants' narratives and during observational qualitative research encounters. Additionally, in order to identify precarity, researchers must have in-depth knowledge of prevailing ideologies and available supports, including those designed for income support, housing and long-term care. A knowledge of international long-term care policies can help researchers adopt a more critical perspective on the policies that influence the lived experience of study participants (for an example, see Portacolone, 2018). In sum, the researcher plays a critical role in the identification of precarity.

This paper contributes to the study of precarity by identifying factors that go beyond those typically found in the field of employment. We call for future interdisciplinary collaborations to better identify and measure precarity in ageing studies and more broadly in the social sciences. One suggestion is to draw on labour studies and the Employment Precarity Index (Lewchuk, 2017) to develop a multidimensional measure that classifies persons as 'secure', 'stable', 'vulnerable', or 'precarious' based on assessment of a series of parameters. This type of approach might align with the markers described earlier in this chapter: (a) uncertainty; (b) limited access to appropriate services; (c) importance of maintaining independence; and (d) cumulative pressures.

Overall, the aim of this chapter has been to facilitate the ability of social scientists to identify and understand the cues of precarity that may appear across the results and data of various projects with low income and marginalized groups of older people. Our team looks forward to future contributions advancing the studies of precarity in the social sciences and in ageing studies, because identifying precarity with well validated measures and frameworks will help us highlight the priorities and concerns of vulnerable populations in a systematic and rigorous fashion. This knowledge is essential to design programmes and social policies at community, provider and system levels to enhance the well-being of these vulnerable populations.

Notes

[1] Spradley (2016) provides an excellent guide to asking questions in ethnographic interviews.

References

Amjad, H., Roth, D.L., Samus, Q.M., Yasar, S. and Wolff, J.L. (2016) 'Potentially unsafe activities and living conditions of older adults with dementia', *Journal of the American Geriatrics Society*, 64(6): 1223–32.

Atkinson, P. and Hammersley, M. (1994) 'Ethnography and participant observation', in: N.K. Denzin and Y.S. Lincoln (eds) *The Sage Handbook of Qualitative Research*, Thousand Oaks, CA: Sage, pp 248–61.

Bauman, Z. (2007) *Liquid Times: Living in an Age of Uncertainty*, Cambridge: Polity.

Beck, U. (1992) *Risk Society: towards a New Modernity*, translated by M. Ritter, London: Sage.

Beck, U. and Beck-Gernsheim, E. (2002) *Individualization: Institutionalized Individualism and Its Social and Political Consequences*, translated by P. Camiller, London: Sage.

Bhattacherjee, A. (2012) *Social Science Research: Principles, Methods, and Practices*, Tampa: University of South Florida.

Bodnar, C. (2006) 'Taking it to the streets: French cultural worker resistance and the creation of a precariat movement', *Canadian Journal of Communication*, 31(3): 675–94.

Bohle, P., Pitts, C. and Quinlan, M. (2010) 'Time to call it quits? The safety and health of older workers', *International Journal of Health Services*, 40(1): 23–41.

Brodaty, H., Heffernan, M., Kochan, N.A., Draper, B., Trollor, J.N., Reppermund, S., Slavin, M.J. and Sachdev, P.S. (2013) 'Mild cognitive impairment in a community sample: the Sydney Memory and Ageing Study', *Alzheimer's & Dementia*, 9(3): 310–17.

Carroll, R. (2002) 'Assassination bears mark of Red Brigades', *The Guardian* [online], 21 March 2002, available from: https://www.theguardian.com/world/2002/mar/21/rorycarroll [Accessed 13 August 2019].

Castel, R. (2003) *L'insécurite sociale. Qu'est-ce qu'être protégé?*, Paris: Le Seuil.

Charmaz, K. (2006) *Constructing Grounded Theory*, London: Sage.

Cohen, L. (1998) *No Aging in India: Alzheimer's, the Bad Family, and Other Modern Things*, Berkeley: University of California Press.

Cooper, C., Tandy, A.R., Balamurali, T.B. and Livingston, G. (2010) 'A systematic review and meta-analysis of ethnic differences in use of dementia treatment, care, and research', *American Journal of Geriatric Psychiatry*, 18(3): 193–203.

Craciun, C. and Flick, U. (2016) 'Aging in precarious times: exploring the role of gender in shaping views on aging', *Journal of Women and Aging*, 28(6): 530–9.

DeVellis, R.F. (2017) *Scale Development: Theory and Applications* (4th edn), Los Angeles: Sage.

Duncan, O.D. (1984) *Notes on Social Measurement: Historical and Critical*, New York: Russel Sage Foundation.

Edwards, J.R. and Bagozzi, R.P. (2000) 'On the nature and direction of relationships between constructs and measures', *Psychological Methods*, 5(2): 155–74.

Elo, S. and Kyngäs, H. (2008) 'The qualitative content analysis process', *Journal of Advanced Nursing*, 62(1): 107–15.

Estes, C.L. (2001) 'Crisis, the welfare state, and aging: ideology and agency in the social security privatization debate', in C.L. Estes and Associates (eds) *Social Policy & Aging: A Critical Perspective*, Thousand Oaks, CA: Sage, pp 95–117.

Ganzeboom, H.B.G., De Graaf, P.M. and Treiman, D.J. (1992) 'A standard international socio-economic index of occupational status', *Social Science Research*, 21(1): 1–56.

Glaser, B.G. and Strauss, A.L. (2010) *The Discovery of Grounded Theory: Strategies for Qualitative Research*, New Brunswick, NJ: Aldine Transaction.

Hill, L. and Walton, I. (2013) 'Screening for dementia: diagnosis... and then what?', *Progress in Neurology and Psychiatry*, 17(2): 8.

Hinton, L., Franz, C. and Friend, J. (2004) 'Pathways to dementia diagnosis: evidence for cross-ethnic differences', *Alzheimer Disease & Associated Disorders*, 18(3): 134–44.

Jamieson, L. and Simpson, R. (2013) *Living Alone: Globalization, Identity and Belonging*, Basingstoke: Palgrave Macmillan.

Klinenberg, E. (2012) *Going Solo: the Extraordinary Rise and Surprising Appeal of Living Alone*, New York: Penguin.

Leonard, P. (1997) *Postmodern Welfare: Reconstructing an Emancipatory Project*, Thousand Oaks, CA: Sage.

Lewchuk, W. (2017) 'Precarious jobs: where are they, and how do they affect well-being?', *Economic and Labour Relations Review*, 28(3): 402–19.

MacKenzie, S.B., Podsakoff, P.M. and Jarvis, C.B. (2005) 'The problem of measurement model misspecification in behavioral and organizational research and some recommended solutions', *Journal of Applied Psychology*, 90(4): 710–30.

Miles, M.B. and Huberman, A.M. (2014) *Qualitative Data Analysis: a Methods Sourcebook* (3rd edn), Thousand Oaks, CA: Sage.

Ortiz, F. and Fitten, L.J. (2000) 'Barriers to healthcare access for cognitively impaired older Hispanics', *Alzheimer Disease & Associated Disorders*, 14(3): 141–50.

Pope, C. and Mays, N. (1995) 'Reaching the parts other methods cannot reach: an introduction to qualitative methods in health and health services research', *BMJ*, 311: 42–5.

Portacolone, E. (2011) 'The myth of independence for older Americans living alone in the Bay Area of San Francisco: a critical reflection', *Ageing & Society*, 31(5): 803–28.

Portacolone, E. (2013) 'The notion of precariousness among older adults living alone in the U.S.', *Journal of Aging Studies* 27(2): 166–74.

Portacolone, E. (2018) 'On living alone with Alzheimer's disease', *Care Weekly*, 2: 50–3.

Portacolone, E., Johnson, J.K., Covinsky, K.E., Halpern, J. and Rubinstein, R.L. (2018) 'The effects and meanings of receiving a diagnosis of mild cognitive impairment or Alzheimer's disease when one lives alone', *Journal of Alzheimer's Disease*, 61(4): 1517–29.

Portacolone, E., Rubinstein, R.L., Covinsky, K.E., Halpern, J. and Johnson, J.K. (2019) 'The precarity of older adults living alone with cognitive impairment', *The Gerontologist*, 59(2): 271–80.

Pruchno, R. and Carr, D. (2017) 'Successful aging 2.0: resilience and beyond', *Journals of Gerontology Series B: Psychological Sciences & Social Sciences*, 72(2): 201–3.

Shih, R.A., Concannon, T.W., Liu, J.L. and Friedman, E.M. (2014) 'Improving dementia long-term care: a policy blueprint', *Rand Health Quarterly*, 4(2): 2.

Sibley, A., MacKnight, C., Rockwood, K., Fisk, J., Gauthier, S., Guzman, D.A. and Hogan, D.B. (2002) 'The effect of the living situation on the severity of dementia at diagnosis', *Dementia and Geriatric Cognitive Disorders*, 13(1): 40–5.

Silverstein, M. and Giarrusso, R. (2011) 'Aging individuals, families, and societies: micro–meso–macro linkages in the life course', in R.A. Settersten Jr and J.L. Angel (eds) *Handbook of Sociology of Aging*, New York: Springer, pp 35–49.

Spradley, J.P. (2016) *The Ethnographic Interview*, Long Grove, IL: Waveland.

Vandenberghe, F. (2007) 'Avatars of the collective: a realist theory of collective subjectivities', *Sociological Theory*, 25(4): 295–324.

Vinson, L.D., Crowther, M.R., Austin, A.D. and Guin, S.M. (2014) 'African Americans, mental health, and aging', *Clinical Gerontologist*, 37(1): 4–17.

PART III

Austerity, care and social responses to precarity

8

Reconstructing dependency: precarity, precariousness and care in old age

Michael Fine

Introduction

Like ageing, care is a complex, embodied and uncertain phenomenon in which social and biological processes are tightly linked (Fine, 2007; Tronto, 1993). Consequently, the forms care takes vary not just for individuals or for gender or social class cohorts, but between communities and across different points in history (Fineman, 2002). In the human biography, the need for supportive care and support is closely tied to age. Our dependence on care varies in intensity through the life course, requiring extensive care in infancy as well as at different points in our lives, including during sickness or as a result of disability in adulthood. The likelihood of reliance on care, in the sense of personal assistance provided with the intention of enabling, supporting and enhancing life, tends to increase with advanced age. Late life is particularly likely to be associated with increased vulnerability, the result of physical ageing and disease as well as the uncertain and insecure social situation of older people. Appropriate responses involving the provision of care on a secure and personal basis are required. Without them, life may cease to be viable. Yet the sources of care are fungible and its quality and character variable. Whether care is provided, and if so how and by whom, are essentially social questions.

The need for care in old age is, however, commonly understood as a health and medical issue. This is a shorthand way of saying that a physical pathology develops for which a specialized diagnosis and appropriate clinical response is required. Medical research on this need has long been closely linked to the concepts of frailty and age-related decline (Collard et al, 2012; Grenier and Hanley, 2007), with evidence showing that patterns of need are both variable and dynamic (Fried,

2000; Higgs and Gilleard, 2014). Increasing attention is also being paid to a newly emergent explanation for this association, the self-described 'geroscience hypothesis' (Huffman et al, 2016; Sierra and Kohanski, 2017), which identifies biological ageing at the level of chromosomes and cells as the common and underlying cause of the health problems and multiple comorbidities associated with advancing age.[1] Proponents of the 'geroscience hypothesis' argue that it has the potential to shift the emphasis away from seeing need as a form of pathology to understanding it as a product of the normal biology of ageing, and possibly, to intervening over time to prevent decline. The discourse and the understanding of care needs that flow from it, however, remain essentially biomedical, lacking any sociological perspective.

The more recently developed body of critical care theory, in contrast, has broadly emphasized the social act of caregiving (Fine, 2018). Addressing what had long been neglected or rendered invisible, this work has sought to gain recognition for the taken-for-granted care work undertaken by women in particular, and to understand the assumptions and social constructs that lie behind the provision of care, especially the issues of gender and the socioeconomic circumstances of caregivers (Fine, 2007; Knijn and Kremer, 1997; Lewis, 2007). An important stream of this work has been concerned with the ethics of care, which also places a strong emphasis on active caregiving (Lloyd, 2004).

Care for older people shares many of the characteristics of care for children and those needing care at other ages: it is a prototypical expression of interpersonal dependency, a social response to provide for the bodily and other support needs of those unable to look after themselves each day. The range and types of care provided to those who need it in old age vary considerably. They range from the requirement to provide basic intermittent assistance with domestic support at the lower levels of need, through to technically demanding care on an ongoing basis that requires levels of advanced professional competency at the higher end. Together, the impact on need and care provision of continual development in medical capabilities, along with the massive variability and inequality in social circumstances, and the increasing reliance on market mechanisms for financing and organizing support in advanced old age, marks aged care as a particularly complex social challenge. The demographic and economic pressures to provide for historically unprecedented and still-growing numbers of older recipients further mark out the contemporary crisis of aged care.

The crises of the unstable and increasingly insecure systems of care for older people experienced under the public and private welfare markets of the 21st century are not inherent, but a product of the precarious employment and the labour market in global capitalism. Drawing on the analysis of what Ebert (2011) has termed the 'precarious work-society', I argue in this chapter that the forms in which care is now made available for older people – the unequal, unstable and inadequate systems of public and private finance to pay for care, the uncertain and changing availability of staff, the increasing lack of state regulation and standards (Wilson and Ebert, 2013) – are increasingly shaped by the precarious conditions of the market. The dangers of becoming dependent on the actions of others and the unknowable experience and outcomes for recipients and their family caregivers, express macroeconomic, demographic and technological changes that, as Kalleberg (2009; 2012) and others have shown, have been reshaping work and employment on a global scale. This extends from the macro conditions of international trade and national economies through to the employment of labour and the organization of support services at local and regional level, through to the micro levels of interpersonal interaction. At a time in which formal care services and facilities for older people have been undergoing almost constant change and are faced with accelerated commercialization, informal care and familial support is also facing unprecedented pressure and is increasingly shaped by market developments.

This chapter explores the potential for the development of critical approach to care based on the concepts of precarity and precariousness. Although now widely used in research on labour markets and in the humanities, precarity has only recently begun to be applied to the study of old age. The concepts have the potential, it is argued, to draw attention to both the socially constructed uncertainties of care provision conditioned by the labour market and corporate practices on the one hand, and the uncertainties of physical ageing and the ontological vulnerabilities that arise from our bodily existence on the other. Yet, uncertainty also confronts those who provide care in an unpaid capacity, just as surely as it shapes the employment and lives of those paid to provide care. The precarious conditions of work reflect the financial fragility of the economic supports and the changing and unequal markets that increasingly underpin the way care is provided to the increasing numbers of people who live extended lives today.

In the next part of this chapter the use of the concepts of precarity and precariousness and their current use and recent application to ageing are reviewed. Following this, the way that critical care theory has developed over the past thirty years is reviewed, examining how authors have sought to engage with changing conditions, policies and markets. The discussion then returns to address the potential of incorporating the concepts of precarity and precariousness to the analysis of care in old age. The chapter argues that viewing care for older people as precarious serves to make sense of the ambivalence with which it is received by those who require it, just as it helps make visible both the hidden links between the global reach of precarious work society and the uncertain and unevenly distributed risks of needing ongoing care in old age.

Precarity and precariousness

The term 'precarious' was widely used to describe and condemn the conditions of uncertain and insecure employment encountered by agricultural, industrial and transport workers in the UK, Australia and the US throughout the 19th and early 20th centuries (Quinlan, 2012). The concept of 'precarity' was also known and used as early as the 1950s (Millar, 2017). After falling from general use for some decades following the introduction of the welfare state, both terms are in again in common use.

Millar (2017, p 3) identifies three competing approaches that have come to dominate current debates. The first, which sees precarity as a labour condition, offers considerable potential as a theoretical tool with which to understand developments in aged care. The second, in which precarity is understood as an 'ontological experience', straddles sociopolitical, biological and existential dimensions, suggesting a link between human physical vulnerability and the availability and provision of care. Each of these concepts is considered in greater depth later in this chapter. The third approach, developed by Guy Standing (see further Chapter 5) combines 'precarious' with 'proletariat', arguing that what Standing terms the 'precariat' may be seen as the 'the new dangerous class', raising the possibility of a new class-like coalition that will fight to change existing social and economic conditions.

This chapter gives particular attention to the implications for care provision arising from these different approaches, beginning with the impact of precarious forms of employment for the organization and delivery of care.

Precarious work

Because providing care is a form of work, precarity arising from developments in the organization of employment and the labour market are of fundamental importance to understanding the way that care operates. Accompanying the processes of globalization and broad neoliberal economic reforms to social policy since the 1980s has been a series of moves away from direct public provision and certainty of entitlement towards marketization, flexibility and individualized consumer choice (Esping-Andersen, 1999; Fine and Davidson, 2018; Sturgeon, 2014; Yeandle et al, 2012). Further changes in state funding and direct provision of secure residential institutions and other more 'traditional' forms of support, including multi-generation family-based care, has added to the insecurity and increasing inequality that increasingly evident in the delivery of aged care (Brennan et al, 2012; see also Chapter 9).

The precarious conditions of employment are also reflected in the gender of the care workforce. Much of the growth in female employment over the past 50 years has been through the expansion of the service economy. Insecure and poorly remunerated employment is common in many countries in the field of aged care (Armstrong and Armstrong, 2005; Aronson and Neysmith, 1996; Glucksmann and Lyon, 2006). A considerable body of research also documents the increasing significance of low-paid, migrant and minority women in care work in most advanced economies (Ehrenreich and Hochschild, 2002; Yeates, 2009).

Precarity and the human condition

Grounded in the concept of embodiment, the second approach is broadly and most effectively developed in the work of Judith Butler (2004; 2011). It has been influential among activists and across the humanities, especially cultural and performance studies but also well beyond this. Butler's approach draws together political with philosophical and ethical concerns. For Butler (2004; 2011), precariousness is a common human condition, a vulnerability that arises from the necessity of our existence as visceral, embodied social beings. From this perspective, we are able to acknowledge that we are both dependent on others and made vulnerable to the actions of others. As a result, we may lose those we depend on or hold dear, those with whom we have formed relationships. This is a double-edged sword, because our exposure to others also carries with it the risk of violence, betrayal, neglect or exploitation. The recognition and response to the vulnerability of others arises from our inherent interdependence as a basic condition for our existence. Acknowledging this underpins a sense of hope, just as it provides the basis for joint ethical action and the possibility of solidarity.

Applying this approach to ageing and care also illuminates the social structural positions and identities that both caregivers and recipients experience. Those who are unable to sustain personal independence in activities of daily living due to their need for care are made to depend on the assistance provided others and are commonly denied personal recognition, excluded from social activities and interactions (Grenier et al, 2017a; Higgs and Gilleard, 2015). This experience of devaluation and loss is one shared by age care workers and informal carers, who, it has been argued, are seen as doing compassionate but unpleasant and 'dirty' work best kept out of sight (Lawler, 1991; Twigg, 2000). The sense of precariousness that arises from the visceral, bodily impossibility of choosing to simply ignore these needs, and from the structural marginality and devaluation of the task of providing necessary support, is truly an ontological experience made manifest as a socioeconomic identity and political position.

There are a number of areas of resonance between these two broad approaches as identified by Millar (2017) that pertain to care in old age. In the existing and continually developing body of work often referred to as 'care theory', there are repeated references to the need for care as a necessary social response to human vulnerability and as an expression of the social bond – an acknowledgement of the dependency and interdependency between people (Fine, 2007; Fine and Glendinning, 2005; Tronto, 1993; 2017). This suggests the potential of a precarity perspective to enrich care theory, an issue pursued in the next section.

Precarity, ageing and care

The case for applying the concept of precarity to ageing and aged care has been made by Grenier et al (2017b). These authors argue that a key value of the approach when applied to ageing concerns the focus on social structure and attention to factors beyond the control of individuals. Here, it is argued that

> extended consideration of precarity renders visible the relationship between structures, life events, and everyday experiences of aging; highlights the shared experiences of risk and insecurity with regards to disadvantage and care; and underscores the political imperative for addressing inequality.... It offers the means to understand risk as produced within the contemporary socio-cultural, economic and political environment, and work against the victim blaming that is promoted through the neoliberal

> emphasis on the self-reliant citizen. It also calls into question the sustainability and future implications of systems that presume the availability of informal supports (family, friends, community volunteers) and/or unrecognized or poorly paid forms of care. (Grenier et al, 2017b, p 13)

In advancing precarity as a perspective on the risks of ageing and a guide to future interventions, the authors join others who contest prevailing views of successful and active ageing as the consequence of individual choice and personal responsibility (Holstein and Minkler, 2003; Katz and Calasanti, 2015). Risk among those of advanced age is not a matter of choice. Nor can it be reduced, it is argued, to an outcome of lifestyle options of individuals. It is instead produced by the sociocultural, economic and political environment, requiring political actions to address issues concerning inequality. Similarly, in responding to vulnerabilities and needs, a social and more collective response is required in contrast with the more individualistic and consumer-based approach associated with the privatization of care. Rather than there being a uniformity that accompanies ageing, precarity focuses on the production of differences between social groups and individuals that shape different forms and levels of risk, as well as the effective response to the insecurities and disadvantages that arise.

Physical and cognitive impairments such as dementia raise further questions that, it is argued, can be best understood as a product of precarious risks faced as one grows older. How does the concept of precarity affect the way we recognize and interact with the person with dementia and the condition they experience? How might our understanding of the nature of support needed be affected when dementia is understood as a form of economic and existential precariousness rather than as a failure to age actively? Grenier et al (2017a) argue that there are significant potential benefits associated with rejecting the dominant view of ageing and dementia as a form of failed stage of life and accepting and responding to them as a part of normal ageing:

> Shifting the focus from constructs that reinforce the negative valuations of age, to a recognised shared vulnerability, acceptance of the limitations of life and death, and shared political responsibility can help to unhinge dementia and impairment from a 'frailed' and 'failed' late life into a foundation from which to develop new types of care relationships. (Grenier et al, 2017a, p 327)

To understand ageing and dementia in this way invokes the precariousness of vulnerability and suffering, suggesting the need to create approaches in which care provides new possibilities for life and interpersonal relationships. Providing and relying on care, in this view, should not be seen as a negative from of dependency to be avoided at all costs, but as a recognition that life requires social collaboration, and that, properly organized, care can open new potentials for living with others.

To propose that seeing precarity and care in this way could lead to such positive outcomes is in many ways remarkable – it is a promise close to intellectual alchemy. Is precarity theory so powerful that its use could transform our understanding of age-related suffering, decline and dependency? Could it serve to guide future research and inform programmes for practical action that could lead to tangible improvements in the way that care is provided to those of us who require it in old age, as well as those who provide it? Before returning to consider the potential of this theoretical and conceptual approach, the next section of this chapter examines key contributions from critical care theory.

Understanding critical care theory

Linguistically, 'care' is an emotive, value-laden and contested term, difficult to define and analyse as social expectations and understandings transform and take different forms in a range of contexts (Fine, 2007). Care is a complex social phenomenon in other ways, too, being shaped and reshaped by and through historical and cultural change. It is at once a mental phenomenon concerned with an emotional and ethical engagement with another (to care *about* another), an active form of work and activity (to care *for* another) and an interpersonal relationship. The concept of care also covers a range of quite distinct practices or forms of delivery – from traditional maternal nurturance and familial support, to support provided to people at home or in large social institutions, to a wide range of contemporary clinical, professionalized and commercial types of service. It has also been reimagined many times over in response to emerging technologies and changing economic conditions at local, national and global levels, as well as medical developments, demographic change and political circumstances. As Hochschild (1995) observes, the ideals and expectations held about care closely reflect the social context from which they arise, with discussion of care commonly invoking strong feelings, from warmth to coldness.

Care remained a largely neglected academic topic, taken for granted or deemed insufficiently worthy of theoretical consideration until the rise of contemporary feminism in the late 1960s and 1970s. Since then critical care theory has developed strongly, as analysts from a wide range of disciplines sought to understand and adapt to changing circumstances. Over time, new insights and perspectives developed, often in response to policy or the technologies of service delivery. Many of these changes seem, at times, to be without a clear direction – there is, for example, only limited evidence of 'progress' or progressive evolution in either the practice or theory of care over this time. Yet in developed capitalist countries at least, one direction of change stands out: care has become increasingly public, as argued elsewhere (Fine, 2007). It was, until recently, considered to be a 'private' matter, something best undertaken within the home as far as possible. But over recent decades care provisions have increasingly come to be organized outside the home and beyond the family, with services provided by paid staff organized and financed through the state, market or community. Similarly, public interest in the visibility of care issues in the media and debates about economic value has increased manyfold.

For feminists, early interest in care arose in the late 1970s and early 1980s, arising from a concern with the unpaid work carried out by women within the family. Care came to be equated with the household duties of married women. According to Hilary Land, these duties included 'caring for their children, their elderly or sick relatives and, of course, their husbands' (Land, 1978, p 360) as well as other forms of unpaid care such as care of the elderly and of children with disabilities (Finch and Groves, 1983). In this view, care came to be considered in Hilary Graham's deservedly famous description as the 'labour of love' (Graham, 1983) provided at home, informally, by unpaid and unrecognized female relatives of the recipients. Domestic care of husbands, children, disabled family members and the aged, in this discourse, was a form of burdensome responsibility undertaken mainly by women as a familial duty towards others. Even when this work was undertaken in a paid capacity, many of the same demeaning characteristics were seen to adhere. For example, writings in nursing from the 1970s onwards depicted care in a focused and very gender-specific way (Benner, 1984; Lawler, 1991; Leininger, 1988; Watson, 1979), as a specialized professional skill undertaken mainly by women.

Different voices

By the 1990s, a range of different voices had begun to emerge and engage in the conversation about care. An important note of dissent came from disability rights authors, including sociologists such as Jenny Morris (1993; 1996), Colin Barnes (1998) and Tom Shakespeare (2000), who contested the use of the concept of care on the basis that the valorization of the concept privileged the perspective of those who provide it at the expense of the recipients. People with disabilities were represented in care theory not as active agents but simply as 'burdens'.

In the United States, feminist political philosophers sought to extend the debate. Joan Tronto (1993), for example, denoted care as 'a species activity', an orientation to the world:

> On the most general level, we suggest caring be viewed as a species activity that includes everything that we do to maintain, continue and repair our 'world' so that we can live in it as well as possible. That world includes our bodies, ourselves, and our environment, all of which we seek to interweave in a complex, life-sustaining web. (Tronto, 1993, p 103)

This approach lifted the concept of care to the level of a philosophical ideal, a feminist-inspired alternative goal to the supposed masculine goal of competitive individualism. In doing so, it built on the ethics of care approach that had grown from the work of Carol Gilligan (1982; Noddings, 1984). Noting how there was no recognition given to the need for care in either mainstream political theory or constitutional manifestos, such as that of the United States or the UN Declaration of Human Rights, Tronto (1993; 2002) argued for care to be elevated to a central, shared culture and moral value.

Citizenship and migration

A number of European care researchers and political philosophers also sought to extend the understanding of care into the political sphere around the same time, acknowledging both *receiving* as well as *giving* care as part of a model of citizenship rights (Knijn and Kremer, 1997; Sevenhuijsen, 1993; Williams, 2001). This new approach drew on and extended the approach that was then developing across the Atlantic, responding too to the restructuring and seeming retreat of the European welfare state that had provided public health and social care services, but seemed to be increasingly reliant on the market and family. Fiona Williams (2001) neatly outlined what amounts to a simple charter of care rights: the right to give care; the right to receive care; and the right to care for oneself. Breaking down the sense of care as an active (caregiver)–passive (recipient) relationship, this line of argument also recognized the reciprocal and embodied character of care. Caring relationships came to be considered as often complex, reciprocal and mutually supportive rather than simple binary relationships between an active carer and a passive and dependent care recipient (Morris, 2001; Fine and Glendinning, 2005). Subsequent research on care has placed ever greater emphasis on the agency and recognition of the care recipient (Lloyd, 2000; 2004; Needham, 2011; Rostgaard, 2006; Yeatman et al, 2009).

A parallel stream of scholarship began to emerge in the late 1990s, first in the US and then later from other countries, that reflected the growth in the private employment market for domestic care workers and domestic assistants. Based initially on empirical ethnographic research, it focused on documenting and analysing the insecure and exploitative employment of low-paid female care workers from African American, Hispanic and migrant backgrounds. Among the latter were care workers from the Philippines, the Caribbean, Latin America, Asia and elsewhere, frequently working without official work visas and with little or no legal protection (Hondagneu-Sotelo, 2000; Parreñas, 2001). Researchers soon documented similar practices in other countries, such as Hong Kong, Singapore, China, Canada and most European nations, including the Nordic states, commonly linked to temporary migration visas that precluded family migration, forcing the women to leave their own family behind (Isaksen, 2010; Michel and Peng, 2012; 2017; Williams, 2012).

Such domestic care workers are typically engaged privately, often by well-educated and professional women needing relief from care of children or ageing parents at home so they can undertake employment of their own. Unable to bring their own family, the migrant care workers are forced to find caregivers in their home land for their own children and ageing parents, leading to the phenomenon described as 'global care chains' (Ehrenreich and Hochschild, 2002). As Hondagneu-Sotelo (2000, p 161) argues, 'the work of caregiving and cleaning, once relegated to wives, mothers and grandmothers, is increasingly commodified and purchased on a global market'.

This form of poorly paid domestic work undertaken in exploitative circumstances, often referred to as the 'commercialisation' or 'commodification of domestic work' (Anderson, 2002), has also been incorporated into publicly funded care programmes (Ungerson and Yeandle, 2006), displacing or limiting the expansion of formally provided, more professional aged care services. Increasingly forms of such work have expanded as a result of the design of welfare programmes, as is the case in Italy, where Bettio et al (2006) have described how having a 'migrant in the family' to provide care has become common, often paid for by cash benefits provided to families as an accepted way to sustain the ideals of family care. This model is by no means restricted to Southern Europe (Michel and Peng, 2012).

A key lesson from the perspective of citizenship and migration is that care can no longer be understood (if it ever could) as a form of unpaid work that is independent from developments in the market and the state. Globalized patterns of migration, along with changing opportunity structures for women, intersect with the changing demographic profile that arises from increased ageing and reduced fertility, shaping expectations, practices and the interpersonal relationships of care on a household as well as a global scale. There remains considerable scope for a more analytic approach based on the concept of precarity that can draw attention to the political-economic and relational aspects of care.

Care, power and dependency

The philosopher Eva Fedor Kittay (1999) identifies another important distinction – between natural and social constructed dependencies – that suggests an important direction this more analytic development might follow. Kittay (1999) places dependency and considerations of power at the centre of analysis of care:

> Dependents require care ... questions of who takes on the responsibility of care, who does the hands-on care, who sees to it that caring is done and done well, and who provides the support for the relationship of care and for both parties to the caring relationship – these are social and political questions.... How a social order organizes care of these needs is a matter of social justice. (Kittay, 1999, p 1)

Like Judith Butler's discussion of vulnerability and precariousness, Kittay argues that dependency is both a fundamental condition of human existence and a socially created relationship (Feder and Kittay, 2002). In this way she builds on a rich tradition of scholarship concerned with the social construction of dependency (Baltes, 1996;

Fineman, 2002; Fraser and Gordon, 1994; Gibson, 1998; Nussbaum, 2002; Townsend, 1981; Walker, 1982). Physical dependency on actions by others is evident at crucial points in the life course that Martha Fineman has called the 'inevitable dependencies' of life (Fineman, cited in Kittay, 1999, p 30). Political, sociocultural, economic and moral conditions at different points in history and in different contexts shape these dependencies and the social response to them (Kittay, 1999, p 29). Gender is historically – but not inevitably – part of these arrangements, as 'care of dependents is work ... traditionally engaged in by women' (Kittay, 1999, p 30).

Kittay's analysis (1999) provides an account of care that may be thought of as a dual system of dependency. The first component involves, at its most basic level, two people: the caregiver (or 'dependency worker', in Kittay's terms) and the recipient (or 'charge'). Each is bound together through the relationship of physical or embodied dependency in which the charge depends on her caregiver for regular assistance with essential life tasks (or activities of daily living). The second component is the system of support through which the dependency worker is maintained in the larger world, in which the caregiver is dependent on a third party – the provider – for her own support (Fine, 2005). The primary dependency of the charge on the caregiver arises in the case of the object from the charge's limited capacity for daily survival and maintenance. This is a form of physical or embodied dependence. The dependency worker, committed to the well-being of her charge, in turn experiences a secondary dependency as a result of her dependence on the provider. This dependency is socially constructed, arising from the social arrangements in which the dependency worker uses her time to support the charge.

Conclusion

Given its origin in feminism and the urgency with which it has been necessary to address the inequality faced by women, critical care theory has generally emphasized the issues associated with providing care as the brief overview presented in the previous section has shown. Over time the focus has extended from the social situation and experiences of unpaid and exploited family caregivers to those of poorly paid, insecure care workers and care professionals. This approach acknowledges the injustice of globalized inequality alongside the inequalities arising from gender. Despite the important critique offered by social disability theorists and the increasing attention given to care recipients in other more recent research on care, it remains a challenge to find a way of theorizing care in a way that truly recognizes the position and experience of both caregivers and recipients, and the capricious, unpredictable and unjust impact that the social practices of care may have for each party. Understanding care in old age in terms of precarity demands that we engage with both the provision and receipt of care. In doing so, precarity reveals many of the realities that existing approaches to care currently neglect, ignore or deliberately gloss over.

Central to this approach must be an acknowledgment of the way in which changes to the employment market have promoted casualized, temporary and insecure work. As care of older people has increasingly gone public, extended beyond the household and family, it has increasingly become a prime site for economic rationalization and cost control (see Chapter 4). Efforts to reduce costs to government and enhance corporate and managerial control of care work have extended to global levels and are no longer restricted to local and national initiatives, as deregulation of competition, globalized sourcing of care workers and marketization have become widespread responses to the need to ensure social support for different target groups at times of extreme personal vulnerability for the welfare capitalist regimes of the OECD (Fine and Davidson, 2018; Kalleberg, 2009; Shutes and Chiatti, 2012; see also Chapter 9). The ongoing impact such developments have had on the workforce are directly translated into the way that care is delivered. The integrating social relationships on which care has traditionally rested have come under increasing stress, under the pressure of increasingly deregulated market competition.

The impacts of the labour market on the way that care is provided are readily apparent. Less immediately visible is the impact of the long-term dependency of care recipients. As Kittay's work shows, these also transfer to those who provide care as they, in turn, are made dependent. Each of the primary parties involved in the caregiving relationship is thus liable to be marginalized and to experience a denial of the social recognition and the possibilities of active social participation that are the hallmarks of full citizenship.

Clearly this is not inevitable. Understanding the precarious nature of this situation indicates ways in which it is possible to confront it. The forms that such dependency takes and how it is managed, however, are not given, but are produced by the (typically hidden) politics and economic underpinnings of the social relationships. Acknowledging the precarious character of care in old age not only helps both parties and their advocates identify the points of weakness, conflict and complaint, but also suggests ways in which it is possible to respond to them.

As Judith Butler (2004) points out, precarity and precariousness is produced by unequal and unjust social arrangements, as well as by the vulnerability that arises from our embodied existence. Precarity helps focus on both the inevitable bodily expressions of dependency and the socially constructed forms that are most readily amenable to change. Yet despite the emphasis placed on interpersonal duty in many discussions of caring, the provision of personal support to those who require it in old age is shaped by economic and social forces on a global scale that produce precarious situations and undermine certainty (see Chapter 10).

Few, if any, older people actively seek to become recipients of formal care (Harrison et al, 2014; Moen, 1978). While care at home, provided as part of longer-term intimate family relationships, has often been found to have a greater degree of acceptance than residential care, both by the very old who require ongoing assistance and at the level of shared social norms (Weicht, 2010; 2015), receiving care itself is commonly understood as a loss of agency and personhood, not least by those who require it most (Higgs and Gilleard, 2015, pp 112–13; Lloyd et al, 2014). Long regarded as a private matter, an exchange that occurred within the intimacy of the domestic sphere, care for aged people is clearly now a global public and corporate concern. The rise of ageing populations, the increasing prevalence of disability and the increased reliance on formalized child care arrangements to support working mothers (Fine, 2007; Kittay et al, 2005) draw attention to the importance of fostering what Kittay et al and others have called 'a global ethic of long term care'. Yet neither these imperative to provide care nor the precarity that existing social and economic arrangements produce can give any reassurance that the resultant provisions truly meet the intent of such moral injunctions.

For those seeking to go beyond the glib salesmanship of consumer marketing, understanding the precarity of care in old age offers a uniquely potent antidote. Precarity promises to distinguish the potential conflicts between those who have and those who do not have real economic power. It also provides a way of examining the cleavages between those who seek to maximize control over care workers – for example, by being held responsible as employers for controlling personal budgets over which they may have little real control – and those who are reliant on the precarious employment that such arrangements typically produce. These issues will become increasingly urgent to address given the trends discussed in this chapter, setting an important agenda for researchers and policymakers alike.

Notes

1. 'The "geroscience hypothesis" posits that manipulation of ageing will delay (in parallel) the appearance or severity of many chronic diseases because these diseases share the same underlying major risk factor (age). The hope is that this will lead to health improvements in the older population with perhaps greater efficiency than can be achieved through the successful cure and management of diseases of ageing as they arise individually or as comorbidities' (Sierra and Kohanski, 2017, p 1).

References

Anderson, B. (2002) 'Just another job? The commodification of domestic labor', in B. Ehrenreich and A.R. Hochschild (eds) *Global Woman: Nannies, Maids and Sex Workers in the New Economy*, New York: Metropolitan Books, pp 104–14.

Armstrong, P. and Armstrong, H. (2005) 'Public and private: implications for care work', *Sociological Review*, 53(supplement 2): 167–87.

Aronson, J. and Neysmith, S.M. (1996) '"You're not just in there to do the work": depersonalizing policies and the exploitation of home care workers' labor', *Gender & Society*, 10(1): 59–77.

Baltes, M.M. (1996) *The Many Faces of Dependency in Old Age*, Cambridge: Cambridge University Press.

Barnes, C. (1998) 'The social model of disability: a sociological phenomenon ignored by sociologists?', in T. Shakespeare (ed.) *The Disability Reader: Social Science Perspectives*, London: Cassell, pp 65–78.

Benner, P. (1984) *From Novice to Expert: Excellence and Power in Clinical Nursing Practice*, Menlo Park, CA: Addison-Wesley.

Bettio, F., Villa, P. and Simonazzi, A. (2006) 'Changing care regimes and female migration', *Journal of European Social Policy*, 16(3): 271–85.

Brennan, D., Cass, B., Himmelweit, S. and Szebehely, M. (2012) 'The marketisation of care: rationales and consequences in Nordic and liberal care regimes', *Journal of European Social Policy*, 22(4): 377–91.

Butler, J. (2004) *Precarious Life: the Powers of Mourning and Violence*, London: Verso.

Butler, J. (2011) 'For and against precarity', *Tidal: Occupy Theory, Occupy Strategy*, 1: 12–13.

Collard, R.M., Boter, H., Schoevers, R.A. and Voshaar, R.C.O. (2012) 'Prevalence of frailty in community-dwelling older persons: a systematic review', *Journal of the American Geriatrics Society*, 60(8): 1487–92.

Ebert, N. (2011) 'Precarious work societies', *Exchange*, 5: 6–10.

Ehrenreich, B. and Hochschild, A.R. (eds) (2002) *Global Woman: Nannies, Maids and Sex Workers in the New Economy*, New York: Metropolitan Books.

Esping-Andersen, G. (1999) *Social Foundations of Postindustrial Economies*, Oxford: Oxford University Press.

Feder, E.K. and Kittay, E.F. (2002) 'Introduction', in E.F. Kittay and E.K. Feder (eds) *The Subject of Care: Feminist Perspectives on Dependency*, Lanham, MD: Rowman & Littlefield, pp 1–13.

Finch, J. and Groves, D. (eds) (1983) *A Labour of Love: Women, Work and Caring*, London: Routledge & Kegan Paul.

Fine, M. (2005) 'Dependency work: a critical exploration of Kittay's perspective on care as a relationship of power', *Health Sociology Review*, 14(2): 146–60.

Fine, M.D. (2007) *A Caring Society? Care and the Dilemmas of Human Service in the 21st Century*, Houndmills: Palgrave.

Fine, M.D. (2019) 'Care and caring', in M. Payne and E. Reith-Hall (eds) *The Routledge Handbook of Social Work Theory*, London: Routledge, pp 83–94.

Fine, M. and Glendinning, C. (2005) 'Dependence, independence or inter-dependence? Revisiting the concepts of "care" and "dependency"', *Ageing and Society*, 25(4): 601–21.

Fine, M. and Davidson, B. (2018) 'The marketization of care: global challenges and national responses in Australia', *Current Sociology*, 66(4): 503–16.

Fineman, M.A. (2002) 'Masking dependency: the political role of family rhetoric', in E.F. Kittay and E.K. Feder (eds) *The Subject of Care: Feminist Perspectives on Dependency*, Lantham, MD: Rowman & Littlefield, pp 215–45.

Fraser, N. and Gordon, L. (1994) 'A genealogy of dependency: tracing a keyword of the U.S. welfare state', *Signs*, 19(2): 309–36.

Fried, L.P. (2000) 'Epidemiology of aging', *Epidemiologic Reviews*, 22(1): 95–106.

Gibson, D.M. (1998) 'The problem of dependency: construction and reconstruction', in D.M. Gibson (ed.) *Aged Care: Old Policies, New Problems*, Melbourne: Cambridge University Press, pp 184–211.

Gilligan, C. (1982) *In a Different Voice: Psychological Theory and Women's Development*, Cambridge, MA: Harvard University Press.

Glucksmann, M. and Lyon, D. (2006) 'Configurations of care work: paid and unpaid elder care in Italy and the Netherlands', *Sociological Research Online*, 11(2): 1–15.

Graham, H. (1983) 'Caring: a labour of love', in J. Finch and D. Groves (eds) *A Labour of Love: Women, Work and Caring*, London: Routledge & Kegan Paul, pp 13–30.

Grenier, A. and Hanley, J. (2007) 'Older women and "frailty": aged, gendered and embodied resistance', *Current Sociology*, 55(2): 211–28.

Grenier, A., Lloyd, L. and Phillipson, C. (2017a) 'Precarity in late life: rethinking dementia as a "frailed" old age', *Sociology of Health & Illness*, 39(2): 318–30.

Grenier, A., Phillipson, C., Laliberte Rudman, D., Hatzifilalithis, S., Kobayashi, K. and Marier, P. (2017b) 'Precarity in late life: understanding new forms of risk and insecurity', *Journal of Aging Studies*, 43: 9–14.

Harrison, F., Low, L.-F., Barnett, A., Gresham, M. and Brodaty, H. (2014) 'What do clients expect of community care and what are their needs? The Community care for the Elderly: Needs and Service Use Study (CENSUS)', *Australasian Journal on Ageing*, 33(3): 208–13.

Higgs, P. and Gilleard, C. (2014) 'Frailty, abjection and the "othering" of the fourth age', *Health Sociology Review*, 23(1): 10–19.

Higgs, P. and Gilleard, C. (2015) *Rethinking Old Age: Theorising the Fourth Age*, London: Palgrave Macmillan.

Hochschild, A.R. (1995) 'The culture of politics: traditional, postmodern, cold-modern, and warm-modern ideals of care', *Social Politics*, 2(3): 331–46.

Holstein, M.B. and Minkler, M. (2003) 'Self, society, and the "new gerontology"', *The Gerontologist*, 43(6): 787–96.

Hondagneu-Sotelo, P. (2000) 'The international division of caring and cleaning work: transnational connections or apartheid exclusions?', in M. Harrington Meyer (ed.) *Care Work: Gender, Labor and the Welfare State*, New York: Routledge, pp 149–62.

Huffman, D.M., Justice, J.N., Stout, M.B., Kirkland, J.L., Barzilai, N. and Austad, S.N. (2016) 'Evaluating health span in preclinical models of aging and disease: guidelines, challenges, and opportunities for geroscience', *Journals of Gerontology Series A: Biological Sciences & Medical Sciences*, 71(11): 1395–406.

Isaksen, L.W. (ed.) (2010) *Global Care Work: Gender and Migration in Nordic Societies*, Lund: Nordic Academic Press.

Kalleberg, A.L. (2009) 'Precarious work, insecure workers: employment relations in transition', *American Sociological Review*, 74(1): 1–22.

Kalleberg, A.L. (2012) 'Job quality and precarious work: clarifications, controversies, and challenges', *Work and Occupations*, 39(4): 427–48.

Katz, S. and Calasanti, T. (2015) 'Critical perspectives on successful aging: does it "appeal more than it illuminates"?', *The Gerontologist*, 55(1): 26–33.

Kittay, E.F. (1999) *Love's Labor: Essays on Women, Equality, and Dependency*, New York: Routledge.

Kittay, E.F., Jennings, B. and Wasunna, A.A. (2005) 'Dependency, difference and the global ethic of longterm care', *Journal of Political Philosophy*, 13(4): 443–69.

Knijn, T. and Kremer, M. (1997) 'Gender and the caring dimension of welfare states: toward inclusive citizenship', *Social Politics*, 4(3): 328–61.

Land, H. (1978) 'Who cares for the family?', *Journal of Social Policy*, 7(3): 357–84.

Lawler, J. (1991) *Behind the Scenes: Nursing, Somology and the Problem of the Body*, Melbourne: Churchill Livingstone.

Leininger, M.M. (ed.) (1988) *Care: the Essence of Nursing and Health*, Detroit: Wayne State University Press.

Lewis, J. (2007) 'Gender, ageing and the "new social settlement": the importance of developing a holistic approach to care policies', *Current Sociology*, 55(2): 271–86.

Lloyd, L. (2000) 'Caring about carers: only half the picture?', *Critical Social Policy*, 20(1): 136–50.

Lloyd, L. (2004) 'Mortality and morality: ageing and the ethics of care', *Ageing & Society*, 24(2): 235–56.

Lloyd, L., Calnan, M., Cameron, A., Seymour, J. and Smith, R. (2014) 'Identity in the fourth age: perseverance, adaptation and maintaining dignity', *Ageing & Society*, 34(1): 1–19.

Michel, S. and Peng, I. (2012) 'All in the family? Migrants, nationhood, and care regimes in Asia and North America', *Journal of European Social Policy*, 22(4): 406–18.

Michel, S. and Peng, I. (eds) (2017) *Gender, Migration, and the Work of Care: a Multi-Scalar Approach to the Pacific Rim*, Cham: Palgrave Macmillan.

Millar, K.M. (2017) 'Toward a critical politics of precarity', *Sociology Compass*, 11(6): e12483.

Moen, E. (1978) 'The reluctance of the elderly to accept help', *Social Problems*, 25(3): 293–303.

Morris, J. (1993) '"Us" and "them"? Feminist research and community care', in J. Bornat, C. Pereira, D. Pilgrim and F. Williams (eds) *Community Care: a Reader*, Houndmills: Macmillan, pp 156–66.

Morris, J. (ed.) (1996) *Encounters with Strangers: Feminism and Disability*, London: Women's Press.

Morris, J. (2001) 'Impairment and disability: constructing an ethics of care that promotes human rights', *Hypatia*, 16(4): 1–16.

Needham, C. (2011) *Personalising Public Services: Understanding the Personalisation Narrative*, Bristol: Policy Press.

Noddings, N. (1984) *Caring: a Feminist Approach to Ethics and Moral Education*, Berkeley: University of California Press.

Nussbaum, M. (2002) 'Care, dependency, and social justice: a challenge to conventional ideas of the social contract', paper presented at the UNRISD Public Meeting on Ageing, Development and Social Protection, Madrid, 8–9 April.

Parreñas, R.S. (2001) *Servants of Globalisation: Women, Migration and Domestic Work*, Stanford: Stanford University Press.

Quinlan, M. (2012) 'The "pre-invention" of precarious employment: the changing world of work in context', *Economic and Labour Relations Review*, 23(4): 3–24.

Rostgaard, T. (2006) 'Constructing the care consumer: free choice of home care for the elderly in Denmark', *European Societies*, 8(3): 443–63.

Sevenhuijsen, S. (1993) 'Paradoxes of gender: ethical and epistemological perspectives on care in feminist political theory', *Acta Politica*, 28(2): 131–49.

Shakespeare, T. (2000) *Help*, Birmingham: Venture Press/British Association of Social Workers.

Shutes, I. and Chiatti, C. (2012) 'Migrant labour and the marketisation of care for older people: the employment of migrant care workers by families and service providers', *Journal of European Social Policy*, 22(4): 392–405.

Sierra, F. and Kohanski, R. (2017) 'Geroscience and the trans-NIH Geroscience Interest Group, GSIG', *GeroScience*, 39(1): 1–5.

Standing, G. (2011) *The Precariat: the New Dangerous Class*, London: Bloomsbury Academic.

Sturgeon, D. (2014) 'The business of the NHS: the rise and rise of consumer culture and commodification in the provision of healthcare services', *Critical Social Policy*, 34(3): 405–16).

Townsend, P. (1981) 'The structured dependency of the elderly: a creation of social policy in the twentieth century', *Ageing and Society*, 1(1): 5–28.

Tronto, J.C. (1993) *Moral Boundaries: a Political Argument for an Ethic of Care*, New York: Routledge.

Tronto, J. (2002) 'The value of care: a response to "Can Working Families Ever Win?"', *Boston Review*, 27(1), available from: https://bostonreview.net/archives/BR27.1/tronto.html [Accessed 12 August 2019].

Tronto, J. (2017) 'There is an alternative: *homines curans* and the limits of neoliberalism', *International Journal of Care and Caring*, 1(1): 27–43.

Twigg, J. (2000) *Bathing: the Body and Community Care*, London: Routledge.

Ungerson, C. and Yeandle, S. (eds) (2006) *Cash for Care in Developed Welfare States*, Houndmills: Palgrave Macmillan.

Walker, A. (1982) 'Dependency and old age', *Social Policy and Administration*, 16(2): 115–35.

Watson, J. (1979) *Nursing: the Philosophy and Science of Caring*, Boston: Little, Brown and Company.

Weicht, B. (2010) 'Embracing dependency: rethinking (in)dependence in the discourse of care', *Sociological Review*, 58(supplement 2): 205–24.

Weicht, B. (2015) *The Meaning of Care: the Social Construction of Care for Elderly People*, London: Palgrave Macmillan.

Williams, F. (2001) 'In and beyond New Labour: towards a new political ethics of care', *Critical Social Policy*, 21(4): 467–93.

Williams, F. (2012) 'Converging variations in migrant care work in Europe', *Journal of European Social Policy*, 22(4): 363–76.

Wilson, S. and Ebert, N. (2013) 'Precarious work: economic, sociological and political perspectives', *Economic and Labour Relations Review*, 24(3): 263–78.

Yeandle, S., Kröger, T. and Cass, B. (2012) 'Voice and choice for users and carers? Developments in patterns of care for older people in Australia, England and Finland', *Journal of European Social Policy*, 22(4): 432–45.

Yeates, N. (2009) *Globalizing Care Economies and Migrant Workers: Explorations in Global Care Chains*, New York: Palgrave Macmillan.

Yeatman, A., Dowsett, G.W., Fine, M. and Guransky, D. (2009) *Individualization and the Delivery of Welfare Services: Contestation and Complexity*, Houndmills: Palgrave Macmillan.

9

From precarious employment to precarious retirement: neoliberal health and long-term care in the United States

Larry Polivka and Baozhen Luo

Introduction

Until about 35 years ago the health care system in the United States was made up largely of relatively small, fee-for-service providers, non-profit community hospitals and modestly sized private insurance companies, including the non-profit Blue Cross Blue Shield companies. Beginning in the late 1970s, however, the health care system gradually underwent a qualitative change in its fundamental economic characteristics. This change is often referred to as the corporatization of US health care, as predicted by Paul Starr in his 1982 book *The Social Transformation of American Medicine* (Starr, 1982).

The focus of this chapter is the spread of corporatization to publicly funded health care programmes, mainly Medicare and Medicaid, after 2000, and the emergence of neoliberal health and long-term care (LTC) in the US. One of the major characteristics of neoliberalism is the privatization – or what David Harvey (2007) calls 'accumulation through dispossession' – of the public sector, by corporate acquisition of their assets and services. Privatization of the public side of the American health care system began slowly after 2000, but accelerated rapidly after the passage of the Affordable Care Act (ACA), or what became known as Obamacare, in 2010. Corporate health interests now control most public health care services in the US through proprietary health maintenance organizations' (HMOs) domination of the Medicaid and the Medicare Advantage programmes (Henry J. Kaiser Family Foundation, 2019).

The implications of these trends are discussed for the growing number of workers who are precariously employed and retirees (current and future), for whom neoliberal health care threatens to undermine their economic and emotional security in their later years. The chapter uses the concept of the precariat to refer to the growing percentage of the labour force receiving relatively low wages, few if any retirement and health benefits, and who have no guarantees regarding continuing employment (Standing, 2011). Precariously employed workers are located disproportionately in the services sector, especially in the food services, cleaning and maintenance, caregiving, and retail sales industries. Many contract workers in the gig economy of Uber and Lyft drivers and other workers with unstable jobs and limited benefits are also members of the precariat work force.

As these workers enter retirement, many will carry their precarious economic status with them in the form of low savings, increasingly limited private pension coverages, and greater dependence on public programmes (Social Security, Medicare and Medicaid) to a greater extent than retirees in the past. Changes affecting these programmes, especially those affecting the health sector, are likely to make retirement a more precarious experience for increasing numbers of future retirees (Lorey, 2015).

The importance of research and theoretical work focused on the growing precarity of life for older persons is summarized in the following passage from Grenier et al (2017):

> The uniqueness of late life where precarity is concerned is the following: where one may move in and out of situations or precariousness throughout life, the need for care (often experienced in relation to age and/or time spent in situations of disadvantage) marks a point of change. It is the shortage of 'time left'—or a lack of opportunity to alter circumstances via the labor market—combined with health and social inequities, and/or the need for care that must be purchased from the market, that can produce or extend insecurities in later life. That is the intersection of time and age produce new forms of insecurity beyond work, as the aging body requires formal and informal forms of support for which limited resources may be available. Further, given the impact of austerity, this may lead precarity to become a permanent rather than temporary condition in late life. (Grenier et al, 2017, p 12)

This chapter takes the view that the growing threat of precarity in later life is in substantial measure a result of the emergence of neoliberal capitalism over the last 40 years, together with changes in the role(s) of the state that have accompanied and supported neoliberalism. These changes are addressed in the first section of the chapter by drawing on Streeck's (2016) theory of the neoliberal 'consolidation state', which, as will be argued in this chapter, provides rich insights into the nature and origins of these changes. The second section addresses broad trends in health care policy and politics and then focuses more narrowly on specific health care programmes in the United States. The focus of the third section is primarily on the growing control of the corporate health industry over the Medicaid programme, and the emerging effects of this trend in neoliberal health care on access and quality of care in the programme.

Corporate health and the expansion of the consolidation state

The increasing for-profit corporate control of the United States health care system, including the huge public programmes Medicare and Medicaid, demonstrates the extent to which the political centre has shifted to the right over the last 40 years – and, more specifically, how this has resulted in the control the corporate health sector exercises over the federal government and many governments at the state level. Health care is now the largest sector of the economy in the US, measuring over 18 per cent of gross domestic product (GDP) (Petty, 2014). This sector is set to continue to grow rapidly with the ageing of the population, increasing acquisitions and mergers that facilitate the growth of monopoly control, and advances in the effectiveness of care through science and technology. These trends will likely enhance the power of corporate health, increasing its leverage over health care policy at the federal and state levels. This influence is likely to further blur the boundaries between the private corporate and public sectors in a fashion similar to that which has occurred in the financial sector, consolidated by the no-strings-attached bailout of the financial sector by the federal government following the financial collapse of 2008 (Polivka, 2012). The blurring of boundaries between the corporate health sector and the government has been occurring since the 1980s, but accelerated following the implementation of the Medicare Advantage and the Part D Medicare drug programmes in 2006, and then surged with the implementation of the ACA in 2014 (Geyman, 2018).

The neoliberal irony here is that as the federal health care programmes, Medicare and Medicaid, grew at unprecedented rates after 2006, federal and state government control over these programmes *declined* as the power of corporate health grew. The costs of these programmes for the federal and state governments are increasing faster than any other major parts of their budgets, but substantive policy and operational control of them is shifting to the corporate sector. This trend is consistent with what Streeck (2016) calls the 'consolidation state', or what might also be referred to as the neoliberal corporate state: a state with the organizing mission to serve the interests of the most powerful corporate actors through privatization, deregulation, shifting taxes from the wealthy to workers and providing corporate bailouts as needed (Streeck, 2016). These policies are not unique to the neoliberal states of the last 40 years, but they have become far more pronounced and critical to the generation of corporate profits during this period. In the field of health care, these policies have become especially important in the period since 2010 (Petty, 2014).

Streeck's (2016) concept of the consolidation state is based on Hayek's advocacy for a large state role in protecting the interests of capital *against* public policies favourable to the interests of the larger public. This model of the state in a capitalist society is designed to *protect* corporate interests from regulatory intrusions, public programmes like Social Security and Medicare that provide workers with a social wage, and high taxes on wealth to fund such programmes. On the other hand, the Hayekian state is equipped to enforce regulations consistent with corporate interests, especially those of monopoly firms, to collect enough tax or debt-based revenues to fund corporate bailouts as necessary, and to impose austerity budgets that protect the capacity of the state to pay for bailouts, keep tax rates on the wealthy low and pay for enough of the public debt to keep interest rates on the debt from becoming too high (Streeck, 2014). The consolidation state is designed to serve corporate interests by containing public debt, much of which was generated in recent years by government efforts to bring the financial crisis and the Great Recession under control, and to ensure that taxes on wealthy households and corporate profits are kept low and not increased to reduce deficits and pay for interest on the debt (Streeck, 2016).

The consolidation state increasingly functions less like a sovereign institution and more like a corporate firm. Streeck (2016) argues that this means that the fundamental mission of the state under neoliberalism is to protect financial markets from democracy, rather than the social democratic state mission of protecting democracy from the market: 'Whereas the politics of democratic capitalists was to protect society from the vagaries of the market (Polanyi), the politics of the consolidation state protects financial markets from what are for them the vagaries of democratic politics' (Streeck, 2016, p 134).

The consolidation state, which emerged in the US in the 1980s, is an unprecedented experiment involving the massive privatization of programmes created to protect individuals against a range of social risks, to provide health care and education, and to build and administer physical infrastructures. It has become the vehicle for the sweeping commodification of the public sector, which directly and indirectly contributes to the growth of precarity among workers and retirees. The model for the consolidation state was created during the Clinton Administration after it embraced an austerity regime in 1993, which was maintained until the end of Clinton's term in 2001. This regime included a welfare reform initiative that greatly reduced spending on poverty relief after 1996:

> The fact that the reform was pushed through by a Democratic president only reinforced its confidence-building effect. Further contributing to it was that the gradual progress towards a balanced budget, and then towards a budget surplus at the end of Clinton's second term, achieved through spending cuts rather than revenue increases. In fact, shrinking the deficit by shrinking public spending was accompanied by substantial tax cuts which, while repeatedly renewing the deficit, created pressures for more spending cuts once 'fighting the deficit' had been established as the supreme principle of the new regime. (Streeck, 2016)

For the consolidation state, debt service and other activities needed to manage the debt are top priorities. Public investment of most kinds, including education, poverty reduction and infrastructure, become at best secondary concerns. This focus on debt management, in combination with austerity budgets, is likely to put entitlements like Social Security at risk as they become more politically vulnerable to 'complaints about old commitments suffocating spending for the future and strangling "fiscal democracy" by denying governments political discretion … result[ing] in less generous benefits for subsequent generations' (Streeck, 2016, p 137). Streeck views this as a process that is likely to further delegitimize social policies aimed at groups such as older people.

At the same time as austerity budgets are gradually reducing funding for public investments in both the physical and social infrastructures, governments are relying increasingly on private sector firms to administer formerly public services:

> While typically subject to regulation, private providers are likely soon to become powerful players in the political arena where they will ally with the upwardly mobile middle class and its liberal-conservative parties. The evolving connections of the new firms with the government, often taking the form of a revolving-door exchange of personnel, and their campaign contributions will further cement the shift from a redistributive towards a neoliberal state that abandons to civil society and the market its responsibility to provide for social equity and social cohesion. (Streeck, 2016, p 138)

All of the wealth-preserving and enhancing functions of the consolidation state are growing threats to the economic security of future retirees, especially the vast majority of retirees who will depend on programmes such as Social Security, Medicare and Medicaid to meet their financial and health care needs. The consolidation state is, in short, a powerful vehicle for putting older persons at increasing risk of a precarious retirement. The public retirement programmes are becoming more important as a source of economic security in retirement as workers experience growing precarity in their employment, including the decline of private pensions and savings along with wage stagnation. The consolidation state, with its priorities of debt service, austerity budgets, low taxes on wealth, and growing privatization of public assets and services, is creating the social and economic conditions for a precarious retirement for most low and middle income workers.

The corporate health part of the consolidation state is inconsistent with the kinds of austerity budgets and tax policies that have been constructed by corporate elites over the past 30 years. Privatization of other services, such as education, welfare and housing, has almost invariably been associated with stagnant or reduced budgets at the federal and state levels. This has not, however, been the case, as a rule, with health care budgets, especially those of Medicare and Medicaid, both of which have increased steadily and at rates well above the consumer price index for decades. These budgets will in all probability increase at an even higher rate for the next several years, with corporate health interests exercising even greater fiscal influence than in the past as their role in both programmes becomes more dominant.

The most likely neoliberal option for eventually containing these costs to government is to adopt policies comparable to those imposed by the government of the UK over the last several years on the National Health Service and the long-term care services system. This would entail continuing the privatization of the Medicare and Medicaid programmes, accelerating the privatization of the Veterans Administration programme and, at the same time, beginning to reduce budget increases even as the number of beneficiaries in each of these programmes continues to grow.

This neoliberal privatization within an austerity policy regime for health care will be substantially more challenging politically to implement compared to the other policy domains such as education and welfare, but the magnitude of the gap between demand (costs) and available revenues is likely to create an unprecedented fiscal crisis of the state necessitating at least an attempt to implement the 'British option': that is, to privatize the programmes as fast as possible while reducing funding. This is precisely what former Speaker of the House Paul Ryan has proposed for Medicare – by converting it into vouchers to subsidize the purchase of private insurance – and for the Medicaid programme, by converting it into a capped block grant to the states' programmes. The effort to make these changes has been made more urgent by the huge 2017 tax cut legislation, which will increase the deficit by US$1.5 trillion over ten years and by the largest defence budget (US$715 billion) in several years.

The country where neoliberal long-term care policies are most comparable to those unfolding in the US is the UK, which has been attempting to privatize long-term care services for the past several years (Humber, 2017). A major characteristic of this initiative is the extent to which these services, both in-home and residential care, are being financialized at a rapid rate, and in the face of deteriorating financial conditions experienced by care providers (De Freytas-Tamura, 2018; Garside, 2017). Private equity firms and hedge funds now have major stakes in the British social care system as provider firms have used loans and investments to expand their service capacities and, increasingly, to stay in business as their debt burdens grow while public and private sources of revenue fail to keep pace (De Freytas-Tamura, 2018; Garside, 2017).

Debt levels in the British residential care sector are very high and the shares of several large residential care firms are officially rated as junk bonds, or sub-investment grade. In 2013, over 700 companies had liabilities worth more than their assets. The National Care Association has stated that a quarter of independent sector care providers are at serious risk of being forced out of the market due to their unmanageable debt levels and lack of government funding which will cause the loss of 40,000 beds in the independent care market, materially increasing the precariousness of long-term care for the elderly and disabled in the UK (Garside, 2017; De Freytas-Tamura, 2018; Quilter-Pinner and Hochlaf, 2019). Humber (2017) notes that

> the shortage of available beds in the care sector has a knock-on effect in hospitals which are increasingly having to retain patients who would be discharged if a place in a community setting could be found. This so-called 'bed blocking' crisis is an expression of the broader problems in the social care sector, and a direct consequence of the marketization of services. Buyouts, bond issues, refinancing and other corporate and ownership strategies make the residential care sector very difficult for local authorities to monitor or control, even if they wanted to. (Humber, 2017, para. 42)

The UK government is attempting to address the growing social care crisis, caused by a rapidly growing population of people with long-term care needs and insufficient public resources, by supporting the development of increasingly large corporate health care systems with responsibilities for both social and health care services. This neoliberal initiative could not be more perfectly designed to reflect the emergence of the consolidation state in Britain and to make the lives of older people increasingly precarious.

Caught between the austerity budgets that fail to provide sufficient funding to serve the population with long-term care needs and highly privatized and financialized in-home and residential care services sectors that are beginning to unravel, Britain is arguably the leading example of how fragile the claim of neoliberal policy advocates have proven to be in practice. Increasingly, there is the likelihood of pressure to 'bail out' a number of large care home companies that cannot meet their debt payments, but in the absence of plans for how the large increases in care needs over the next ten years will be met. The expanding involvement of investment firms in long-term care services in the US could well create the kind of funding and quality issues there that now confront Britain and its older citizens, whose future have been made increasingly precarious as a result (Rau, 2018).

Neoliberal health care in the United States

The history of health reform

The health care economy in the US has changed substantially over several decades with arguably the most important change occurring in the late 1970s and early 1980s with the rapid rise of corporate health firms, especially insurance and pharmaceutical companies. Paul Starr described this change in its early stages in *The Social Transformation of American Medicine* (1982), a history of medicine and the health care system in the US from the turn of the 20th century until the early 1980s. Physicians essentially controlled the system through their fee-for-service practices for most of the 20th century. Private insurance corporations, however, began to emerge as a major force in US health care during and after the second world war, as large employers began to offer health insurance to their employees (Hacker, 2002). Physicians, mainly through the American Medical Association, had successfully resisted efforts by reform advocates and policy makers to move toward the kind of universal public health programmes that were implemented by European countries after the war, which left an opening for corporate health firms, mainly insurance companies, to gain a foothold in the system, gradually marginalizing the power of physicians (Quadagno, 2005).

President Franklin D. Roosevelt had begun to push for a national health programme towards the end of the war, but died before he could gain momentum for his proposal. President Harry Truman picked up Roosevelt's initiative for reform but, even with strong labour union support, was unable to overcome the opposition of the American Medical Association and wealthy conservative opponents of Roosevelt's New Deal who spent millions on a campaign to convince the public that Truman's plan was a communist plot to bring more socialism to America (Gaffney, 2015).

Since the end of the Second World War, insurance companies have been able to use the leverage provided by Congress when it made employer funds used for employee health insurance exempt from taxes, to rapidly tighten their grip on the health care system in the US and begin the process of displacing physicians from their decades-long role as the most powerful group in American health care (Quadagno, 2005). As most of the countries of Europe were moving toward some form of universal health care, the US, after Medicare and Medicaid, was essentially moving in the opposite direction. Insurance companies gradually became the main payers for medical care, and pharmaceutical companies began to grow as research produced more effective medication and hospitals expanded and developed large hospital networks and systems on an increasingly extensive basis (Petty, 2014; Woolhandler and Himmelstein, 2017).

In 1964, the Democratic Party led by Lyndon B. Johnson won control of the presidency and Congress by decisive margins, which they used to pass legislation setting up the Medicare and Medicaid programmes. Following implementation in 1966, these programmes provided many older Americans, as well as the poor, with health insurance for the first time, materially reducing the level of precarity among retirees. Health reform advocates felt that a national health programme providing universal coverage for all Americans would follow closely on the creation of these programmes (Quadagno, 2005).

The creation of Medicare and Medicaid, however, was the last time serious reform proposals were considered in the US until the ACA was initiated by the Obama Administration in 2009 and 2010 (Woolhandler and Himmelstein, 2017). Deteriorating economic conditions caused by rising inflation related to deficit funding of the Vietnam War, and the 1973 Organization of the Petroleum Exporting Countries restrictions on production that drove the cost of oil to unprecedented levels, gave greater credibility to the conservative argument that universal health care was unaffordable (Stein, 2010). This argument was given momentum by newly emerging corporate interests dedicated to reducing the size of the public sector, its role in the economy and the taxes required to fund public programmes. This increasingly organized corporate resistance had long opposed the expansion of the public sector beginning with the New Deal programmes of the 1930s (Phillips-Fein, 2009). More moderate members of the corporate elite were increasingly drawn to this agenda, and as the economy faltered, labour became more assertive and their profit margins were threatened by rising costs and wage increases (Stein, 2010). Defenders of the Keynesian compromise between labour and capital and a strong public sector, who had played the leading role in the shaping economic and social policies from 1933 to the early 1970s, began to lose their grip on the levers of power by the late 1970s (Polivka, 2012). One of the first policy casualties of this shift in the ideological and political cultures of the US was any possibility of further progress in the creation of a universal health care system.

The Clinton Administration attempted to revive health care reform with a focus on both expanded coverage and cost containment through an administrative process called managed competition that supporters of the proposal had a very difficult time explaining and defending.

The proposal was essentially an expansion of the existing private insurance system with a complicated mechanism for encouraging regional competition among insurance plans that would theoretically contain costs as coverage was expanded (Starr, 2013). The proposal, after an elaborate year-long planning effort, was too opaque for even Democratic Party policy makers to spend much political capital on and could not survive the withering advertisements paid for by corporate interests, mainly the health insurance companies (Skocpol, 1997).

These companies had grown much stronger economically and politically since the last major debate on health care reform in the early 1970s. The corporatization of health care had advanced to the point that by 1993 and 1994, corporate health was one of the most formidable sectors of the corporate world; far more capable of defending their interests than they had been previously (Skocpol, 1997). The major reason behind the surge in political influence and power was the rapid development of the managed care or health maintenance organizations (HMO) model of delivering and paying for medical services under a capitated rate covering members of the HMO. The initial legislation setting up the regulatory structure for managed care was passed during the Nixon Administration in 1973 (Gaffney, 2015; Woolhandler and Himmelstein, 2017). This legislation largely limited health maintenance organizations to administration by non-profits such as the Kaiser Permanente and Puget Sound Health system programmes, which had administered managed care effectively for decades prior to 1973.

In 1981, however, the anti-government, pro-corporate administration of President Reagan, who claimed the conservative economist Frederick Hayek as his inspiration, changed the original HMO legislation, ending federal grant support for non-profit HMOs and restrictions on proprietary status, and promoting the role of private investors (Wilentz, 2008). Over 80 per cent of managed care organizations were non-profit until 1982; by the late 1980s most were for-profit and increasingly under the control of large corporate insurers like United Health, Aetna and Cigna (Geyman, 2004).

The rationale for the expansion of corporate health management organizations was drawn largely from the work of conservative economists including Frederick Hayek, Milton Friedman and Mark Pauly. According to these critics, the best way to contain health care costs without restricting access and threatening quality of care was through private corporations competing in free markets to increase the number of members in their HMOs (Gaffney, 2015). This approach to administering health care was responsive to Hayek and Friedman's theory that the value of any good or service could only be determined through the price setting mechanisms of the market unfettered by regulations and public subsidies that would restrict competition, the principle means of determining real value (Gaffney, 2015). This pro-market model of health care was also consistent with Pauly's (2010) concept of moral hazard, which claimed that free or highly subsidized health care would incentivize people to consume more health care than they really needed and needlessly drive up costs of care.

The clearest example of this theory in practice is the Consumer Directed Health Care (CDHC) programme that employer-based insurance plans are increasingly offering beneficiaries. This model of health insurance, which is more directly targeted at the moral hazard of excessive consumption than most managed care models, usually takes the form of a plan that covers catastrophic care or the cost of care after the patient's out-of-pocket costs have exceeded some annual limit, usually between US$1,500 and US$2,500 for individuals and over US$4,000 for families (Gaffney, 2015). These plans are increasingly being purchased and now cover over 20 per cent of beneficiaries in the private, mostly employer, insurance market. A tax exempt medical savings account is usually included in CDHC plans. Beneficiaries can use these accounts to cover out-of-pocket costs incurred before reaching their deductible ceilings.

Even without support in the health services research literature, the Consumer Directed Health Care model in some form is becoming a major vehicle for health insurance in the United States. The number of beneficiaries in such plans has grown steadily since 1996, when the Federal Legislation setting up medical savings accounts as a tax deductible method of paying for medical care was passed. Furthermore, regular insurance plans offered in the private sector have been increasing the level of deductibles steadily for the last several years, driving up out of pocket costs for individuals and families (Johnson, 2017).

The Affordable Care Act

The ACA, in its main features, is a modest health care reform programme that was consciously designed to be consistent with the neoliberal focus on financing and delivering health care through private insurance markets. Regardless of feverish Republican objections, and the Trump Administration's efforts to dismantle it, the ACA is not a national health insurance programme that departs in any significant manner from the country's deeply neoliberal health care system (Petty,

2014; Woolhandler and Himmelstein, 2017). Whatever may have been President Obama's initial vision for the ACA, fundamental principles extremely favourable to the corporate health sector, were agreed to by the Administration, corporate health lobbyists and Congress. Three main factors were at work.

First, the Administration removed the public option from their proposal, which meant that the federal government would not be able to offer either a new public insurance programme or a Medicare or Medicaid buy-in option in the insurance exchanges established by the American Care Act (also ACA); only private plans would be available (Geyman, 2018). Powerful corporate opposition to a public option provision in the ACA was driven by the fear among insurance companies and other health care companies that it would prove popular with the public and pave the way to some form of single payer health care system in the United States. Critics of the Obama Administration's strategy on this aspect of the ACA debate continue to think that the Administration could have struck a better bargain with the corporate health sector by insisting on an expansion of the Medicare programme for those 65 and older to the 55–64 age population in lieu of a more comprehensive public option.

Second, the Administration agreed to an individual mandate requiring all Americans to have insurance in some form or pay a penalty through the tax reporting system. The insurance companies insisted that the mandate was necessary in order to offset the costs of new regulations required by the Administration. These would end the use of pre-existing medical conditions to exclude people from coverage through unaffordable premiums, co-payments and deductibles, rescissions in coverage when medical costs became high and allow children to remain on their parent's insurance plans until they were 26 years old (Petty, 2014). These and other progressive provisions of the ACA are now in jeopardy as the Trump Administration's attempts to dismantle them, or at least, make them substantially more difficult for the public to gain and maintain access to them.

The third principle agreed to by the Administration was to *exclude* provisions that would allow the federal government to negotiate the price of drugs, as it does in the Medicaid and Veterans health programmes with the pharmaceutical industry (Gaffney, 2015). This pro-corporate provision substantially limited the scope of the reform legislation from the beginning. It also ensured that it would be a fundamentally neoliberal pro-corporate in design and as such, vulnerable to the kind of rollback efforts now underway in the Trump Administration. It should be noted, however, that these efforts have met considerable resistance at the federal and state levels as public support for the ACA has grown significantly since 2016 and the failure of the Republican-controlled Congress to repeal the ACA. These efforts are likely to continue over the next two years, but it is increasingly doubtful that they will succeed in the absence of strong public support for them. This does not mean, however, that the Trump Administration will not be able to limit the reach and erode the quality of the ACA through administrative interventions or failures to execute the law properly.

This fact reflects how much has changed from Medicare and Medicaid, the Kennedy universal health care plan period of the 1960s and early 1970s, to the kind of reform that was considered realistic to propose in 2010. The hold of corporate health on the health care system of the United States had increased enormously in the intervening decades and the industry's political power was much greater in 2010 than in the period before 1970. The power of corporate health grew especially fast after 1982 and the Reagan neoliberal turn in US politics and economic policy (Petty, 2014; Gaffney, 2015). By 2010, it was qualitatively more difficult to pass any reform legislation that might conflict with the corporate agenda. Consequently, the ACA not only avoids conflict with corporate interests, it gives those interests a major boost by increasing the number of people the insurance companies insure and increasing their control over the Medicaid programme through managed care contracts with the states.

Medicaid and long-term care

Corporate health control of the Medicaid programme is more extensive than the industry's control of the Medicare programme through the Medicare Advantage (plans offered by private companies approved by Medicare). Over 70 per cent of all Medicaid beneficiaries are now members of mostly for-profit HMOs (Rudowitz and Antonisse, 2018) – a percentage that has grown rapidly since 2000. The ACA expansion of the Medicaid programme has added 10 million to Medicaid, making it the largest insurance programme in the United States with 74 million beneficiaries (Rudowitz and Antonisse, 2018). With 80 per cent of these beneficiaries in HMOs, the Medicaid programme has become a very significant source of profit for the corporate health sector and led to a deep industry interest in the 20 per cent who remain in the fee-for-service system. Much of this 20 per cent includes older and younger low-income and low-wealth beneficiaries with long term care needs (Polivka and Luo, 2017).

The Medicaid long-term care programme consisted of institutional (nursing home) care almost entirely until the mid-1980s when states began to use Home and Community Based Services (HCBS) allowed under a new waiver programme established by Congress in 1981. The waiver allowed the states to use funds that would have otherwise gone for nursing home care to be used for alternative in-home and community residential services to individuals meeting the financial and level of care eligibility requirements for Medicaid supported nursing home care (Polivka and Zayac, 2008). The Home and Community Based Services (HCBS) Medicaid programme grew slowly from the 1980s through the 1990s. The services were largely administered through the non-profit ageing services network which had been established under the Older Americans Act of 1966 as part of the Johnson Administration's Great Society initiative to expand the New Deal (Polivka and Zayac, 2008).

By 2000, several states had very substantially reduced their dependence on nursing homes for the delivery of long-term care through the expansion of Medicaid waiver funded HCBS programmes. Within a decade almost half the states were serving over half of their Medicaid LTC beneficiaries in the community leading to a reduction of the nursing home population from 1.6 million in 2000 to 1.4 million by 2010 (Polivka and Zayac, 2008). These numbers were clear evidence of the non-profit ageing network's capacity to decisively shift LTC from nursing home domination to a far more balanced and more efficient LTC system increasingly featuring in-home and community residential care that older people and younger disabled persons greatly preferred to nursing home placement (Polivka and Luo, 2017). This demonstrated capacity to reduce nursing home use and to serve LTC recipients more cost effectively in the community did not go unnoticed by insurance companies looking to expand their HMO participation in the Medicaid programme from acute care to LTC.

According to Estes (2014), this expansion is now occurring for two major reasons: first, corporate insurers and managed care organizations were historically sceptical that Medicaid supported long-term care services could be made profitable because of relatively low funding levels, the complicated trajectories of care for people with long term care needs, the lack of potential for achieving increased efficiencies in these services, and the profits that greater efficiency could generate. This perception, however, changed when it became evident that community based non-profit organizations were successfully diverting impaired persons from nursing homes to less expensive community-based programmes, which reduced costs and generated savings, some or all of which could be converted to profits under corporate administration of the Medicaid long-term care system.

The second reason identified by Estes (2014) is the emergence of the neoliberal, pro-corporate ideology that emerged in the 1980s, which became dominant at both the federal and state government levels by the end of the Clinton Administration. This ideology claimed that by outsourcing public programmes to the private sector (privatization) governments would be able to take advantage of free markets and light regulation to save money for taxpayers and improve the quality of services in competitive market environments. This ideology has proven durable even in the absence of much documented evidence to support it.

Over 30 years of experience and research findings showed that the ageing network, with its service delivery and case management capacities and comparatively low costs, could build and administer the infrastructure for HCBS programmes and create well-balanced long-term care systems much less dependent on expensive home care. These capacities, which were built over a 30 year period and largely funded through Medicaid waivers, are amply documented in three comprehensive and comparative analyses of state long-term care systems conducted by the American Association of Retired Persons between 2011 and 2017 (Reinhard et al, 2014). These reports show that many states have dramatically transformed their LTC systems over the last three decades with the use of Medicaid waiver funds largely administered by non-profit Ageing Networks and their non-profit organizations in states across the country. The reports identify the top ten LTC states by ranking their performance five sets of criteria covering such measures as access to care, quality of care, costs, etc. All ten of the top-ranked states in 2017 have strong ageing networks and other non-profit participants in their HCBS systems; none of them are administered by corporate HMOs in managed long-term care (MLTC) systems. In fact, two states (Iowa and Kansas) that were ranked in the top ten in 2011, fell into the third quintile by 2017 following the implementation of HMO administered MLTC programmes after 2012 (Reinhard et al, 2017).

Documentation, however, of the non-profit sector's ability to create and administer cost effective community based LTC systems has not been sufficient to keep them from being replaced in a growing number of states by HMO administered or MLTC programmes. In the absence of supportive empirical evidence, the principle rationale offered by proponents of the corporate MLTC model is essentially ideological. They make the neoliberal case for corporate management of the Medicaid LTC programme by claiming that as competing organizations in a free market for publicly funded LTC services, they will be incentivized to achieve the kinds of efficiencies the non-profit sector cannot, allowing them to cut or at least contain costs and generate profits without undermining access to care or its quality (Polivka and Zayak, 2008). This ideology based rationale is barely plausible. The non-profit Aging Network organizations in most of the states have administered their Medicaid LTC programmes efficiently over the last 25 years as shown in the AARP state LTC reports and it strains credulity to argue that for-profit corporations could provide services in MLTC programmes at a lower cost without limiting access and quality of services (Polivka and Luo, 2017).

In the three states that have made the most aggressive efforts to change from an Ageing Network administered LTC programme to a corporate one, the results would seem to strongly justify scepticism about the neoliberal rationale for privatizing public programmes. Iowa and Kansas have slipped badly in the AARP ranking of state LTC programmes since launching their corporate programmes; Florida, which began its corporate programme in 2013 now has over 60,000 people on its wait list for Medicaid LTC services (Polivka-West, 2017). Furthermore, evaluations of the Florida programme have shown that the programme is not reducing costs for Medicaid LTC services compared to the previous Aging Network administered programme. A major part of the original neoliberal rationale for the programmes claimed that market driven efficiencies would inevitably reduce costs (Polivka-West, 2017). Instead, the HMOs insist that they are underfunded and will need substantial increases to continue participating in the programme (Chang, 2015).

The HMOs in Iowa and Kansas have made similar claims about inadequate funding, raising the question of whether Medicaid will ever have enough funding to meet the financial demands of the for-profit HMOs or will policy makers be forced to let the HMOs limit access and quality of services in order to ensure profitability and keep the HMOs in the Medicaid LTC programme. The HMOs would seem to have an advantage over policymakers in that in states like Kansas, Iowa and Florida the AN capacity to run the Medicaid HCBS programme they built before the HMOs were given control may have eroded to the point that returning the programme to their administration is not feasible absent a major and expensive rebuilding effort. This means that these and other states adopting the corporate MLTC model in Medicaid do not have enough political leverage to hold the HMOs accountable for the delivery of cost effective services to enough beneficiaries to keep wait lists from growing as rapidly as they have in Florida. This may not, however, be a politically sustainable situation and public resistance generated by media accounts of denied or poor quality services could force policy makers to pay the HMOs substantially more, further undermining the cost reduction part of the rationale for the corporate MLTC model.

The failure of policy makers in these and other states moving toward corporate Medicaid LTC to anticipate and better prepare for these developments reflects their deep affinity for neoliberal ideology and its application to public policy. It also reflects the power of health care corporations at the Federal and state levels to use the neoliberal ideology to transform the Medicaid programme and create profit-making opportunities with their managed care programmes. This transformation was largely complete in the acute care part of the Medicaid programme in most states by 2015 and is now under way in LTC in a growing number of states. The Trump Administration and the Republican-led Congress and policy makers in many states, however, have placed a high priority on cutting or sharply restricting growth in Medicaid. If they are successful in achieving these priorities the budget for Medicaid LTC could be tightened substantially over the next decade putting HMO profitability in the Medicaid programmes under growing pressure and increasing the probability that the corporate HMOs will abandon the Medicaid programme, especially the LTC part of the programme, leaving policy makers with a harsh dilemma: either raise Medicaid spending to pay the HMOs what they want or allow the LTC programme to deteriorate, even as the need for LTC services is set to double in the US over the next 20 years and as precarity among older people increases (Polivka and Luo, 2017).

Conclusion

The health care system in the US has grown enormously over the last several decades and is now the largest industry in the US economy – representing around 18 per cent of GDP. This growth has been driven by the rapidly rising prices of pharmaceuticals and medical procedures, many of which are now dependent on advanced medical technologies, and by population growth, especially among older cohorts with greater needs for chronic care and long-term care. This growth has occurred in both the private and the public sectors of the health care system as corporate health firms and the Medicare, Medicaid and Veterans Administration programmes have grown rapidly since 1980.

Even though the public sector programmes have more than doubled in costs and persons served over the last 20 years, corporate health firms, mainly the six big insurance companies, have increasingly gained control of these programmes through contracts with the federal and state governments to administer about one-third of the Medicare programme (Medicare Advantage), over 75 per cent of the Medicaid programme, through HMOs for both acute and long-term care, and a growing share of the VA health care programme. The community-based portion of the LTC Medicaid programme had historically been administered through the non-profit Aging Network at the state and local levels. This began to change very rapidly ten years ago, however, when corporate health firms, mainly large insurance companies, began to administer managed LTC programmes through HMOs under contracts with a growing number of state governments. The ACA (Obamacare) actually accelerated this shift in the Medicaid programme to greater corporate control by expanding contracts with corporate health firms, while simultaneously increasing the population receiving health insurance by 24 million through expansion of the Medicaid programme and the creation of subsidized private insurance exchanges for those newly eligible coverage groups outside the Medicaid programmes. This means that very substantial increases in public health care funding has resulted in a significantly more neoliberal, corporate controlled health care system, especially in LTC, than existed before implementation of the ACA in 2014.

These trends are contributing to the growing precarity of life in old age for Americans. As governments at every level continue to look for ways to achieve austerity goals (reduced social and health spending and tax cuts mainly for the wealthy) in their annual budgets, they are also pursuing privatization through contracts, in many cases, with for-profit firms to provide increasingly less regulated social and health services. A large percentage of the privatized funds must be spent to meet profit expectations and cover high administrative costs, which means that funds for health care for older beneficiaries of the Medicare and Medicaid programmes are increasingly under pressure at both the sources of appropriation and of expenditure. This is a clear recipe for the growth of precarity among older people, who are dependent on these publicly funded health care programmes for meeting virtually all of their health and long term care needs.

These trends in the direction of greater precarity are consistent with Streeck's concept of the consolidation state in the neoliberal political economies of the US and the majority of European countries. The consolidation state is designed to serve the interests of capital, especially finance capital, by implementing austerity budgets, maintaining a regime of low taxes on wealth, prioritizing the financing of state deficits and debt, and privatizing as many profitable public services and assets as possible. The mission of the consolidation state is to protect capital from the democratically determined interests of the public rather than protecting the public and democracy from capital.

As the consolidation state tightens its grip on the entire public sector, the precarity of later life is likely to grow as the already extensive privatization of health and long-term care services is expanded and the original purpose to serve the sick and frail as effectively as possible is subverted by the pursuit of corporate profits through commodification of the need for care. Other features and functions of the consolidation state such as austerity budgets and cuts in regulations designed to ensure service quality and the financialization of services, in place of public funding, are also threatening the well-being of older people and increasing their exposure to precarity. These policies are putting public health care, long-term care and other programmes supporting older persons in jeopardy, creating a glide path toward the extension of precarious employment into a precarious retirement for millions of people in a relentlessly neoliberal political economy.

References

Chang, D. (2015) 'Florida says privatizing Medicaid cut costs, but insurers say they're underpaid by state', *Miami Herald* [online], 17 July, available from: https://www.miamiherald.com/news/health-care/article27532903.html [Accessed 12 August 2019].

De Freytas-Tamura, K. (2018) 'Britain was a pioneer in outsourcing services. Now, the model is "broken"', *The New York Times* [online], 31 January, available from: https://www.nytimes.com/2018/01/31/world/europe/britain-outsourcing-elderly-care.html [Accessed 12 August 2019].

Estes, C.L. (2014) 'The future of aging services in a neoliberal political economy', *Generations*, 38(2): 94–100.

Gaffney, A. (2015) 'The neoliberal turn in American health care', *International Journal of Health Services*, 45(1): 33–52.

Garside, J. (2017) 'Private equity firm made struggling care home operator take costly loan', *The Guardian* [online], 8 November, available from: https://www.theguardian.com/news/2017/nov/08/private-equity-terra-firma-care-home-four-seasons-loan [Accessed 12 August 2019].

Geyman, J.P. (2004) *The Corporate Transformation of Health Care: Can the Public Interest Still Be Served?*, New York: Springer.

Geyman, J. (2018) 'Crisis in U.S. health care: corporate power still blocks reform', *International Journal of Health Services*, 48(1): 5–27.

Grenier, A., Phillipson, C., Laliberte Rudman, D., Hatzifilalithis, S., Kobayashi, K. and Marier, P. (2017) 'Precarity in late life: understanding new forms of risk and insecurity', *Journal of Aging Studies*, 43: 9–14.

Hacker, J.S. (2002) *The Divided Welfare State: the Battle over Public and Private Social Benefits in the United States*, Cambridge: Cambridge University Press.

Harvey, D. (2007) *A Brief History of Neoliberalism*, Oxford: Oxford University Press.

Henry J. Kaiser Family Foundation (2019) *An Overview of Medicare* [online], 13 February, available from: https://www.kff.org/medicare/issue-brief/an-overview-of-medicare [Accessed 12 August 2019]

Humber, L. (2017) 'Neoliberalism and the crisis in health and social care', *International Socialism* [online], 155, available from: http://isj.org.uk/neoliberalism-and-the-crisis-in-health-and-social-care/ [Accessed 12 August 2019].

Johnson, C.Y. (2017) 'Out-of-pocket health spending in 2016 increased at the fastest rate in a decade', *The Washington Post* [online], 6 December, available from: https://www.washingtonpost.com/news/wonk/wp/2017/12/06/out-of-pocket-health-spending-in-2016-increased-at-the-fastest-rate-in-a-decade/ [Accessed 12 August 2019].

Lorey, I. (2015) *State of Insecurity: Government of the Precarious*, translated by A. Derieg, London: Verso.

Pauly, M.V. (2010) *Health Reform without Side Effects: Making Markets Work for Individual Health Insurance*, Stanford: Hoover Institution Press.

Petty, S. (2014) 'The neoliberal restructuring of healthcare in the US', *International Socialist Review* [online], 94, available from: https://isreview.org/issue/94/neoliberal-restructuring-healthcare-us [Accessed 12 August 2019].

Phillips-Fein, K. (2009) *Invisible Hands: the Businessmen's Crusade against the New Deal*, New York: W.W. Norton.

Polivka, L. (2012) 'The growing neoliberal threat to the economic security of workers and retirees', *The Gerontologist*, 52(1): 133–44.

Polivka, L. and Zayac, H. (2008) 'The aging network and managed long-term care', *The Gerontologist*, 48(5): 564–72.

Polivka, L. and Luo, B. (2017) 'Neoliberal long-term care: from community to corporate control', *The Gerontologist*, 59(2): 222–9.

Polivka-West, L. (2017) 'Medicaid managed long term care in Florida', *Claude Pepper Center* [online], available from: https://claudepeppercenter.fsu.edu/wp-content/uploads/2016/06/Medicaid-Managed-Long-Term-Care-in-Florida-Issue-Brief-December-2017-by-LuMarie-Polivka.pdf [Accessed 12 August 2019].

Quadagno, J.S. (2005) *One Nation, Uninsured: Why the U.S. Has No National Health Insurance*, New York: Oxford University Press.

Quilter-Pinner, H. and Hochlaf, D. (2019) *Social Care: Free at the Point of Need: The Case for Free Personal Care in England* [online], London: Institute of Public Policy Research, available from: https://www.ippr.org/files/2019-05/social-care-free-at-the-point-of-need-may-19.pdf [Accessed 12 August 2019].

Rau, J. (2018) 'Care suffers as more nursing homes feed money into corporate webs', *The New York Times* [online], 2 January, available from: https://www.nytimes.com/2018/01/02/business/nursing-homes-care-corporate.html [Accessed 12 August 2019].

Reinhard, S.C., Kassner, E., Houser, A., Ujuari, K., Mollica, R. and Hendrickson, L. (2014) *Raising Expectations: a State Scorecard on Long-Term Services and Supports for Older Adults, People with Physical Disabilities, and Family Caregivers* (2nd edn), Washington, DC: AARP Public Policy Institute [online], available from: https://www.aarp.org/home-family/caregiving/info-2014/raising-expectations-2014-AARP-ppi-health.html [Accessed 13 March 2017].

Reinhard, S., Accius, J., Houser, A., Ujvari, K., Alexis, J. and Fox-Grage, W. (2017) *Picking Up the Pace of Change, 2017: a State Scorecard on Long-Term Services and Supports for Older Adults, People with Physical Disabilities, and Family Caregivers*, Washington, DC: AARP Public Policy Institute [online], available from: http://www.nasuad.org/node/69541 [Accessed 12 August 2019].

Rudowitz, R. and Antonisse, L. (2018) *Implications of the ACA Medicaid Expansion: a Look at the Data and Evidence*, Henry J. Kaiser Family Foundation [online], available from: https://www.kff.org/medicaid/issue-brief/implications-of-the-aca-medicaid-expansion-a-look-at-the-data-and-evidence/ [Accessed 12 August 2019].

Skocpol, T. (1997) *Boomerang: Health Care Reform and the Turn against Government*, New York: W.W. Norton.

Standing, G. (2011) *The Precariat: the New Dangerous Class*. London: Bloomsbury Academic.

Starr, P. (1982) *The Social Transformation of American Medicine: the Rise of a Sovereign Profession and the Making of a Vast Industry*. New York: Basic Books.

Starr, P. (2013) *Remedy and Reaction: the Peculiar American Struggle over Health Care Reform* (rev. edn), New Haven: Yale University Press.

Stein, J. (2010) *Pivotal Decade: How the United States Traded Factories for Finance in the Seventies*, New Haven: Yale University Press.

Streeck, W. (2014) *Buying Time: the Delayed Crisis of Democratic Capitalism*, translated by P. Camiller, London: Verso.

Streeck, W. (2016) *How Will Capitalism End? Essays on a Failing System*, London: Verso.

Wilentz, S. (2008) *The Age of Reagan: a History, 1974–2008*, New York: HarperCollins.

Woolhandler, S. and Himmelstein, D.U. (2017) 'The Affordable Care Act: how Nixon's health reform proposal became Democrats' albatross', *International Journal of Health Services*, 47(4): 612–20.

10

Austerity and precarity: individual and collective agency in later life

Chris Phillipson

Introduction

Earlier chapters have reviewed the way in which the concept of precarity has been used to identify new forms of insecurity affecting the lives of older people. An underlying cause of the changes described arose from the financial crisis of 2008 and the implementation of public policies built around economic austerity (see further Tooze, 2018). The purpose of this chapter is to examine the impact of these developments and to assess potential areas of challenge and resistance on the part of older people. For many countries, the issues surrounding the growth of more precarious lives – at all points of the life course – has been embedded in a process – pre- and post-2008 – of marginalizing the language and narrative of the welfare state, alongside associated ideas of social inclusion and social security. Blackburn (2006, p 5) makes the point that an ageing society 'requires new welfare principles not their repudiation'. However, the reality has been the gradual erosion of welfare support as well as the social solidarity that gave it legitimacy (McKibbin, 2017). Both aspects underline the extent of the crisis facing societies undergoing demographic change: in the case of Europe, one set of welfare institutions is being abandoned, with their replacement coming in the form of a precarious set of arrangements characterized by reduced state involvement, privatization of care and pensions, and greater responsibilities placed upon women for unpaid work within the home and community (Cooper and Whyte, 2017; Taylor-Gooby et al, 2017; Toynbee and Walker, 2017).

This chapter examines the context for the rise of precarity in the lives of older people, as well as responses and alternative areas of practice. The chapter is divided into five sections. First, it presents a discussion of the link between precarity and changes in the welfare state and austerity policies imposed by governments in the Global North. Second, it considers the impact of the decline of areas of social support and the emergence of what Streeck (2016) has termed an 'under-institutionalized' society. Third, the changes outlined are linked to the influence of neoliberal policies with their emphasis on personal responsibility for managing transitions through the life course. Fourth, the chapter considers the basis for 'collective' forms of agency, underpinned by a recognition of issues concerning the provision of universal basic services, substantive equality and collective engagement. A concluding section summarizes the key arguments and issues highlighted in the chapter.

Precarity and austerity

A starting point for the discussion concerns the way in which the experience of ageing has been steadily isolated from institutions that had previously been central to providing support in later life. The key changes relate to the removal of what might be termed the 'pillars' around which the idea of 'old age' was constructed during the 20th century, illustrated by the decline of the welfare state, the replacement of retirement with the idea of an 'extended working life', and the abandonment of equality as a primary economic and social objective (Gamble, 2016; Macnicol, 2015; Phillipson, 2013; Rosanvallon, 2013).[1] For Marshall (1950), the welfare state was crucial in adding a third dimension to the historical evolution of citizenship (following on from civil or political rights), with social rights in the form of pensions, health and education. Gamble (2016, p 38) summarizes the underlying assumptions behind state intervention as follows:

> The moral case for providing welfare collectively emphasizes the vulnerability of the majority of citizens to misfortunes and risks beyond their control – such as illness, unemployment, or incapacity. It appeals to the idea of solidarity: those most able and fortunate have a duty to assist those most in need or suffering misfortune. By pooling resources and risks, everyone can be helped at the point of their lives when they most need it.

The economic and political environment characteristic of neoliberalism has produced a fundamental challenge to the idea of the 'social' or 'welfare' state. This development preceded the economic crisis of 2008 but has accelerated since that time, driven by what Klein (2007) views as the 'shock doctrine' tactics associated with what she terms 'disaster capitalism'. This phenomenon is defined by Klein (2007, p 2) as the systematic use of 'public disorientation following a collective shock – wars, coups, terrorist attacks, market crashes, or natural disasters – to push through radical corporate measures – often called "shock therapy"'. In the context of population ageing, such policies have been especially associated with the impact of economic austerity, introduced and promoted throughout Europe to address rising national budget deficits and debts.

Teeple (2017, p 26) summarizes the main austerity measures as amounting to a 'mix of state spending cuts in salaries, staff, pensions, and services – including reductions in health care, education, and unemployment insurance – and a further restructuring of the labour market to increase "flexibility"'. He observes that austerity policies have involved a 'massive shift of wealth from the public to the private sector in order to save global financial corporations from themselves. In this context, the crisis presented an opportune moment to accelerate the process of dismantling the Keynesian welfare state and increasing the opportunities for accumulation' (Teeple, 2017, p 33).[2]

Although in the case of pensions, and only in some countries, there has been a degree of protection for older people,[3] the reverse has been the case in respect of health and social care (Taylor-Gooby et al, 2017). Cuts in home care provision, combined with deinstitutionalization, have greatly increased pressures on groups such as minority women and older people caring for their partners (Bassel and Emejulu, 2017). Kröger and Bagnato's (2018, p 212) survey of countries across Europe concluded that 'cuts in home-based and institutional care provisions have pushed responsibilities back to the family in different parts of Europe'. They further note that

> the widely adopted 'ageing in place' principle has not delivered on its promises.... Based on this approach, institutional provisions have been cut in different parts of the continent but as this has not been accompanied by major investments in home care provisions, long-term care has failed to meet people's needs. Access to home care has instead become stricter in several countries and the range of home care services has been narrowed. (Kröger and Bagnato, 2018, p 213)

The process described has been especially severe in Southern Europe, with the economic crisis undermining an already limited formal care sector (Stuckler and Basu, 2013). But even in countries with what had been 'advanced' welfare provision, austerity policies have introduced major cuts to key areas of health and social care (see further Chapter 9). In the UK, Humphries et al (2016) tracked cuts to local authority funding over the period 2010–16, finding a 26 per cent decline in elderly people receiving support, with projections that an increasing proportion of people will find themselves effectively removed from the care system. Austerity policies may in fact provide a partial explanation for what appears to be a slowdown (for example, in the case of England and Wales) in the rate of improvement in life expectancy, and even a possible reversal at older ages (Hiam et al, 2017; see also Stuckler and Basu, 2013). Hiam et al (2017) comment that

> the fact that [cuts to services] have systematically harmed women more than men, and the very elderly more than the younger elderly, suggests that it is those who have less access to resources of all kinds that have been hardest hit. Elderly women are far more likely to live alone and to be poor as compared with elderly men. People aged over 85 tend to be frailer and, crucially, more likely to be dependent on a well-functioning health and social care system. (Hiam et al, 2017, p 3; see also Office for National Statistics, 2018; 2019)

The decline of the 'social'

The changes described have been implicated in a broader range of concerns associated with the impact of neoliberal policies, notably in respect of growing inequality (Joyce and Xu, 2019), the commercialization of everyday life, and the penetration of corporate and finance capital with state actors (Brown, 2015). Streeck (2016, p 14) describes neoliberalism as leading to an '*under-institutionalized*' society (author's emphasis), producing a failure 'to provide its members with effective protection and proven templates for social action and social existence'. He further suggests that

> As collective institutions are eroded by market forces, accidents are to be expected all the time, while collective agency to prevent them is lost. Everybody is reduced to fending for themselves.... Individualization of risk breeds individualization of protection, by competitive effort … and, if at all, private insurance – or … by older, pre-modern social ties like family. In the absence of collective institutions, social structures must be devised individually bottom-up, anticipating and accommodating top-down pressures from

'the markets'. Social life consists of individuals building networks of private connections around themselves, as best they can with the means they happen to have at hand. (Streeck, 2016, pp 40–2)

Population ageing, on the basis of the analysis in the previous section, is taking place with social institutions that are in retreat or in the process of being 'dismembered' (Sassen, 2014, p 5). Judt (2015, p 308) argues that 'the new master narrative – the way we think about the world – has abandoned the social for the economic'. Brown (2015, p 176) goes further in arguing that neoliberalism must be seen not simply as an economic policy, but as a 'governing rationality that disseminates market values and metrics to every sphere and construes the human itself exclusively as homo oeconomicus' (see further Davies, 2015).

Standing (2016, p 187) makes the point that the 'social commons', the 'facilities and amenities essential to normal living [but] provided outside of the private market', are now being eroded through the forces of privatization and commodification (see also Meek, 2014; Wainwright, 2018). Standing (2016, p 205) views 'the depletion of the commons' as a 'hidden part of the austerity agenda'. But in countries such as the UK the impact has been of major significance, introducing new layers of precarity and destabilizing communities.

Precarity can be understood – as the various chapters in this book demonstrate – at many different levels, but changes to the micro- and meso-institutions that support everyday life are of crucial importance (Portacolone, 2013; see further Chapter 7). To take one example, bus services – upon which older people tend to rely upon more than other social groups – have been cut in the UK to the level of the 1980s (National Audit Office, 2014). Other areas that have been substantially reduced include housing services, cultural and leisure services, and adult education (Toynbee and Walker, 2017). Such changes have substantially eroded the availability of *collective spaces*. For example, public libraries – nearly 627 of which closed in England, Wales and Scotland over the period 2012–18 – are a notable example (see further Klinenburg, 2019). The loss or depletion of public space reinforces the move to reconfigure ageing as an individual as opposed to collective or social responsibility.

Agency and active ageing

The changes affecting the social infrastructure supporting everyday life illustrate longer-term trends towards what has been termed the 'individualization of old age' (Settersten and Trauten, 2009; Vickerstaff and Cox, 2005). In contrast with what Townsend (1981) termed the 'structured dependence' associated with ageing in the 20th century, older people are now 'tasked' with the responsibility for creating the environment in which their own ageing can be managed. This process has been supported through the adoption in many countries of policies associated with 'active' or 'successful ageing' (Foster and Walker, 2015). Frameworks for 'growing old' have been ordered (or reordered) around 'third age' issues of health and wellness, with older people expected to live out their later years as 'productive' and 'active' citizens (Gilleard and Higgs, 2005). This shift in emphasis can itself be linked to views that have tended to emphasize individual agency as detached from, albeit constrained by, social institutions (see, for example, Elder, 1998). Older people – 'freed' from what have come to be viewed as the 'over-socializing' supports associated with state welfare – must take charge of shaping appropriate transitions from work to retirement, or 'choosing' to undertake caring roles within the family or performing volunteer work within the community (Gratton and Scott, 2016).

However, a contrasting view would emphasize the importance of social structures in organizing the agency of individual actors, and by extension influencing the potential for 'active' or 'successful' ageing. Dannefer and Huang (2017, p 5) make the point that 'much ... agentic action is inevitably directed toward the reproduction of existing patterns of social life. Although this is not necessarily an unhealthy state of affairs, it does make clear that the majority of agentic acts performed by a person and by all members of a cohort have the effect of simply reproducing one's habitus, the existing world-taken-for-granted, the world of everyday life'. However, it is precisely the transformation of the 'world of everyday life' for many groups of older people (notably female carers, older workers and minority women) that has been highly disruptive for the enactment of individual agency. The withdrawal of key social institutions associated with retirement and the welfare state has been matched by pressures within the field of employment and upon neighbourhood-level supports. Giddens (1976, p 161) highlights the extent to which 'structures must not be conceptualized as simply placing constraints on human agency, but as *enabling*' (my emphasis). But the argument here is that the effects of austerity and neoliberal policies have been highly *disabling* for vulnerable groups within the older population. McBride and Mitrea (2017) argue that

> austerity intensifies precarity (through its effects on lower growth and subsequently lower quality jobs, shrinking

the state, and raising unemployment) and, through its own narrative of reduced consumption and individual responsibility, puts more pressure for individuals on individuals to be resilient, 'lower their expectations' and survive rather than strive to change austere trajectories. (McBride and Mitrea, 2017, p 102; see also Bassel and Emejulu, 2017)

This pressure to 'lower expectations' is especially relevant to older people facing cuts to welfare provision at national and local levels. Elderly people have had to 'accept' the rationing of social care with public support for home care (in countries such as the UK) restricted to those with very high levels of need or falling within particular medical categories (see further Chapter 4); they have had to 'accept' the postponement of retirement with the raising of pension ages (see further Chapter 5); and they (women especially) have had to accept increased care responsibilities for parents and partners. Following Brown (2015), within the context of 'active' or 'successful' ageing, taking 'responsibility' has become the basis for reframing social policy in later life:

> Responsibilization tasks the worker, student, consumer, or indigent person with discerning the correct strategies of self-investment and entrepreneurship for thriving and surviving; it is in this regard a manifestation of human capitalization. As it discursively denigrates dependency and practically negates collective provisioning for existence, responsibilization solicits the individual as the only relevant and accountable actor. (Brown, 2015, pp 132–3)

The developments outlined amount to a reshaping of later life in ways which will almost certainly produce highly unpredictable outcomes. Thus, precisely at the point in life where *certainty* becomes a desirable quality, daily life – and the support upon which it relies – appears as progressively more random and capricious. But this raises the issue of how to rebuild institutions in ways that can address the expanding range of social needs arising from different kinds of demographic change. A welfare state in the form that developed in the second half of the 20th century seems unlikely to re-emerge. However, the options presently on offer may leave many older people abandoned within the community, dependent upon their families for support, or warehoused within institutional settings. The next section of this chapter sets out an alternative approach, based upon the potential for developing collective forms of organization within communities.

Collective responses to individual ageing

One response to the changes discussed in this chapter concerns the need for further development of critical perspectives that identify new ways of linking the individual to the collective, and which counter the undermining of social support that has taken place over the past decade. Such an approach might start with what Wright (2010) has termed an 'emancipatory social science', one that 'seeks to generate scientific knowledge relevant to the collective project of challenging various forms of human oppression'. Wright (2010, p 10) argues that 'the word *emancipatory* identifies a central moral purpose in the production of knowledge – the elimination of oppression and the creation of conditions for human flourishing. And the word *social* implies the belief that human emancipation depends upon the transformation of the social world, not just the inner life of persons'. Among the tasks Wright (2010, p 10) identifies for fulfilling the mission of an emancipatory social science are: first, identifying the ways in which 'existing social institutions and social structures systematically impose harms on people'; second, 'developing credible alternatives to existing social structures that would eliminate, or at least significantly mitigate, the harms identified in the diagnosis and critique'.

What could be the goal of what might be termed an '*emancipatory gerontology*' (emphasis added; Estes and DiCarlo, 2019) for future agendas on ageing? Three themes might be considered in response to the issues identified in this chapter: first, linking debates around ageing with ideas associated with implementing what has been termed 'Universal Basic Services' (UBS); second, ensuring recognition of *substantive equalities* by means of challenging both past and present experiences of discrimination; and third, identifying new sources of *collective engagement* among different groups of older people.

On the first issue, a precondition for developing new policies and institutions might be made through reconnecting to the original vision of a welfare state responsible for promoting the well-being of all its citizens. The tendency for capitalism to convert 'public services into commodities' (Navarro, 1976) has significantly increased over the past two decades, with the increasing penetration of multinational corporations into the health and social care system (Humber, 2017). The evidence, as summarized earlier, suggests that, taking the example of the UK, this process has had the greatest effect on older people from the poorest socioeconomic groups, with the decline in services in areas of high deprivation[4] creating the kind of 'no care zones' described by Estes et al (1993) in the US. Older people share this experience, of course, with many other groups affected by the implementation of austerity policies (McGarvey, 2018; O'Hara, 2015), highlighting the need for interventions that address basic needs across the life course. Here, the implementation of what has been termed 'Universal Basic Services' must be regarded as precondition for addressing the issues identified in this chapter and elsewhere in this book. Percy (2017, p 11) defines UBS as 'a collection of 7 free public services that enable every citizen to live a larger life by ensuring access to safety, opportunity and participation'. He writes,

> We repurpose the idea of public services to look at the feasibility of extending the same principles of universal access, free at the point of need, which we already manifest in our National Health Service, our public education, our democracy, and our legal services (albeit with variable quality). To the 3 existing public services we add Shelter, Food, Transport and Information. In some fashion these have been, or are, delivered as limited public services, but to reap the maximum returns all of these need to be elevated to more fully fledged Basic Services. (Percy, 2017, p 11)

Portes (2017, p 23) argues that the UBS model, by ensuring that every citizen has access to a range of services, is consistent with a 'capabilities' approach to addressing inequality:

> That is, the role of the state is to ensure an equitable distribution of not (just) money but the opportunity to participate and contribute to society. For that to be meaningful there are likely to be certain services everyone should be able to access. In this model poverty is not directly a matter of relative (or absolute) income but of access to opportunities, the prerequisites for which will change over time, and ensuring such access is the responsibility of the state. (Portes, 2017, p 23)

Second, the case for adopting the UBS model has been reinforced by the way the social or welfare state is being reconstructed, with the language of 'entitlement' and 'welfare' increasingly associated with 'moral failure' and 'inadequacy' (Armstrong, 2017; McGarvey, 2018).

This is a radically changed dynamic to that which characterized state intervention during the previous century (Gamble, 2016). Sassen (2003, p 18) argues that 'the development of welfare states in the twentieth century became a crucial institutional domain for granting entitlements to the poor and disadvantaged'. At the same time, the formal or legal equalities that emerged during this period are now challenged by the precarious circumstances, reviewed in different chapters in this book, faced by workers, carers, migrants, minority women and other social groups (see also Bassel and Emejulu, 2017; Bloodworth, 2018; Lewis et al, 2015; Standing, 2011). This process is accelerating pressures for ensuring *substantive equalities*, defined as the recognition of social processes that lead to inequality, of which the claims of those facing discrimination in the health and social care system are a notable example. Indeed, it might be argued that the failure to advance substantive equality is having devastating consequences for older people experiencing the application of labels such as frailty and dementia in conditions of austerity: such identities *undermining* and *devaluing* the people to whom they are applied (Grenier et al, 2017). Moreover, work towards substantive equalities is pressing given *past* as well as *current* experiences of discrimination. Understanding lifelong experiences of racism is especially important in the context of the health and social care needs of minority ethnic groups and minority women in particular, where racism linked with ageism will do much to shape attitudes and experiences in later life (Bassel and Emejulu, 2017; Phillipson, 2015).

Third, what Sassen (2003, p 24) refers to as the 'destabilization of the meaning of citizenship', with pressures from globalization and the consolidation of the market economy, is coming at a time when the possibilities of *exclusion* are being increased through cuts in support to vulnerable populations. At the same time, Sassen (2003, p 23) observes that given the role of the state in a neoliberal economy, there is a reduction in 'the likelihood that state institutions will do the type of legislative and judiciary work that has led to formal inclusions'. This raises the question of the extent to which citizens themselves (and older people in particular) can be empowered to develop new forms of social inclusion, within local communities but with implications for the practice of citizenship at national levels and beyond.

The policy implications of living in a more precarious environment suggests the need for consideration of what Dannefer and Huang (2017) have termed 'collective agency' – or the pursuit of collectively shared objectives – as a response to the politics of individualism associated with austerity and cuts to the welfare state. The implication of this view is that we need to conceptualize and recognize areas of practice – actual and emergent – that can promote solidarity at the neighbourhood and wider urban levels, but which can in turn influence national debates about the future of policies towards older people.

A potential way forward, following Cooper (2014), is that of identifying and promoting what she describes as '*everyday utopias*' [emphasis added], these defined as 'networks and spaces that perform regular daily life … in a radically different fashion'. Cooper suggests that 'everyday utopias are fruitful places from which to think differently and imaginatively about concepts [such as property, care, markets, work and equality … in counter-normative ways'. And she suggests that they work 'by creating the change they wish to encounter, building new ways of experiencing social and political life'. Analysing a number of different types of schemes (radical schools, local exchange trading schemes), she argues that these are not 'expressions of an ideal self-sufficient life' but are 'more akin to hot-spots of innovative practice' … 'engaged in the work of "civil repair"' (Cooper, 2014, p 9). Similarly, Segal (2018, p 200), in her overview of utopian approaches, draws on the work of Marxist feminists Katherine Gibson and Julie Graham to point out that 'market transactions are never completely hegemonic when the overall economy consists of a variety of transactions'. Segal comments that 'this is what feminists have always highlighted in revealing the variety and extent of unpaid care work … [as well as] other alternative economic practices, from gift giving and volunteering to barter and theft, alongside the occupation of public spaces, both for play and socializing, as well as for nurturing a politics of defiance' (Segal, 2018, p 200; see also Monbiot, 2017).

Some of the debates around developing new forms of collective engagement have been linked to the idea of building what Wright (2010) and Neamtan (2005) have termed a 'social economy': 'economic activity that is directly organised and controlled through the exercise of some form of social power [that is] rooted in the voluntary association of people in civil society and … based on the capacity to organize people for collective action of various sorts' (Wright, 2010, p 193). The approach outlined by Wright and others underlines the need to examine the scope and relevance of alternative social and economic practices and their potential contribution to developing new forms of public policy in the field of ageing. A range of alternative practices exist or are emerging among groups of older people, these including: co-housing groups; the 'Village' movement; environmental action groups; transgender groups; care cooperatives; and co-research and co-production.[5] The examples that have begun to emerge offer valuable ways forward; taken together, they even suggest alternative ways of 'thinking about' and 'practicing' ageing: areas of innovation (even 'cultures of resistance') that can feed back into proposing a different kind of welfare state, different forms of citizenship and different ways of experiencing later life.

However, despite the importance of the activities listed, limitations should also be noted. Buffel and Phillipson (2018), for example, writing about initiatives to develop 'age-friendly communities', note that the movement has tended to marginalize black and minority ethnic groups, and those within the lesbian, gay, bisexual, transsexual and queer (LGBTQ) communities. Lehning et al (2017, p 53) express concern about the extent to which age-friendly initiatives are 'failing to address the specific needs of racial and ethnic minorities or those with low incomes; this is of particular concern, given these subgroups of older adults are likely to live in particularly un-ageing-friendly, under-resourced neighbourhoods'. This last point identifies the challenge of developing alternative economic and social practices in the context of the serious problems facing urban environments, notably widening inequalities, rapidly expanding numbers of people – from all age groups – without a home;[6] and the closure of facilities for people with addiction and mental health problems. Dawson (2017) identifies the rise of what he terms 'extreme cities', with a new precariousness affecting urban life given the impact of climate-change induced disasters. Cities, Dawson (2017, p 5) argues, 'are the defining social and ecological phenomena of the twenty-first century: they house the majority of humanity, they contribute the lion's share of carbon to the atmosphere, and they are peculiarly vulnerable to climate chaos'. Evidence is already available of the disproportionate impact of hurricanes (Katrina in New Orleans in 2005), heatwaves (in Chicago in 1995 and France in 2003) and tsunamis (in Tōhoku, Japan in 2011) on older people. Such developments, given the retreat of state support and public services, underline the urgent need for new forms of collective agency that can respond to the public health and environmental crises facing vulnerable communities (see further Wallace-Wells, 2019).

Conclusion

This chapter has examined the extent to which economic and social pressures have created a precarious environment for growing old in the 21st century. The retreat of the institutions associated with the welfare state, retirement and the pursuit of equality have introduced major risks to the various transitions negotiated through middle and later life. The institutions, as developed in the 20th century, were themselves criticized in a variety of ways, notably for the extent to which they imposed various forms of 'dependency' (Estes, 1979; Townsend, 1981; Walker, 1980); for their failure to combat discrimination and ageism (Macnicol, 2006); and for their exploitation of women as carers (Estes, 2006; Calasanti, 2010). But they were also vital in laying the basis for the development of social rights common to all citizens, underpinned by the activities and responsibilities of the state. As Gamble (2016, p 14) puts it,

> Citizens depended upon one another; their fate was inextricably bound up with all other citizens of the community, this meant that the state, too, had both an obligation to maximise the potential of every citizen and an interest in doing so. Providing the best possible education, the best health care, the best opportunities for creativity and training – all these became both what modern citizens expected and modern governments strove to deliver.

But the speed of unravelling of welfare and other state responsibilities is striking, especially when set beside the relatively slow pace of their evolution over the course of the 19th and 20th centuries (Timmins, 1996). John Myles (1984) highlighted the extent to which older people were the major beneficiaries of an expanding welfare state; by implication they have been among the prime losers as key areas of provision have been lost or rationed – this coming at a time of accelerated growth in population ageing, not least among those entering their eighties and beyond. However, the extent of change has been concealed by a debate about how older people, and the 'boomer generation' in particular, have received 'unfair' support in contrast with other age groups, due to a combination of benefits received over the life course and 'ring-fenced' protection within old age itself. The importance of the boomer or 'generational warfare' argument has been that it appears to fill a vacuum left by the retreat of the welfare state, providing a moral case for abandoning provision now deemed as 'too expensive' for a group who had, it was argued, received an 'excess' of support over their life course.[7]

This last argument grabbed attention in part because the alternative view was both more complex and raised broader concerns about support for older people. The complexity was reflected in the widening economic and social inequalities *within* the older population, these reflected most especially in ethnic, income and gender divisions but also in differences in access to health and social care. A narrative that focused on the idea of a 'generational divide' helped foreclose discussions about the implications of welfare state restructuring, and its consequences for *all* generations. But an alternative idea may be that while growing old does in numerous ways reflect cumulative advantages and disadvantages gathered through the life course, the dismantling of state support and the shift towards individualization poses threats across a range of age and social groups (see further Meek, 2018). It is here that we would argue that the idea of 'precarity' is worthy of application to issues facing older people in the 21st century. Lorey (2015, p 1) takes the view that 'precarization is not an exception, it is rather the rule. It is spreading even in those areas that were long considered secure. It has become an instrument of government and, at the same time, a basis for capital accumulation that serves social regulation and control'. She further argues that

> precarization means more than insecure jobs, more than the lack of security given by waged employment. By way of insecurity and danger it embraces the whole of existence, the body, modes of subjectivation. It is threat and coercion, even while it opens up the possibilities of living and working. Precarization means living with the unforeseeable, with contingency…. In the course of the dismantling of the welfare state and the rights associated with it, a form of government is established that is based on the greatest possible insecurity, promoted by proclaiming the alleged absence of alternatives. (Lorey, 2015, pp 1–2)

It is the development of new forms of vulnerability that has become a characteristic feature of later life (as well as other life course transitions): whether as regards the threat to pensions, the uncertainty over the provision of care or the labelling of older people as a burden on society. None of these insecurities will necessarily be experienced by all older people or to the same degree. They may strike for a relatively large or relatively small proportion of later life; and the extent of resistance that people have will vary a great deal – again, the cumulative dimension of advantage or disadvantage will be a significant factor. But it might be argued that a very large proportion of people – of all generations – are affected by the last point Lorey (2015) makes, namely, the apparent absence of alternatives. The danger being suggested is that the loss of the welfare state becomes 'accepted' and 'normalized', reinforced by the continued denigration of 'public' and 'social' provision. It is here that the idea of 'precarity' may provide a way forward, providing both a framework for critical perspectives and a basis for developing alternatives to the crisis facing many groups of older people.

Notes

1. This historical shift is outlined in Phillipson (2013).
2. For a review of the broad impact of austerity on groups across the life course, see Cooper and Whyte (2017). Tribe (2017, p 46) has made the point that 'the real problem is … not so much that the 1 per cent are accumulating ever greater amounts of wealth; rather, that such accumulation is linked to the private appropriation of social wealth. Further, the consolidation of their power inflicts policies on the rest of society that impoverish the environment and social circumstances in which we all live'.
3. In many European countries the thrust of policy has been to protect pensioners e.g. by inflation-proofing the basic state pension. In the UK, in the mid-1990s, pensioners had the highest rates of poverty apart from children, with three in ten pensioners living in poverty. By 2011–12, this had fallen to only 13 per cent, mainly driven by improvements in support for single older people (and through fewer older people renting properties). However, figures for the UK (2016–17) show a reversal in this trend, mainly arising through cuts to additional benefits to supporting older people, and increases in housing costs (Joseph Rowntree Trust, 2018). The situation facing older people in South Mediterranean countries is especially serious in some cases: economic sanctions applied to Greece post-2008 have had a significant impact on older people, with pensions nearly halved before 2015 and with further cuts of 10–20 per cent due in 2019 (Varoufakis, 2018). Spain has stopped the inflationary indexing of pensions thus reducing their purchasing power. Spain is an example of a country where with very high levels of unemployment affecting families, there is substantial evidence of older people pooling their resources to help unemployed younger family members. Even the Scandinavian countries have made important changes to their welfare state, notably in moving from defined benefit to defined contribution pensions. And the move to raise pension ages across OECD countries essentially amounts to a substantial cut in pensions – affecting women in particular.
4. In the UK, evidence from the Health Survey for England indicates that a third of men 65 and over living in the most deprived areas (33 per cent) have an unmet need for at least one so-called 'activity of daily living' compared with 15 per cent in the least deprived; in the least deprived

areas the figure falls to 15 per cent; the equivalent figures for women are 42 per cent and 22 per cent (Savage, 2017).
5   For a review of these areas, see Buffel et al (2018).
6   For a discussion on this issue, see Grenier (2019); Nagourney (2016).
7   For presentation of this theme, see Willetts (2010); for a critique of this approach, see Segal (2014); Hills (2015).

References

Armstrong, S. (2017) *The New Poverty*, London: Verso.

Bassel, L. and Emejulu, A. (2017) *Minority Women and Austerity: Survival and Resistance in France and Britain*, Bristol: Policy Press.

Blackburn, R. (2006) *Age Shock: How Finance Is Failing Us*, London: Verso.

Bloodworth, J. (2018) *Hired: Six Months Undercover in Low-Wage Britain*, London: Atlantic Books.

Brown, W. (2015) *Undoing the Demos: Neoliberalism's Stealth Revolution*, New York: Zone Books.

Buffel, T. and Phillipson, C. (2018) 'A manifesto for the age-friendly movement: developing a new urban agenda', *Journal of Aging and Social Policy*, 30(2): 173–92.

Buffel, T., Handler, S. and Phillipson, C. (eds) (2018) *Age-Friendly Cities and Communities: a Global Perspective*, Bristol: Policy Press.

Calasanti, T. (2010) 'Gender and ageing in the context of globalization', in D. Dannefer and C. Phillipson (eds) *The Sage Handbook of Social Gerontology*, London: Sage, pp 137–49.

Cooper, D. (2014) *Everyday Utopias: the Conceptual Life of Promising Spaces*, Durham, NC: Duke University Press.

Cooper, V. and Whyte, D. (eds) (2017) *The Violence of Austerity*, London: Pluto.

Dannefer, D. and Huang, W. (2017) 'Precarity, inequality, and the problem of agency in the study of the life course', *Innovation in Aging*, 1(3): 1–10.

Davies, W. (2015) *The Limits of Neoliberalism: Authority, Sovereignty and the Logic of Competition*, London: Sage.

Dawson, A. (2017) *Extreme Cities: the Peril and Promise of Urban Life in the Age of Climate Change*, London: Verso.

Elder, G.H., Jr (1998) 'The life course as developmental theory', *Child Development*, 69(1): 1–12.

Estes, C.L. (1979) *The Aging Enterprise*, San Francisco: Jossey-Bass.

Estes, C. (2006) 'Critical feminist perspectives, aging, and social policy', in J. Baars, D. Dannefer, C. Phillipson and A. Walker (eds) *Aging, Globalization and Inequality: the New Critical Gerontology*, Amityville, NY: Baywood, pp 81–102.

Estes, C.L. and DiCarlo, N.B. (2019) *Ageing A–Z: Concepts toward Emancipatory Gerontology*, New York: Routledge.

Estes, C.L., Swan, J.H. and Associates (1993) *The Long-Term Care Crisis: Elders Trapped in the No-Care Zone*, Newbury Park, CA: Sage.

Foster, L. and Walker, A. (2015) 'Active and successful aging: a European policy perspective', *The Gerontologist*, 55(1): 83–90.

Gamble, A. (2016) *Can the Welfare State Survive?*, Cambridge: Polity.

Giddens, A (1976) *New Rules for Sociological Method: a Positive Critique of Interpretative Sociologies*, New York: Basic Books.

Gilleard, C. and Higgs, P. (2005) *Contexts of Ageing: Class, Cohort and Community*, Cambridge: Polity.

Gratton, L. and Scott, A. (2016) *The 100-Year Life: Living and Working in an Age of Longevity*, London: Bloomsbury.

Grenier, A. (2019) *Homelessness in Late Life: Experiences of Unequal Aging*, Montreal: McGill–Queens University Press [forthcoming].

Grenier, A., Lloyd, L. and Phillipson, C. (2017) 'Precarity in late life: rethinking dementia as a "frailed" old age', *Sociology of Health & Illness*, 39(2): 318–30.

Hiam, L., Dorling, D., Harrison, D. and McKee, M. (2017) 'Why has mortality in England and Wales been increasing? An iterative demographic analysis', *Journal of the Royal Society of Medicine* 110(4): 153–62.

Hills, J. (2015) *Good Times, Bad Times: the Welfare Myth of Them and Us*, Bristol: Policy Press.

Humber, L. (2017) 'Neoliberalism and the crisis in health and social care', *International Socialism* [online], 155, available from: http://isj.org.uk/neoliberalism-and-the-crisis-in-health-and-social-care/ [Accessed 13 August 2019].

Humphries, R., Thorlby, R., Holder, H., Hall, P. and Charles, A. (2016) *Social Care for Older People: Home Truths* [online], London: Nuffield Trust, available from: https://www.nuffieldtrust.org.uk/research/social-care-for-older-people-home-truths [Accessed 13 August 2019].

Joseph Rowntree Foundation Analysis Unit (2018) *UK Poverty 2018: a Comprehensive Analysis of Poverty Trends and Figures*, York: Joseph Rowntree Foundation [online], available from: https://www.jrf.org.uk/report/uk-poverty-2018 [Accessed 13 August 2019].

Joyce, R. and Xu, X. (2019) *Inequalities in the Twenty-First Century: Introducing the IFS Deaton Review* [online], London: Institute for Fiscal Studies, available from: https://www.ifs.org.uk/inequality/chapter/briefing-note/ [Accessed 13 August 2019].

Judt, T. (2015) *When the Facts Change: Essays 1995–2010*, edited by J. Homans, London: William Heinemann.

Klein, N. (2007) *The Shock Doctrine: the Rise of Disaster Capitalism*, London: Allen Lane.

Klinenberg, E. (2019) *Palaces for the People: How Social Infrastructure Can Help Fight Inequality, Polarization, and the Decline of Civic Life*, New York: Penguin Random House.

Kröger, T. and Bagnato, A. (2018) 'Care for older people in early twenty-first-century Europe: dimensions and directions of change', in F. Martinelli, A. Anttonen and M. Mätzke (eds) *Social Services Disrupted: Changes, Challenges and Policy Implications for Europe in Times of Austerity*, Cheltenham: Edward Elgar, pp 201–18.

Lehning, A.J., Smith, R.J. and Kyeongmo, K. (2017) '"Friendly" initiatives: an emerging approach to improve communities for vulnerable populations', *Journal of Policy Practice*, 16(1): 46–58.

Lewis, H., Dwyer, P., Hodkinson, S. and Waite, L. (2015) *Precarious Lives: Forced Labour, Exploitation and Asylum*, Bristol: Policy Press.

Lorey, I. (2015) *State of Insecurity: Government of the Precarious*, translated by A. Derieg, London: Verso.

Macnicol, J. (2006) *Age Discrimination: an Historical and Contemporary Analysis*, Cambridge: Cambridge University Press.

Macnicol, J. (2015) *Neoliberalising Old Age*, Cambridge: Cambridge University Press.

Marshall, T.H. (1950) *Citizenship and Social Class and Other Essays*, Cambridge: Cambridge University Press.

McBride, S. and Mitrea, S. (2017) 'Internalizing neoliberalism and austerity', in S. McBride and B.M. Evans (eds) *The Austerity State*, Toronto: University of Toronto Press, pp 98–122.

McGarvey, D. (2018) *Poverty Safari: Understanding the Anger of Britain's Underclass*, Edinburgh: Luath Press.

McKibbin, R. (2017) Book review of Dismembered: How the Attack on the State Harms Us All by Polly Toynbee and David Walker – review', *The Guardian* [online], 11 May, available from: https://www.theguardian.com/books/2017/may/11/dismembered-attack-state-polly-toynbee-review [Accessed 13 August 2019].

Meek, J. (2014) *Private Island: Why Britain Belongs to Someone Else*. London: Verso.

Meek, J. (2018) 'NHS SOS', *London Review of Books*, 40(7): 17–30.

Monbiot, G. (2017) *Out of the Wreckage: a New Politics for an Age of Crisis*, London: Verso.

Myles, J. (1984) *Old Age in the Welfare State: the Political Economy of Pensions*, Lawrence: University of Kansas Press.

Nagourney, A. (2016) 'Old and on the street: the graying of America's homeless', *New York Times* [online], 31 May, available from: https://www.nytimes.com/2016/05/31/us/americas-aging-homeless-old-and-on-the-street.html?emc=eta1&_r=0 [Accessed 15 August 2019].

National Audit Office (2014) *The Impact of Funding Reductions on Local Authorities*, London: National Audit Office [online], available from: https://www.nao.org.uk/report/the-impact-funding-reductions-local-authorities/ [Accessed 13 August 2019].

Navarro, V. (1976) *Medicine under Capitalism*, New York: Praeger.

Neamtan, N. (2005) 'The social economy: finding a way between the market and the state', *Policy Options*, July/August, pp 74–6.

Office for National Statistics (2018) *Changing Trends in Mortality in England and Wales: 1990 to 2017 (Experimental Statistics)*, London: Office for National Statistics [online], available from: https://www.ons.gov.uk/peoplepopulationandcommunity/birthsdeathsandmarriages/deaths/articles/changingtrendsinmortalityinenglandandwales1990to2017/experimentalstatistics [Accessed 13 August 2019].

Office for National Statistics (2019) *Health State Life Expectancies by National Deprivation Deciles, England and Wales, 2015 to 2017*. London: Office for National Statistics [online], available from: https://www.ons.gov.uk/peoplepopulationandcommunity/healthandsocialcare/healthinequalities/bulletins/healthstatelifeexpectanciesbyindexofmultipledeprivationimd/2015to2017 [Accessed 13 August 2019].

O'Hara, M. (2015) *Austerity Bites: a Journey to the Sharp End of Cuts in the UK*, Bristol: Policy Press.

Percy, A. (2017) 'Universal Basic Services: a larger life for the ordinary person', in H. Moore, J. Portes, H. Reed and A. Percy, *Social Prosperity for the Future: a Proposal for University Basic Services*, London: UCL Institute for Global Prosperity [online], pp 9–16, available from: https://ubs-hub.org/igp-report-2017/ [Accessed 13 August 2019].

Phillipson, C. (2013) *Ageing*, Cambridge: Polity.

Phillipson, C. (2015) 'Placing ethnicity at the centre of studies of later life: theoretical perspectives and empirical challenges', *Ageing and Society*, 35(5): 917–34.

Portacolone, E. (2013) 'The notion of precariousness among older adults living alone in the U.S.', *Journal of Aging Studies*, 27(2): 166–74.

Portes, J. (2017) 'Universal Basic Services: discussion paper', in H. Moore, J. Portes, H. Reed and A. Percy, *Social Prosperity for the Future: a Proposal for University Basic Services*, London: UCL Institute for Global Prosperity [online], pp 17–27, available from: https://ubs-hub.org/igp-report-2017/ [Accessed 13 August 2019].

Rosanvallon, P. (2013) *The Society of Equals*, translated by A. Goldhammer, Cambridge, MA: Harvard University Press.

Sassen, S. (2003) 'The participation of states and citizens in global governance', *Indiana Journal of Global Legal Studies*, 10(5): 5–28.

Sassen, S. (2014) *Expulsions: Brutality and Complexity in the Global Economy*, Cambridge, MA: Belknap Press.

Savage, M. (2017) 'Social care postcode gap widens for older people', *The Guardian* [online], 16 December, available from: https://www.theguardian.com/society/2017/dec/16/social-care-for-elderly-postcode-gap-grows [Accessed 20 April 2018].

Segal, L. (2014) *Out of Time: the Pleasures and the Perils of Ageing*, London: Verso.

Segal, L. (2018) *Radical Happiness: Moments of Collective Joy*, London: Verso.

Settersten, R.A., Jr and Trauten, M.E. (2009) 'The new terrain of old age: hallmarks, freedoms, and risks', in V.L. Bengtson, D. Gans, N.M. Putney and M. Silverstein (eds) *Handbook of Theories of Aging* (2nd edn), New York: Springer, pp 455–69.

Standing, G. (2011) *The Precariat: the New Dangerous Class*, London: Bloomsbury Academic.

Standing, G. (2016) *The Corruption of Capitalism: Why Rentiers Thrive and Work Does Not Pay*, London: Biteback.

Streeck, W. (2016) *How Will Capitalism End? Essays on a Failing System*, London: Verso.

Stuckler, D. and Basu, S. (2013) *The Body Economic: Why Austerity Kills*, London: Allen Lane.

Taylor-Gooby, P., Leruth, B. and Chung, H. (eds) (2017) *After Austerity: Welfare State Transformation in Europe after the Great Recession*, Oxford: Oxford University Press.

Teeple, G. (2017) 'Austerity policies: from the Keynesian to the corporate welfare state', in S. McBride and B.M. Evans (eds) *The Austerity State*, Toronto: University of Toronto Press, pp 25–43.

Timmins, N. (1996) *The Five Giants: a Biography of the Welfare State*, London: Fontana.

Tooze, A. (2018) *Crashed: How a Decade of Financial Crises Changed the World*, London: Penguin Random House.

Townsend, P. (1981) 'The structured dependency of the elderly: a creation of social policy in the twentieth century', *Ageing & Society*, 1(1): 5–28.

Toynbee, P. and Walker, D. (2017) *Dismembered: How the Attack on the State Harms Us All*, London: Guardian Books.

Tribe, K. (2017) 'Inequality', in P. Hudson and K. Tribe (eds) *The Contradictions of Capital in the Twenty-First Century: the Piketty Opportunity*, New York: Agenda, pp 29–52.

Varoufakis, Y. (2018) 'Why we founded new political party MeRA25 to challenge austerity in Greece', *New Statesman* [online], April 18, available from: https://www.newstatesman.com/world/europe/2018/04/why-we-founded-new-political-party-mera25-challenge-austerity-greece [Accessed 20 January 2019].

Vickerstaff, S. and Cox, J. (2005) 'Retirement and risk: the individualisation of retirement experiences?', *Sociological Review*, 53(1): 77–95.

Wainwright, H. (2018) *A New Politics from the Left*, Cambridge: Polity.

Walker, A. (1980) 'The social creation of dependency in old age', *Journal of Social Policy*, 9(1): 45–75.

Wallace-Wells, D. (2019) *The Uninhabitable Earth: Life after Warming*. New York: Penguin Random House.

Willetts, D. (2010) *The Pinch: How the Baby Boomers Took Their Children's Future – and Why They Should Give It Back*, London: Atlantic.

Wright, E.O. (2010) *Envisioning Real Utopias*, London: Verso.

11

Conclusion: Precarity and ageing in the 21st century

*Chris Phillipson, Amanda Grenier
and Richard A. Settersten Jr*

Introduction

This book has explored the extent to which the concepts of 'precarity' and 'precariousness' can provide new insights into the way in which inequalities and insecurities may be experienced across the life course. A dominant theme of the chapters has been the impact of various changes that have affected the lives of older people in the 21st century, these including the decline of the social or welfare state, the move to extend working life, the pressures faced by caregivers and the vulnerabilities of late old age. Of course, as many of the contributors suggest, not all older people are affected in the same way, with significant variations according to race, ethnicity, gender, social class and sexual orientation. But relatively few people are likely to escape the experience or feeling of insecurity at some point in later life, and for many these may become deeply rooted in everyday life.

As a general argument, then, and for different reasons, we think ideas associated with 'precarity' and 'precariousness' are valuable for students of ageing and policymakers to consider. First, they extend our understanding of the many sources and forms of insecurity that may affect the lives of older people. These have been illustrated in this book through, for example, discussions relating to migration (Kobayashi and Kahn), care work (Fine), cuts to health and social care (Polivka and Bao; Portacolone), and the influence of life course transitions in creating precarity and responses to it (Settersten). Second, later life may bring distinctive features in respect of changes to mental and physical health. As noted in many of the chapters, however, these are often best understood in terms of lives that, from childhood onwards, may face numerous threats to independence and security (see, for example, the chapters by Settersten and Grenier). Third, on an optimistic note, the idea of precarity may also be used to point the way to new forms of resistance developed by individual older people and by larger social groups (an aspect identified in the chapters by Katz and Phillipson). Thus, the debate about precariousness is not only about understanding new vulnerabilities but also about the emergence of collective organizations in response, both across and within generations (see later in this chapter).

One additional observation about the benefits of viewing ageing through the lens of precarity is its potential to extend debates within the field of critical gerontology (see the introductory chapter). The issues discussed in this book might be said to have been anticipated by critical perspectives that emerged in the 1970s and 1980s (see, for instance, Estes, 1979; Townsend, 1981; Walker, 1980), and which were subsequently extended in theories of cumulative advantage/disadvantage (Dannefer, 2003), studies on the relationship between globalization and inequality (Baars et al, 2006), critical perspectives on gender and ageing (Calasanti, 2010), and related work.

Over the past decade, critical gerontology has expanded into new areas, including cultural gerontology (Katz, 2018; Twigg and Martin, 2015), migration (Torres, 2019), ageing and urbanization (Buffel et al, 2018), and frailty (Grenier et al, 2017). However, notwithstanding the importance of these topics, links between cultural, economic and social ties in the construction of ageing have often been ignored. This may be viewed in part as reflecting uncertainty about how to respond to the social crisis created by the financial crash of 2008; in part, also, through the fragmentation of critical perspectives over the period since the 1980s. We think that the work on precarity can itself make an important contribution to further research on critical gerontology: by restoring linkages between work on political economy, social structure, and issues of meaning, embodiment and identity in later life; and by making more visible the different types of social and cultural changes affecting older people, driven by the diversity of ageing populations, processes of individualization and widening social inequalities.

This concluding chapter highlights some of the economic, social and political factors that create precarity in the lives of older people. This will be done by first tracing some of the linkages between the context of austerity and economic crisis and broader questions about the future of the welfare state; and then by demonstrating how taking the example of later life can bring new insights into our understanding of the nature of precarity.

Austerity and precarious institutions

The argument of this book is that concepts of 'precarity' and 'precariousness' provide an important aid to understanding the consequences of the 'new times' faced by older people: not only the resulting tensions and contradictions in their lives but also the potential for challenging and resisting the various pressures on everyday life. As explained in the chapter by Phillipson, the global financial crisis post-2008 transformed the landscape around which services and supports to older people had been built. The reduction in state responsibilities has been substantial, especially when set beside the framework that had been established in many European countries over the course of the 20th century (Kuttner, 2018).

But this is not simply about there being *fewer* services available (although that is certainly the case), more that what is available, how it is provided and who takes responsibility have radically altered the *social basis* upon which support (of any kind) is provided. Judt connects this problem to privatization, asking,

> What does 'privatization' mean? It removes from the state the capacity and the responsibility for making good the shortcomings of people's lives; it also removes the same set of responsibilities from the conscience of fellow citizens, who no longer feel a shared burden for the common dilemmas. All that remains is the charitable impulse derived from an individual's sense of guilt towards other suffering individuals. (Judt, 2012, p 373)

But if the argument about the weakening (or 'precariousness') of social institutions is accepted, then it also follows that new ways are needed for thinking about and understanding the economic and social changes affecting the lives of older people. In the 21st century, who counts as 'old', who sees themselves as 'old', and who is treated as 'old' becomes open for negotiation in distinctive ways. The contributors to this book have illustrated the questions around age and social responses through a variety of examples, highlighting some of the underlying causes as well. An important theme is the extent to which economic and social trends post-2008 have accelerated processes of individualization, which were apparent in the late 1980s and 1990s but have come sharply into focus in the last decade given the direction of public policy. This development has raised significant issues about the meaning of old age itself, with respect to the challenge to retirement (with the move to extend working life), the differential allocation of resources to social groups (with presumed tension between younger and older generations, but also conflicts related to the inclusion or exclusion of groups based on other kinds of statuses) or pressures on the provision of care (with the devolution of responsibility to privatized forms of support).

A further argument made by contributors to this book is the need to take a 'long view of precarity', which acknowledges that the life course itself has been subject to significant revision and flux as social institutions and networks have become unstable. This has introduced greater individualization, and therefore greater personal risk, in life course trajectories. It has also meant that the 'turning points' people encounter – periods of unemployment, the onset of chronic ill-health, migration or the loss of a partner – may themselves lead to longer periods of instability and uncertainty than was once the case. In the 1990s, researchers argued that the life course had become 'de-standardised' with the loosening of the 'lock-step' of education, work and retirement (Kohli et al, 1991). Three decades later, we can see the 'break-up' more clearly in terms of the consequences arising from the retreat of the state, or the redefinition of what it is that states are supposed to do or provide. Less clear are the consequences for individuals and families as they navigate the distinctive precarities of later life, and in particular from locations of disadvantage and/or fewer financial resources (see further the chapters by Fine, Grenier and Portacolone).

Taking the example of ageing tells us much, therefore, about the experience of life moving into the third decade of the 21st century. We can go further than this, however: ageing, later life, old age, however termed, also brings new insights for researchers and policymakers grappling with the idea of studying and living in a more precarious world. The next section of this chapter summarizes some of the ways in which this might be the case.

What ageing brings to the study of precarity

Beyond the labour market

An important rationale behind this book was the view of the editors that the example of ageing and older people introduced a new perspective on issues related to precarity and precariousness. Much of the research literature on this topic has been influenced – notably through the work of Standing (2011) – by the view that changes in the labour market, associated for example with the growth of short-term forms of employment, have been key factors driving precarity. However, contributors to this book have extended the debate beyond the labour market to examine a wider range of causal factors and consequences. Lain and his colleagues, for example, have drawn out the extent to which precarity may work across multiple domains, illustrated by the changes affecting employment, households and the welfare state (see also Settersten for examples of cross-domain interactions). They have put forward the concept of 'ontological precarity', exploring the extent to which insecurity may be amplified or exacerbated by interactions within and across these three domains.

The book has also extended the idea of precarity by noting its importance to understanding the radical changes affecting care work. Fine, for example, has observed the extent to which changes in the organization of employment have had a profound influence on the provision of formal care, this area becoming a prime site for economic rationalization and cost control (a point further developed in the chapter by Polivka and Luo). One argument in fact is that the care worker can be seen, in various guises, as the 'precariat' par excellence. This point is illustrated in a study by Patel and Moore (2018, p 34), who, noting that 'flexibility and permanent availability have long been the hallmarks of care work', suggest that 'the freelance economy can be read as an expansion of the discipline of care work spread across the entire working world'. Indeed, with the retreat of state welfare, the precariousness of care work comes to the fore, as demonstrated by the growing influence of private equity firms in the provision of home and residential care (Shaxson, 2018).

Cumulative personal and ontological vulnerabilities

A further aim of this book was to contribute to understanding the everyday experiences of older people, especially those from disadvantaged and marginalized groups. Attention to ageing and precarity exposes the deeply personal and ontological experiences of vulnerability that take place across the life course and into late life. Extending the analysis of precarity into late life reveals the extent to which experiences of vulnerability are a shared part of the human condition that do not cease at retirement. Indeed, vulnerability may become even more acute at the onset of the need for care, reinforced by policies or practices that create or sustain inequality (see, for example, the chapters by Portacolone and Grenier). The contributors have drawn attention to distinct forms of precariousness related to living alone, immigration, frailty and the need for care. In some cases, these reflect new challenges facing older people, illustrated by the pressures on those living in urban areas undergoing rapid gentrification (Smith et al, 2018) or those entering the 'no care zones' created by the collapse of home care services (Estes et al, 1993). In others, the precariousness may be considered an ever-present feature that shifts and changes throughout the life course, through encounters that hold the potential to provide relief or more deeply engrain precarity through, for example, sustained unmet need.

One conclusion to be drawn, as regards the cultural and interpretive aspects of precariousness, is how power and privilege, enacted through a range of social relations, relational encounters and institutional/organizational practices, can affect people across the life course and into late life. It is here that the contributions of Butler's (2006; 2009) thinking on precariousness, the construction of devalued subjects and the implications of processes of dehumanization are most acute. The chapters in this book have rendered visible the extent to which the experiences of precarity and precariousness are both individual and deeply political, rooted in economic and political priorities, and often organized around individualized systems of care and cost imperatives. Further, they signal the apprehension that older people, and particularly those from marginal groups who are most reliant on forms of care that are being scaled back, will be abandoned (see also Povinelli, 2011). Taken together, it is the everyday stories of older people's lives that reveal the gross inequalities and injustices of such realities and create significant cause for concern (see, for example, the chapters by Kobayashi and Kahn, Polivka and Bao, and Portacolone).

Precarity and human rights

Taking the perspective of ageing, therefore, allows us to see different areas of social life – beyond those of employment – as contributing to manifestations of precariousness. But insights drawn from the study of later life allow us to go one step further. Studying ageing tells us about distinctive forms of precarity; however, we also learn about new skills and relationships that may be formed in response. Settersten, for example, has highlighted the extent to which personal attributes and capacities, accumulated over the life course, become key ingredients for managing precarity. Katz and Phillipson emphasize the new social and economic organizations and spaces created by older people, part of what Monbiot (2017, p 77) views as the 'explosive revival of civic life'. At both levels – the personal and the organizational – we find older people leading responses to living in a precarious world, reconstructing personal relationships as well as the networks and organizations to which they relate. Such developments reinforce the argument from Esping-Anderson concerning the need, in the context of ageing populations, 'for a sphere which supports the market but is not governed by it, a sphere which allows labour and human needs to be "de-commodified," and acknowledges the priority of individuals' social rights over their market performance' (cited in Gamble, 2016, p 107).

Against this last point, the chapters in this book have demonstrated the extent to which various forms of cultural, economic and social rights have been severely compromised in later life. The changes to the welfare state have curtailed many of the ideals formed in the period following the Second World War, reintroducing 'early industrial notions of a divided citizenry: the citizens who work and the lesser citizens who don't work. Employment thus return[ed] to social policy as a measure of full participation' (Judt, 2012, p 371). In gerontology, this division was noted through Townsend's (1981) attention to the 'structured dependency' of older people, and how problems relating to dependency persisted as a major issue affecting older people in many parts of the world. In the case of more contemporary issues in ageing, this division has been reinforced by concepts within gerontology itself, notably those associated with 'active' and 'successful' ageing (see further Chapter 1).

A product of these developments has been the emergence of the precarious state affecting those labelled with cognitive and related impairments, a state commonly termed the 'fourth age' (Higgs and Gilleard, 2015). But there are now many other groups within the older population – for example, migrants, people in nursing and residential homes (where voting rights are routinely denied), older workers with limited employment rights – who face deprivation of different forms of economic, social and political rights. One response to such challenges might come though the adoption of the type of human rights perspective developed in the work of the late Peter Townsend (2007). Townsend highlighted the importance of measures such as the *European Convention on Human Rights* and the *Universal Declaration of Human Rights* as offering a means of challenging the 'structured dependency' of older people. Use of such rights-based frameworks may become essential given the rise of care organizations operating across national borders, and the drive to deregulate and privatize hitherto public services. In arguing for the establishment of a linkage between studies of ageing and a human rights framework, Townsend concluded that

> Human rights instruments offer hope of breaking down blanket discrimination and of using resources more appropriately, and more generously, according to severity of need. But investment in human rights is not only a moral and quasi-legal salvation from things that are going depressingly wrong. Used best, human rights offer a framework of thought and planning [for] the 21st Century that enables society to take a fresh, and more hopeful, direction. (Townsend, 2007, p 43)

Conclusion

This book has explored precarity and ageing from a range of disciplinary backgrounds, critical perspectives and international contexts. It was our intention to make more visible, and to provide a distinctive approach to understanding, the changing cultural, economic and social circumstances that create precarity across the life course and for older people. Taken together, the chapters offer a detailed exploration of both structured and existential vulnerabilities, and repeatedly challenge the assumption that older people will be protected by existing social programmes or whatever resources they can marshal on their own. We have shown that the concepts of precarity and precariousness bring the potential to rethink ageing and late life in contemporary conditions, but that these concepts require continued critical appraisal, clarification with respect to other aligned constructs, and methodological developments if knowledge is to be harnessed in order to improve well-being and address inequalities among older people.

The chapters have demonstrated that precarity and precariousness invariably have social origins and consequences – often rooted in larger cultural, economic and social circumstances, which brings the potential for malleability and openness to intervention, or which makes these circumstances shared experiences. The chapters have also shown that precarity and particularly precariousness are interpersonal phenomena, often felt acutely in, expressed through or even spread in social relationships. The various contributions have also highlighted the extent to which precarity is often experienced in intersectional ways, at social locations that include age, ethnicity, race, gender, migration status, socio-economic status and other key dimensions of social relations. They have also pointed to particular moments that may heighten insecurities and risks, as well as highlighted how precarity and precariousness may change across the life course and over time. These analyses reveal that older people experience precarity in different ways, whether individually, based on their personal life histories and current circumstances, or systematically, across a range of social locations and geographic contexts. The chapters have further demonstrated that precarity is inherently a political phenomenon and therefore has a natural association with social policies and matters of inequality, due to the ways in which policies either exclude or enhance social protections.

In conclusion, this book argues that understanding the impact of precarity on late life will improve understanding of contemporary forms of risk and insecurity, as well as make a substantial contribution to work in social gerontology and related social science disciplines. Older people in the 21st century face distinctive challenges from the erosion of the welfare state alongside the emergence of more complex transitions running through the life course. The response to this will require new theoretical and policy frameworks to aid understanding of both the challenges and the potential of later life. Perspectives drawn from work on precarity should provide a valuable contribution to tackling the cultural, economic and social issues facing older people in the years ahead.

References

Baars, J., Dannefer, D., Phillipson, C. and Walker, A. (eds) (2006) *Aging, Globalization and Inequality: the New Critical Gerontology*, Amityville, NY: Baywood.

Buffel, T., Handler, S. and Phillipson, C. (eds) (2018) *Age-Friendly Cities and Communities: a Global Perspective*, Bristol: Policy Press.

Butler, J. (2006) *Precarious Life: The Powers of Mourning and Violence*, London: Verso.

Butler, J. (2009) *Frames of War: When Is Life Grievable?*, London: Verso.

Calasanti, T. (2010) 'Gender and ageing in the context of globalization', in D. Dannefer and C. Phillipson (eds) *The Sage Handbook of Social Gerontology*, London: Sage, pp 137–49.

Dannefer, D. (2003) 'Cumulative advantage/disadvantage and the life course: cross-fertilizing age and social science theory', *Journals of Gerontology Series B: Psychological Sciences & Social Sciences*, 58(6): S327–37.

Estes, C.L. (1979) *The Aging Enterprise*, San Francisco: Jossey Bass.

Estes, C.L., Swan, J.H. and Associates (1993) *The Long Term Care Crisis: Elders Trapped in the No-Care Zone*, Newbury Park, CA: Sage.

Gamble, A. (2016) *Can the Welfare State Survive?* Cambridge: Polity.

Grenier, A., Lloyd, L. and Phillipson, C. (2017) 'Precarity in later life: re-thinking dementia as "frailed" old age', *Sociology of Health and Illness*, 39(2): 318–30.

Higgs, P. and Gilleard, C. (2015) *Rethinking Old Age: Theorising the Fourth Age*, London: Palgrave.

Judt, T. with Snyder, T. (2012) *Thinking the Twentieth Century*, London: William Heinemann.

Katz, S. (ed.) (2018) *Ageing in Everyday Life: Materialities and Embodiments*, Bristol: Policy Press.

Kohli, M., Rein, M., Guillemard, A.-M. and Van Gunsteren, H. (eds) (1991) *Time for Retirement: Comparative Studies of Early Exit from the Labor Force*, Cambridge: Cambridge University Press.

Kuttner, R. (2018) *Can Democracy Survive Global Capitalism*, New York: W.W. Norton.

Monbiot, G. (2017) *Out of the Wreckage: a New Politics for an Age of Crisis*, London: Verso.

Patel, R. and Moore, J.W. (2018) *A History of the World in Seven Cheap Things: a Guide to Capitalism, Nature, and the Future of the Planet*, London: Verso.

Povinelli, E.A. (2011) *Economies of Abandonment: Social Belonging and Endurance in Late Liberalism*, Durham, NC: Duke University Press.

Shaxson, N. (2018) *The Finance Curse: How Global Finance Is Making Us All Poorer*, London: Bodley Head.

Smith R.J., Lehning, A.J. and Kyeongmo, K. (2018) 'Aging in place in gentrifying neighborhoods: implications for physical and mental health', *The Gerontologist*, 58(1): 26–35.

Standing, G. (2011) *The Precariat: the New Dangerous Class*, London: Bloomsbury Academic.

Torres, S. (2019) *Ethnicity and Old Age: Expanding Our Imagination*, Bristol: Policy Press.

Townsend, P. (1981) 'The structured dependency of the elderly: a creation of policy in the twenty-first century', *Ageing & Society*, 1(1): 5–28.

Townsend, P. (2007) 'Using human rights to defeat ageism: dealing with policy-induced "structured dependency"', in M. Bernard and T. Scharf (eds) *Critical Perspectives on Ageing Societies*, Bristol: Policy Press, pp 27–44.

Twigg, J. and Martin, W. (eds) (2015) *Routledge Handbook of Cultural Gerontology*, London: Routledge.

Walker, A. (1980) 'The social creation of dependency in old age', *Journal of Social Policy*, 9(1): 45–75.

Index

A
abandonment, concept of 43
Aboriginal communities 43
abuse of immigrant older adults 122
access to services 155–6
acculturation of immigrant older adults 126–7
active ageing 31
   and agency 219–22
acute illnesses 28
adolescence 48–9
Adolescence: Its Psychology and Its Relations to Physiology, Anthropology, Sociology, Sex, Crime, Religion and Education (Hall) 48
Affordable Care Act (ACA, 2010) 130, 131, 191, 202–4, 209
   individual mandate 203
   price of drugs negotiation, exclusion 203–4
   public option, removal of 203
   public support for 204
   Trump's plans to dismantle 203–4
   resistance to 204
age-friendly communities 226
age of uncertainty 148
AGE UK 69
ageing
   double standards 28
   individualization of 220
   pillars 216
   precarity and migration 133–5
   risk and insecurity 12
ageing in place 25
Ageing Networks organizations 206, 207, 209
ageing populations
   and precarity 4–6
ageism 56
   older workers 107

agency and active ageing 219–22
Alzheimer's disease 51, 52, 58–9n8, 152
ambiguity, comfort with 34
American Medical Association 199
National Institute on Ageing (NIH) (US) 50
anticipatory socialization 35
appropriate services, limited access to 155–6
austerity 94, 216–18
   depletion of the commons 219
   erosion of collective spaces 219
   intensification of precarity 220–1
   and precarious institutions 239–40
   in the UK 219
   vulnerable groups, disabling for 220–1

B
Barker hypothesis 21
Barnes, Colin 178
Bauman, Zygmunt 148, 161
Beck, Ulrich 81–2, 148, 161
bed-blocking crisis 198
Beiser, M. 132
Bellagio Initiative 53
Bettio et al 180
Bi, Keith 116
Biagi, Marco 148
biological life 45
Blackburn, R. 215
boomer generation 227
brain ageing 52
Brown, W. 219, 221
Buffel, T. and Phillipson, C. 226
burden
   of frailty 70
   of immigrants 131–2
   people with disabilities 178

burn out 159
Butler, Judith 2, 44, 45, 46, 56, 119, 131–2, 183
  Frames of War 131
  precarious conditions 78
  precariousness 131, 173
  on precarity 74–5

C

Campbell, I. and Burgess, J. 93
Canada
  Canada Health Act (1984) 130
  dependency period for sponsored parents 136
  health and social service programme cutbacks 129
  immigrant older adults 115
    precarity, increasing state of 116–17
  immigrant older women 135
  immigration policies 123
  Minimum Necessary Income (MNI) 136
  Old Age Security (OAS) 120
  points-based system of immigration 129
  Special Senate Committee on Ageing recommendation (2009) 136
Canada Health Act (1984) 130
Canadian Frailty Network 69
capitalism
  converting public services into commodities 222
care 8
  as an academically neglected topic 177
  complexity of 176
  concept of 176
  dependency 169, 180–2, 182
  economic rationalization and cost control 182
  ethics of 170
  and frailty 72, 73
  at home 183
  labour market impacts 182
  labour of love 177
  models of 77
  physical pathology 169
  political context of 75–7
  power and dependency 180–2
  precarious work 172–3
  precarity and ageing 174–6
  precarity and the human condition 173–4
  public responsibility 177, 183
  range and types of 170
  recipients of 183
  residential 183
  residential care sector 197–8
  social care system 197
  as a species activity 178
  state funding cuts 173
  unmet needs 76
  unpaid 109, 177
  see also critical care theory; domestic care workers; health care system (US)
care cooperatives 225
care gaps 76
care rights, charter of 179
care theory 174
caregivers 174
Castel, Robert 148, 161
characteristics, personal 33–4
Childhood and Society (Eriksons, E. & J.) 50
childhood obesity 47–8
children
  as health learners 47
Children of the Great Depression (Elder) 46
Choi, N.G. and Smith, J. 125
Choi, Una 127
choice 31
chronic illnesses 28
citizenship and care 178–80
citizenship, destabilization of meaning 224
cleavages within societies 30
Clinton, Bill 200, 206
co-housing groups 225
co-research and co-production 225–6

Index

cognitive health 51–2
cognitive impairment 152, 154, 159, 175
cognitive losses 25
cognitive memory decline 51–2
Cohen, Patricia 50
cohort influences 26–7
collective agency 224, 225
collective engagement 222
collective responses to individual ageing 222–6
collective spaces 219
commercialisation of domestic work 179–80
commodification of domestic work 179–80
competitive individualism 178
consolidation state 194–8, 210
  debt management 195
  precarious retirement 196
Consumer Directed Health Care (CDHC) programme 202
contratti a termine (work contracts with an end date) 148
contratti precari (precarious contracts) 148
Cooper, D. 225
corporate health firms 199
  power of 204
corporate health management 201–2
corporatization of US health care system 191, 193–8
critical care theory 170, 171–2, 176–81
  care, power and dependency 180–2
  citizenship and migration 178–80
  different voices 178
critical gerontology 5, 238
cross-domain dynamics 21
cultural gerontology 5, 238
cumulative advantage 22, 92
cumulative disadvantage 22, 92, 129
cumulative pressures of precarity 158–60
Curtis et al 120

D

Daly, T. and Armstrong, P. 76
Dannefer, D. 58n5
Dannefer, D. and Wang, W. 220, 224
Dastjerdi, M. and Mardukhi, A. 125–6
Dawson, A. 226
death, denial of 27
debt management 195
decline narrative 79
decline of the social 218–19
deficits model of frailty 70–1
Defined Benefit (DB) pension schemes 108, 111
Defined Contribution (DC) pension schemes 108
dehumanization 131–2
dementia 52, 175–6
demography 20, 27–8
dependence/dependency 78, 169, 227
  and care 180–2
  dual system of 181
despair, crisis of 51
devalued subjects and vulnerability 77–9
diabetes mellitus 117
different voices about care 178
disability as tragedy narrative 79
disadvantage 6, 22, 92, 129
disaster capitalism 216–17
discrimination against immigrant older adults 128–9
dislocation of communities 42–3
'disrupt ageing,' need to 31
divorce 20, 29, 96
  consequences for women 102, 105
domestic care workers 179
  low-paid female 179
  migrant 179
  poorly paid 179–80
dual system of dependency 181
Duncan, O.D. 149

E

Ebert, N. 171
economic exploitation and deprivation 42–4

economic markers of precarity 119–21
Elder, Glen 46
emancipatory gerontology 222
emancipatory social science 222
embodiment, concept of 173
employer ageism 94
employment *see* work
employment precarity 95
Employment Precarity Index 150, 162
Employment Support Allowance 96, 105
environmental action groups 225
environments 26–8
 demography 27–8
 history 26–7
epidemiological transition 28
epigenetics 20–1
Erikson, Erik and Joan 50
Estes, C.L. 205–6
Estes et al 76
ethics, of care 170
Ettlinger, N. 119
European Convention on Human Rights (ECHR) 243
Evans, B. and Reid, J. 55
everyday utopias 225
exclusion 224
 see also social exclusion
existential vulnerability of ageing 77
expulsion from homes 42–3
extreme cities 226

F
fatherhood 29
femininity 29
feminists 177
fertility, declining 20
fetal origins hypothesis 21
figurative methodology 41
financial crisis (2008) 217, 238
Fineman, Martha 78–9, 181
flexibility in labour market 217
flexible work 111

fluid self-definitions 33
foreclosure evictions 43
formative measures 149–50
Foucault, Michel 42, 45
 radical subjectivity 56–7
fourth age of life 24, 51, 243
frail subject 80, 83
frailty 8, 69–70
 and care 72, 73
 concept of 69–70
 deficits model 70–1
 discourses and practices 71
 emergence of 72
 and life course experience 72
 and older women 72–3
 phenotype model 70
 problems and limits of responses to 70–3
 relocation of 79–83
 and risk 81–2
 as a shared experience of vulnerability 80–1
 social conditions and political systems 82–4
 and success 71
 and vulnerability 72, 73
Frames of War (Butler) 131
France, precariat 148
Friedman, Milton 201–2
Fullen, M.C. and Gorby, S.R. 54
futurity 79

G
Gamble, A. 216, 227
gaps in care 76
gender 29–30
generational equity debate 30
geontopower 42, 57n1
Gerontological Society of America 53–4
gerontology 243
geroscience hypothesis 170, 184n1
Gibson, Kathryn 225
Giddens, A. 220
gig economy 192
Gilligan, Carol 178

Index

global capital 42–4
global care chains 179
global precarity 42–3
global wealth, poor to rich 42–3
goals, realistic 33
governmentality 45
Graham, Hilary 177
Graham, Julie 225
Gray, J. 12
Grenier et al 44, 117, 174–5, 175, 192
grounded theory 151
Gullette, Margaret Morganroth 71

H

Hall, G. Stanley 48
Hayek, Frederick 194, 201–2
health care system (UK)
  bailing out of care homes 198
  corporate 198
  failure of neoliberalism 198
health care system (US) 191–3
  Affordable Care Act (ACA, 2010) 130, 131, 191, 202–4, 209
  austerity regime (1993) 195
  British option 197
  change in economic characteristics 191
  Clinton Administration 195
  Consumer Directed Health Care (CDHC) programme 202
  corporate hold over 204
  corporatization of 191, 193–8, 201
  expansion of corporate health management 201–2
  growth of 193
  health maintenance organizations (HMO) model 201
  historic makeup of 191
  insurance companies 199–201
  Kaiser Permanente programme 201
  neoliberal health care 199–208
    health reform, history of 199–202

  nursing homes 205
  privatization of 191, 195–7, 199–201
  Puget Sound Health system programme 201
  see also Medicaid; Medicare
health insurance (US) 130
health literacy issues of immigrant older adults 125
health maintenance organizations (HMOs) 191, 204, 207–8
  model 201
healthcare systems for immigrant older adults 129–31
healthy immigration effect (HIE) 123
heart disease 117
Henderson, J. and Denny, K. 53, 54–5
Hiam et al 218
hidden variables 26
Himmelsbach, Ines 24
history 26–7
Hochschild, A.R. 176
Home and Community Based Services (HCBS) 205, 206
home care aides 156
Hondagneu-Sotelo, P. 179
Hospitality sector, case study 98–111
HRT (hormone replacement therapy) 58n7
human development 41–2, 48
human rights 242–4
Humber, L. 198
Humphries et al 218
Hyman, I. 128

I

immigrant older adults 115, 119
  case study 116
  changes in health status 134
  coping strategies 127
  dependency period for sponsored parents 136
  family reunification 120
  health inequalities 117
  invisibility in public policy 131

immigrant older adults (CONTINUED)
  markers of precarity
    economic 119–21
    psychosocial and cultural 121–7
      abuse and stigma 122
      acculturation 126–7
      health literacy 125
      immigrant status 123–4
      language 124–5
      life course events 124
      loss of status and role 123
      social isolation and loneliness 125–6
  Old Age Security (OAS) 120
  othering practices 128
  politics of precarity 127–31
    immigration policy 129
    systemic racism and discrimination 128–9
  poverty, living in 120
  precarity, risk and vulnerability 116
  predispositions to certain diseases 117
  research 132–3
  sponsored family members 120–1
  sponsored immigrant status 134–5
  visibility in public discourse 131
  vulnerability and social risk 117
immigrant status 123–4
immigration policy, impact on immigrant older adults 129
inadvertent discrimination 128–9
independence 78, 154
  importance of maintaining 157–8
individual choice 175
individual level of precarity 19–20, 20
individualistic ideology 161
individualization 239, 240
  of old age 220
    collective responses to 222–6
inequality/inequalities 6, 30, 175
  capabilities approach to addressing 223
  and frailty 81–2
  growing 218
inevitable dependencies of life 181

inner-individual level of precarity 19, 20
insecurity 93, 148, 237
institutionalized discrimination 129
insurance companies 199–200, 199–201
inter-group relationships 34
interdependence 32, 74, 173
interpersonal nature of precarity 32–3
intersectionality 30, 133–4
intimacy 34
isolation 157–8

J
Jaques, Eliott 50
Johnson, Lyndon B. 200
Judt, T. 4–5, 219, 239

K
Kafer, A. 79
Kaiser Permanente programme 201
Kalleberg, A.L. 171
Kittay, Eva Fedor 180–1
Klein, N. 216–17
Klinenberg, E. 157
Kobayashi, K.M. and Prus, S.G. 135
Kröger, T. and Bagnato, A. 217

L
labour market
  beyond 240–1
  reforms 110–11
Laceuelle, H. 77
Lai, D.W.L. and Surood, S. 122
Lain et al 241
Land, Hilary 177
language issues of immigrant older adults 124–5
Laslett, P. 23, 58n6
later life 23–4, 25, 29, 237
  reshaping of 221
Latino paradox 123
Leahy, Deana 47
Lehning et al 226

levels of precarity 8
　individual 19–20, 20
　inner-individual 19, 20
　supra-individual 20
Lewchuk, W. 150
life course 8, 19
　and crises 46–52
　　adolescence 48–9
　　childhood obesity 47–8
　　cognitive memory decline 51–2
　　mid-life crisis 49–51
　　puberty 49
　　youth 48
　destandardized 240
　fourth age of life 24, 51
　gender 29–30
　immigrant older adults 124
　later life 29
　paradigm of 19
　personal characteristics 33–4
　precarity
　　and environments 26–8
　　interpersonal nature of 32–3
　　later life 23–4, 25
　　levels of 19–21
　　life domains in 21
　　life transitions 24–5
　　long view of 21–3
　and resilience 53–5
　and resistance 55–7
　third age of life 23–4
life domains 8, 21
life expectancy 20, 51
　reversals in 27
　slowdown in rate of 218
life transitions 24–5
linked lives 32
liquid times 42
living alone 157–8, 158–9
living otherwise 57
loneliness 149
　of immigrant older adults 125–6
Long Life, The (Small) 57
long-term care (LTC) systems 204–8, 209
Lorey, I. 45, 228
Low Income Cut-Off 134

M

MacArthur Foundation 50
macro level 151
malnutrition, grandparents/
　great-grandparents history of 20
managed long-term care (MLTC)
　systems 206–8
marginalization 6, 128
marginalized groups 76, 77
Marshall, T.H. 216
masculinity 29
McBride, S. and Mitrea, S. 220–1
measurement 149
Medicaid 191, 193, 193–4
　beneficiaries in HMOs 204
　expansion of 204
　health care budgets 196
　Home and Community Based
　　Services (HCBS) 205, 206
　and long-term care 204–8, 209
　neoliberal, pro-corporate
　　ideology 206–7, 208
　profitability 205–6
　privatization of programmes 197
　setting up of 200
　waiver funds 206
Medicare 191, 193, 193–4
　health care budgets 196
　Medicare Advantage programme
　　191, 193, 204, 209
　privatization of programmes 197
　setting up of 200
memory 51–2
men
　fatherhood 29
　vulnerabilities 30
meso level 151
micro level 151, 161
mid-life crisis 49–51, 58n7
middle age 58n6
Midlife in the United States (MIDUS)
　50–1
migration 8, 115
　ageing and precarity 133–5
　and care 178–80
　context 116–18
　globalized 180

migration (CONTINUED)
   and precarity 119
      policy recommendations 135–6
   see also immigrant older adults
mild cognitive impairment (MCI) 52
military service 22–3
Millar, K.M. 2, 13n1, 74, 94, 172, 174
Mills, C. Wright 34–5
Monbiot, G. 242
moral hazard, concept of 202
Morris, Jenny 178
mortality, sex differential 27
Moztarzadeh, A. and O'Rourke, N. 126
Mukherjee, A.J. and Diwan, S. 126
Myles, John 227

N

Nam et al 120
National Care Association 197–8
nationalism 132
Navarro, V. 136
neoliberal corporate state 194
neoliberalism 31
   all-encompassing 219
   challenge to the welfare state 216
   and precarity 192–3
   privatization of public sector 191
   under-institutionalized society 218–19
   vulnerable groups, disabling for 220–1
Neugarten, B.L. 35, 58n6
New Deal 199
National Health Service (NHS) 69
Nixon, President Richard 201
no care zones 76, 83, 223, 242
nursing homes 205

O

Obama, President Barack 130, 200, 203

Obamacare *see* Affordable Care Act (ACA, 2010)
obesity, childhood 47–8
objective reality 93
old age *see* ageing
Old Age Security (OAS) 120
old age spans 23
Older Americans Act (1966) 205
older workers
   employment precarity 95
   flexible working, right to 111
   grinners 91
   groaners 91
   ontological precarity *see* ontological precarity
   pressures to work longer 91, 92
   unemployed 95
O'Neil, K. and Tienda, M. 120
ontological precarity 9, 91, 93–4, 241
   interaction of domains 96–8
   precarious employment 91, 92, 94–5, 96–8
   precarious households 92, 96, 96–8, 110
   precarious welfare states 92, 95–6, 96–8
ontological vulnerabilities 241–2
othering practices 128
Oxford English Dictionary (OED) 2–3

P

pain 79
Patel, R. and Moore, J.W. 241
path dependency processes 21–2
patient advocates 156
Pauly, Mark 201, 202
Pension Credit 96
pension schemes 108
pensioners, poverty of 229n3
pensions 217
perceptions 34–5
Percy, A. 223
personal characteristics 33–4
personal responsibility 175

Index

personal vulnerabilities 241–2
phenotype model of frailty 70
Phillipson, Chris 43
physical dependency 181
physical impairment 175
physical losses 25
physicians 199
planning 36
political systems 82–4
politics of precarity 127–31
   health care system 129–31
Portes, J. 223
positive ageing 31
Poureslami et al 125
Povinelli, Elizabeth 42, 43
power, and care 180–2
pre-dementia conditions 52
precariat 42, 148, 172, 241
   gig economy 192
   US health care workers 192
Precariat, The (Standing) 91
precarious conditions 75–7, 78, 81
precarious, definition 3
precarious employment 91, 92, 94–5, 96–8
   and care 172–3
   US health care workers 192
precarious households 92, 96, 96–8, 110
precarious institutions 239–40
precarious retirement 196
precarious welfare states 92, 95–6, 96–8
precarious work-society 171
precariousness 56, 74, 131, 173, 238
   burden and dehumanization 131–2
   distinct from precarity 2–3, 44
   feminist readings of 80–1
   in multiple domains 96–8
   as part of living 44
precarity
   and austerity 216–18
   care and ageing 174–6
   concept of 73–5
      cultural studies and philosophy 74
      origins 172
      political science and labour studies 74
   and critical perspectives on ageing populations 4–6
   definition 119
   distinct from precariousness 2–3, 44
   and environments 26–8
   and the human condition 173–4
   and human rights 242–4
   index of 150
   interactions between different domains 97
   interpersonal nature of 32–3
   intersectionality 133–4
   as a labour condition 172
   later life 23–4, 25, 29
   levels 19–21
   life transitions 24–5
   as a lived experience 9, 91, 93, 94
   long view of 21–3, 240
   meaning of 2–4
   and migration 133–5
      policy recommendations 135–6
   as an ontological experience 172
   personal characteristics 33–4
   politics of 127–31
   quantitative and qualitative measures of experiences 134
   recognising and measuring 149–50
   relocating frailty 79–83
   and risk 81
   structural and cultural interpretations 83, 86n5
   studies 150–3
      markers of precarity
         appropriate services, limited access to 155–6
         cumulative pressures 158–60
         independence, maintaining 157–8
         uncertainty 152–3
         questions, cues for 154, 156, 158, 160
      role of researchers 162
   subjective realm 34–6
   see also ontological precarity

precarity thinking, critical trends in 42–6
precarity trap 121
precarization 228
pressures, cumulative 158–60
private companions 76
private insurance corporations 199
privatization 239
    Medicaid 197
productive ageing 31
psychosocial and cultural markers of precarity 121–7
    abuse and stigma 122
    acculturation 126–7
    case studies 121–2
    health literacy 125
    immigrant status 123–4
    language 124–5
    life course events 124
    loss of status and role 123
    social isolation and loneliness 125–6
puberty 49
Puget Sound Health system programme 201

Q

qualitative measures of experiences 134
quantitative measures of experiences 134

R

racism 224
    against immigrant older adults 128–9
radical subjectivity 56–7
Reagan, Ronald 201
reflective capacity 33
reflective measures 149
representational struggles 41
residential care 183
residential care sector (UK) 197–8
    debt levels 197–8
resilience 42, 53–5, 161

resistance 42, 55–7
responsibility 31
retirement 25
    precarious 196
risk 6, 75, 134, 148, 175
    and frailty 81–2
    misunderstanding of 82
    shared and particular 81–2
risk society 42
risk-taking, moderate 33–4
Roberts, Celia 49
Roger et al 122
role, loss of among immigrant older adults 123
Roosevelt, President Franklin D. 199
Rose, Nikolas 45
Ryan, Paul 197

S

safe jobs 94
Sassen, Saskia 42–3, 224
second demographic revolution 28
security 93
Segal, L. 225
self-efficacy 34
self-regulation 33
self-reporting 54
Seneca 34–5
services, limited access to 155–6
shadow of the future 36
shadow of the past 19, 21, 36
Shakespeare, Tom 178
Sheehy, Gail 50
shock doctrine tactics 216–17
Small, Helen 57
social care system (UK) 197
social commons 219
social conditions 82–4
social, decline of the 218–19
social economy 225
social exclusion 6, 224
social forces 19
social imaginary of decline 72
social inclusion 224
social isolation of immigrant older adults 125–6

social policy/policies 152
   reframing 221
social relationships, close 34
social rented accommodation 102
social state 5
Social Transformation of American Medicine, The (Starr) 191, 199
sociological imagination 35
sponsored family members 120–1, 126, 134–5
   dependency period for parents 136
   life course transitions 126–7
Standing, Guy 74, 75, 91, 172, 219
Starr, Paul 191, 199
state intervention 216, 224
State Pension 98
   inadequacy of 102
   in Scandinavian countries 229n3
   in Spain 229n3
State Pension age 95–6
   rises in 104, 111
statecraft 45
statistical panic 57
Statistics Canada (2016) 117, 118
status, loss of among immigrant older adults 123
stigma 149
   of immigrant older adults 122
Stockholm Resilience Centre 53
Streeck, W. 194
   neoliberal state 194–5
   neoliberalism as under-institutionalized society 218–19
structured dependency 220, 243
subjective experience 93
subjective realm 34–6
substantive equalities 222, 224
success, and frailty 71
successful ageing 31, 71, 220
   models of 25
Sun et al 126
support groups 35
supra-individual level of precarity 20

T

Tanner, James Mourilyn 49
   Tanner scale 49
Teeple, G. 217
theoretical constructs 149
third age of life 23–4
Torres, Sandra 134
Townsend, P. 220, 243–4
transgender groups 225
Tronto, Joan 78, 178
Truman, President Harry 199
Trump, President Donald 203–4, 208
turning points 22, 240
Tyler, Imogen 41

U

uncertainty 42, 93
   markers of 152–3
United Kingdom (UK)
   austerity 219
   see also health care system (UK)
United States of America (USA)
   Affordable Care Act (ACA, 2008) 130
   Clinton Administration 200, 206
   health and social service programme cutbacks 129
   health care 193
   health insurance 130
   insurance companies 199–200
   Medicaid 156
   nationalism 132
   neoliberal, pro-corporate ideology 206–7, 208
   New Deal 199
   Nixon Administration 201
   Obama Administration 130, 200, 203
   Reagan Administration 201
   subsidized home care aides 156
   Trump Administration 203–4, 208
   see also health care system (US)
Universal Basic Services (UBS) 222, 223–4
Universal Declaration of Human Rights (UDHR) 243

universal health care 199, 200
unlinked lives 33
unpaid care 109

V
Vang et al 124
Vernon, Dr Martin 85n3
Veterans Administration programme 197
victim blaming 132
Village movement 225
vulnerability 6, 134
    cumulative personal and ontological 241–2
    and devalued subjects 77–9
    feminist readings of 80–1
    and frailty 72, 73, 80–1
    of men 30
    new forms of 228
    relational aspects 78
    social conditions and political systems 82–4
    of women 30
vulnerable subject 78–9

W
Waite, L. 2, 73–4, 93
welfare state 5, 31, 95, 98
    assumptions behind state intervention 216
    changing landscape 92
    importance of 216
    precarious domain for older workers 105
    reconstruction of 223–4
    reductions in provision of 149
    retreat of 148
    see also precarious welfare states
Wild et al 54
Williams, Fiona 179
women
    family relationships and protections 29–30
    mortality rates 27
    social convoys 27–8
Women Against State Pension Inequality campaign 95
Woodward, Kathleen 57
work
    case studies 98–111
    physically demanding 95, 103–4, 111
work intensification 95
World Health Organization (WHO) 53
World Health Organization's Commission on the Social Determinants of Health 129
Worth, N. 93
Wright, E.O. 222, 225

X
Xu, L. 116

Y
youth, crisis of 48

Z
zones of no care 76, 83, 223, 242

www.ingramcontent.com/pod-product-compliance
Lightning Source LLC
Chambersburg PA
CBHW070916030426
42336CB00014BA/2433